OCR
A LEVEL

BRITAIN
1930–1997

Acknowledgements

pp.11,60: Richard Toye: from *Churchill's Empire: The World that Made Him and the World He Made* (Pan, 2011); **p.12: Winston Churchill:** taken from a speech made to the India Empire Society (11 December 1930); **p.13: Winston Churchill:** from a speech given to the West Essex Conservative Association (23 February 1931); **p.13: Arthur Herman:** from *Churchill and Gandhi: The Rivalry That Destroyed an Empire and Forged Our Age* (Arrow, 2009); **p.15: Winston Churchill:** taken from a speech given to the House of Commons on the day Edward VIII abdicated (10 December 1936); **pp.16,23,32: Winston Churchill:** from *The Second World War, Volume 1: The Gathering Storm* (Penguin, 2005); **p.16: Stanley Baldwin:** taken from a speech given in the House of Commons on the problems of rearming Britain (12 November 1936); **p.20: Winston Churchill:** taken from a speech given in the House of Commons on the Munich Agreement (October 1938); **p.22: Neville Chamberlain:** from a letter to his sister (20 March 1938); **p.27: David Irving:** extract from the diary of the Acting Director of Naval Operations from *Churchill's War: The Struggle for Power: 1* (Veritas, 1987); **p.27: Duff Cooper:** from *Old Men Forget* (Faber & Faber, 2011); **p.28: Leo Amery:** from *My Political Life* (Hutchinson, 1953); **pp.28,37,52, 87: John Colville:** from *The Fringes of Power: Downing Street Diaries 1939–1955* (Weidenfeld & Nicolson, 2004); **p.32: Winston Churchill:** from 'Blood, Toil, Tears and Sweat' speech (13 May 1940), taken from *His Finest Hours: The War Speeches of Winston Churchill* by Graham Stewart (Quercus, 2007); **pp.33–34:** cabinet minutes from 1940 from UK War Cabinet, www.ukwarcabinet.org.uk and The National Archives, permission for re-use of all © Crown copyright information is granted under the terms of the Open Government Licence (OGL); **p.34: Baron Hugh Dalton:** from *The Fateful Years: Memoirs, 1931–1945* (Frederick Muller Ltd., 1957); **p.34: Winston Churchill:** taken from the 'We Shall Fight on the Beaches' speech (4 June 1940); **p.35: Winston Churchill:** taken from a speech (20 August 1940); **p.36: David Irving:** from a letter by Sir Dudley Pound from *Churchill's War: The Struggle for Power: 1* (Veritas, 1987); **p.41: Gordon Corrigan:** taken from Field Marshal Wavell's view of Churchill's military outlook from *Blood, Sweat and Arrogance: The Myths of Churchill's War* (Weidenfeld & Nicolson, 2007); **pp.41,56: Lord Alanbrooke:** extract: Britain's most senior soldier records an encounter with Churchill during the El Alamein campaign in North Africa from *Alanbrooke War Diaries 1939–1945: Field Marshall Lord Alanbrooke*, ed. Alex Danchev and Dan Todman (Weidenfeld and Nicolson, 2002); **p.41: Robert Blake and Wm. Roger Louis:** extract: Churchill's Chief of Staff writes to Sir Claude Auchinleck after his appointment to command in the Middle East in July 1941 from *Churchill* (OUP, 1996); **p.41: Robert Blake and Wm. Roger Louis:** extract: Churchill writes to his son, Randolph, from Cairo in October 1941 from *Churchill* (OUP, 1996); **p.44: General Marshall,** memorandum (1 April 1942); **pp.44–45: Lord Alanbrooke:** extract: Sir Alanbrooke, the overall head of the army, expresses doubts about D Day in his diary entry for 5 June 1944 from *Alanbrooke War Diaries 1939–1945: Field Marshall Lord Alanbrooke*, ed. Alex Danchev and Dan Todman (Weidenfeld and Nicolson, 2002); **p.44: Winston Churchill:** extract: Churchill recalls a visit by US envoys, General Marshall and Harry Hopkins, to urge a 'Second Front' in April 1942 from *The Second World War, Volume 4: The Hinge of Fate* (Penguin, 2005); **p.44: Mark Stoler:** report of a meeting between Stimson and Roosevelt (August 1943); **pp.46–47: Bishop George Bell:** Bishop George Bell speaks in the House of Lords about the bombing (9 February 1944); **p.46: James Fyfe:** extract: Churchill writes to Harris on 1 June 1942 from *Great Ingratitude: Bomber Command in World War 2* (GC Book Publishers, 1993); **pp.46,71,75: Nigel Knight:** from *Churchill. The Greatest Briton Unmasked* (David and Charles, 2009), reproduced by permission of the publisher; **pp.47,80: Richard Lamb:** from *Churchill as War Leader: Right or Wrong* (Bloomsbury, 1993); **p.47:** extract: The bombing of Germany: advice given to the British government in 1942 by Lord Cherwell from *History Learning Site* (History Learning Site, 2015), http://www.historylearningsite.co.uk; **p.47: Dietmar Suss:** from *Death from the Skies: How the British and Germans Survived Bombing in World War II* (OUP, 2014); **p.48: Winston Churchill:** from Churchill's speech to the House of Commons (7 February 1945); **p.50: Paul Addison:** extract: Diary of Churchill's secretary after debate on the Beveridge Report from *Churchill on the Home Front, 1900–1955* (Jonathan Cape, 1992); **p.50: Winston Churchill:** taken from a speech to the nation (March 1943); **p.51: Sarah Churchill:** taken from a letter to her father, Winston Churchill, dated April 1945 from *Churchill on the Home Front, 1900–1945* (Jonathan Cape, 1992); **p.51: Winston Churchill:** taken from a speech to the Conservative conference (March 1945); **p.52:** table: Summary of seats won in the 1945 election; **p.52:** table: Summary of votes cast in the 1945 election; **p.54:** Raymond Mortimer: extract: A friend of the Conservative MP Harold Nicholson writes about the election (10 July 1945); **p.55:** Lord Ismay: from *The Memoirs of Lord Ismay* (Heinemann, 1960); **p.55:** Lord Attlee et al.: Aneurin Bevan, as quoted in *Churchill By His Contemporaries. An Observer Appreciation* (Hodder & Stoughton, 1965); **p.55:** Sir Ian Jacob et al.: from *Action This Day: Working with Churchill* (Macmillan, 1968); **p.56:** Lord Alanbrooke: extract: The Chief of the Imperial General Staff records a conference with Churchill (19 August 1943); **pp.59–60:** Winston Churchill: taken from a speech made to the House of Commons in 1945 from *Victory, the sixth volume of Winston Churchill's War Speeches*, Charles Eade (Cassell, 1946); **p.60:** Christopher Catherwood: from *Winston Churchill: The Flawed Genius of World War II* (Berkley, 2010); **p.60: Adolf Hitler:** taken from a speech to the Reichstag (July 1940); **p.60: F.D. Roosevelt:** from a conversation between him and his son (1943); **p.62: Francis L. Loewenheim, Harold D. Langley and Manfred Jonas** from *Roosevelt and Churchill: Their Secret Wartime Correspondence* (Da Capo Press Inc., 1990); **p.63: Joseph P. Lash:** from *Roosevelt and Churchill* (W. W. Norton and Company, Inc., 1980); **p.63:** from The Atlantic Charter (14 August 1941); **p.63:** General Smuts: correspondence between General Smuts and Winston Churchill; **p.68:** Winston Churchill: criticism of US policy; **p.68:** Winston Churchill: thoughts following Hitler's invasion of the USSR (June 1941); **pp.68,76:** Winston Churchill: from *Triumph and Tragedy: The Second World War, Volume 6* (Winston Churchill World War II Collection) (Penguin, 2005); **p.70:** Winston Churchill: from a radio broadcast to the British people after the German invasion of Russia (1941); **p.70:** Alexander Cadogan: extract: Alexander Cadogan describes Churchill's meeting with Stalin in August 1942 (The National Archives), http://blog.nationalarchives.gov.uk; **p.71:** minutes taken from a meeting between Marshal Stalin and Churchill, at the Kremlin (13 August 1942); **p.71: Winston Churchill:** from an account of Churchill's discussion with Stalin from *Memoirs of the Second World War* (Houghton Mifflin, 1996); **p.72:** memorandum from Churchill to General Scobie, the commander of the British forces in Athens (December 1944); **p.76: Winston Churchill:** from a speech at the Yalta Conference, followed by Stalin's response (February 1945); **p.78:** extract: Churchill's attitude to post-war Europe; **pp.78–9:** extract: Churchill speaks at the University of Zürich (September 1946); **p.79: Winston Churchill:** from a memo to members of his cabinet (29 November 1951); **p.80: Winston Churchill:** from 'The Sinews of Peace' speech (March 1946); **p.81:** taken from 'Stalin's Reply to Churchill' from *Pravda* (Pravda, 14 March 1946); **p.83: Charles de Gaulle:** extract from *The Complete War Memoirs of Charles de Gaulle* (Carroll & Graf Publishers, 1998); **p.83: Simon Berthon:** from a telegram dated 6 June 1942, from De Gaulle to the Free French commanders in Africa and the Middle East as quoted in Allies at War (Thistle Publishing, 2013); **p.83: Baron Charles McMoran Wilson Moran:** extract: Churchill's personal doctor recalls Churchill's view of de Gaulle at the Casablanca Conference, 1943 from *Churchill: The Struggle for Survival 1945–60* (Carroll & Graf Publishers Inc, 2006); **p.83: Winston Churchill:** from a letter to the foreign secretary (June 1944); **p.84: Winston Churchill:** from a broadcast by Churchhill after his meeting with Roosevelt at Placentia Bay (24 August 1941); **p.87: Robert Boothby:** taken from a letter to Winston Churchill (9 May 1940); **p.90:** table: The 1951 election results; **pp.90,94: Harold Macmillan:** from the 'Britons have never had it so good' speech (1957), taken from *Access to History: 1945–2007* by Michael Lynch (Hodder Education, 2008); **p.93: Michael Lynch:** table: GDP growth rates, 1951–64; from *Access to History: Britain 1945–2007* (Hodder Education, 2008); **p.96:** table: Unemployment in Britain, 1951–64; **p.96:** quote from R.A. Butler; **p.99:** Lord Denning: from his report on the Profumo Affair (1963), taken from *Britain since 1945: A Political History* by David Childs (Routledge, 2012); **p.101:** from Clause IV of the Labour party about nationalisation; **p.101: Aneurin Bevan:** from *In Place of Fear* (Kessinger Publishing, 2010); **p.102:** table: The 1959 general election results; **p.104: Jeremy Thorpe:** from his observation on Harold Macmillan's 1962 cabinet reshuffle. Adapted from the final line of Charles Dickens' *A Tale of Two Cities*; **pp.104,108: T.O. Lloyd:** from *Empire to Welfare State: English History 1906–85* (OUP, 1986); **p.105:** quote from R.A. Butler; **p.107: Winston Churchill:** opinions on the Conservatives' improvements to the social services (1954); **p.107: Michael Shanks:** from *The Stagnant Society: A Warning* (Pelican, 1964); **p.112:** table: The 1959 and 1964 general election results; **pp.102,113: Harold Wilson:** from 'White Heat of Technology' speech (1 October 1963); **p.117:** table: The March 1966 general election result; **p.118: B.R. Mitchell:** table: The numbers attending university courses in selected years, taken from *British Historical Statistics* (Cambridge University Press, 1988); **p.118:** from Wilson's report to the Commons (April 1965); **p.119: Barbara Castle:** extract taken from her diary (January 1968); **p.124: David Reynolds:** table: Britain's percentage share of world exports of manufactures, taken from *Britannia Overruled, British Policy and World Power in the 20th Century* (Longman, 1991); **p.126: David Butler and Gareth Butler:** table: Workers in selected British occupations, taken from *British Political Facts 1900–1994* (Macmillan, 1994); **p.126: David Butler and Gareth Butler:** table: Membership figures for selected unions, *British Political Facts 1900–1994* (Macmillan, 1994), reproduced with permission of Palgrave Macmillan; **p.127:** table: The June 1970 general election result; **p.129: Edward Heath:** speech to his party conference (1970); **p.131: David Butler and Gareth Butler:** table: Industrial relations under the conservatives, *British Political Facts 1900–1994* (Macmillan, 1994), reproduced with permission of Palgrave Macmillan; **p.132:** table: The February 1974 general election result; **p.133:** cynics commenting on the Social Contract (1973); **p.133:** table: The October 1974 general election result; **p.137:** Harold Wilson's promise (1963); **p.135: James Callaghan:** extract from speech to the Labour Party conference (September 1976); **p.138: Kenneth O. Morgan:** from *Britain Since 1945: The People's Peace* (Oxford Paperbacks, 2001); **p.138: David Childs:** from *Britain Since 1939: Progress and Decline* (Palgrave Macmillan, 2001); **p.143:** table: The 1979 general election result; **p.145:** table: The 1983 general election result; **p.145:** table: The 1987 general election result; **p.148:** table: Unemployment, 1979–90. Economics research by Lewis Goodall, BBC Analysis and Research, original figures from the Office for National Statistics (ONS), permission for re-use of all © Crown copyright information is granted under the terms of the Open Government Licence (OGL); **p.149:** table: Inflation rate (%), 1976–92. Economics research by Lewis Goodall, BBC Analysis and Research, original figures from the Office for National Statistics (ONS), permission for re-use of all © Crown copyright information is granted under the terms of the Open Government Licence (OGL); **p.149:** table: Government spending as a percentage of GDP, 1976–2010. Economics research by Lewis Goodall, BBC Analysis and Research, original figures from the Office for National Statistics (ONS), permission for re-use of all © Crown copyright information is granted under the terms of the Open Government Licence (OGL); **p.154:** David Butler and Gareth Butler: table: Statistics for unemployment, strikes and trade unions in selected years, taken from *British Political Facts 1900–1994* (Macmillan, 1994); **p.160: Sir Geoffrey Howe:** from resignation speech to the House of Commons (13 November 1990); **p.163:** table: The 1997 general election result; **p.164: Eric J. Evans:** from *Thatcher and Thatcherism* (Routledge, 2013); **p.164: Andrew Roberts:** adapted from 'How Margaret Thatcher made Britain great again' from *The Week* (The Week, 25 February 2009); **p.174: Margaret Thatcher:** from a statement to the media (1990); **p.175: Winston Churchill:** opinion on building a special relationship between the British Commonwealth and the United States (March 1946); **p.187: Harold Macmillan:** from the 'Wind of Change' speech (1960); **p.192: Brian Lapping:** from *End of Empire* (Paladin, 1989); **p.193: Niall Ferguson:** from *Empire, How Britain Made the Modern World* (Penguin, 2004).

Every effort has been made to trace or contact all copyright holders, but if any have been inadvertently overlooked the Publishers will be pleased to make the necessary arrangements at the first opportunity.

OCR
A LEVEL

Nicholas Fellows
Mike Wells

BRITAIN 1930–1997

HODDER
EDUCATION
AN HACHETTE UK COMPANY

The Publishers would like to thank the following for permission to reproduce copyright material:

Photo credits p.6 © Adam Woolfitt/Corbis; **p.7 & 88** ©arevhamb – Fotolia; **p.11** © Punch Limited; **p.12** © Eric BVD – Fotolia; **p.14** © The Granger Collection, NYC / TopFoto; **p.16** © Illustrated London News; **p.22** © Illustrated London News; **p.26** © David Low / Solo Syndication; **p.33** © Hulton-Deutsch Collection/Corbis; **p.39** © Hulton Archive/Getty Images; **p.46** © dpa picture alliance / Alamy; **p.53** © Mary Evans Picture Library/Onslow Auctions Limited; **p.54** © Fotomas / TopFoto; **p.65** © Punch Limited; **p.66** Roosevelt and Churchill struggle for control of Africa, 1942 (colour litho), German School, (20th century) / Private Collection / Peter Newark Military Pictures / Bridgeman Images; **p.67** © Everett Collection Historical / Alamy; **p.69** © Corbis; **p.72** © Roger-Viollet / TopFoto; **p.73** © Punch Limited; **p.95** © Popperfoto/Getty Images; **p.98** © Central Press/Hulton Archive/Getty Images; **p.101** © DAVID COLE/REX; **p.116** © David Farrell/Getty Images; **p.129** © ITV/REX; **p.134** © Central Press/ Hulton Archive/Getty Images; **p.136** © United News/Popperfoto/Getty Images; **p.144** © Tim Roney/Getty Images; **p.151** © Les Gibbard, published in The Guardian, 4 December 1981, British Cartoon Archive, University of Kent, www.cartoons.ac.uk.

Every effort has been made to trace all copyright holders, but if any have been inadvertently overlooked the Publishers will be pleased to make the necessary arrangements at the first opportunity.

Although every effort has been made to ensure that website addresses are correct at time of going to press, Hodder Education cannot be held responsible for the content of any website mentioned in this book. It is sometimes possible to find a relocated web page by typing in the address of the home page for a website in the URL window of your browser.

Hachette UK's policy is to use papers that are natural, renewable and recyclable products and made from wood grown in well-managed forests and other controlled sources. The logging and manufacturing processes are expected to conform to the environmental regulations of the country of origin.

Orders: please contact Hachette UK Distribution, Hely Hutchinson Centre, Milton Road, Didcot, Oxfordshire, OX11 7HH. Telephone: +44 (0)1235 827827. Email education@hachette.co.uk Lines are open from 9 a.m. to 5 p.m., Monday to Friday. You can also order through our website: www.hoddereducation.co.uk

© Andrew Boxer, Nicholas Fellows, Mike Wells 2015

First published in 2015 by

Hodder Education,

An Hachette UK Company

Carmelite House

50 Victoria Embankment

London EC4Y 0DZ

Impression number   11

Year   2022

Cover photo © Pictoral Press Ltd/Alamy

Illustrations by Integra Software Services

Typeset in ITC Legacy Serif Std Book 10/13 by Integra Software Services Pvt. Ltd., Pondicherry, India

Printed and bound by CPI Group (UK) Ltd, Croydon CR0 4YY

A catalogue record for this title is available from the British Library

ISBN 9781471837296

Contents

Introduction

This book has been written to support your study of:

■ the British Period Study and Enquiry Unit Y113 and Y143, Britain 1930–1997.

This introduction gives you an overview of:

■ the OCR AS and A Level course
■ how you will be assessed on this unit
■ the different features of this book and how these will aid your learning.

1 The OCR AS and A Level course

This study will form part of your overall History course for the OCR specification, of which there are three Unit Groups and a Topic based Essay. The Unit Groups comprise:

■ British Period Study and Enquiry, which follow chronologically on from each other (Unit Group 1 – AS and A Level).
■ Non-British Period Study (Unit Group 2 – AS and A Level).
■ Thematic Study and Historical Interpretations (Unit Group 3 – A Level only).

This book covers one Period Study Topic (Britain 1951–1997) and one Enquiry Topic (Churchill 1930–1951) from Unit Group 1 of the OCR History specification. You will study both of these for the examination.

During the 1930s Britain experienced both a severe economic depression, and a growing threat from Germany which culminated in the Second World War. The war brought major changes to the country, by both weakening it as a great world power and bringing about major changes to economic and social policy under Labour, from 1945 to 1951. It also brought Winston Churchill, one of its greatest leaders, to power, and his career from 1930 to 1951 forms a major part of this book. In the post-war period Britain lost its empire and appeared to be in political and economic decline. The book explains why the Conservatives dominated the country politically from 1951 to 1964, how political leaders from both major parties after that period dealt with Britain's problems, and also how Margaret Thatcher's election victory in 1979 confirmed the end of the post-war consensus on economic and social policy. The book deals with major events in foreign and colonial policy after 1951 and with the changing relations with Europe.

The chapters in the book correspond to the Key Topics in the specification, with four chapters for each Period Study and three for the Enquiries.

2 How you will be assessed

A Level

Each of the three Unit Groups has an examination paper, whereas the Topic based essay is marked internally but externally moderated.

■ Unit Group 1 – the British Period Study is assessed through two essays, from which you answer one, and the Enquiry is assessed through a source-based question. This counts for 25 per cent of your overall marks.

- Unit Group 2 – the Non-British Period Study is assessed through a shorter answer question and one essay. This counts for 15 per cent of your overall marks.
- Unit Group 3 – the Thematic Study and Historical Interpretations Unit is assessed through two essays which cover at least 100 years, and one in-depth question based on two interpretations of a key event, individual or issue that forms a major part of the theme. This counts for 40 per cent of your overall marks.

For the Topic based essay you will complete a 3000–4000 word essay on a topic of your choice. This counts for 20 per cent of your overall marks.

AS Level

Each of the two Unit Groups has an examination paper:

- Unit Group 1 – the British Period Study is assessed through your choice of one of two essays, and the Enquiry is assessed through two source-based questions. This counts for 50 per cent of your overall marks.
- Unit Group 2 – the Non-British Period Study is assessed through an Essay and an Interpretation Question. The Interpretation Question will come from one of two specified Key Topics. This counts for 50 per cent of your overall marks.

Examination questions for Unit Group 1

For both the AS and A Level you will have been entered for a specific unit and your examination paper will contain only the questions relating to that unit.

There will be two sections in the examination paper. Section A is the Enquiry section and Section B is the Period Study section.

In Section A there will be one set of documents. For the AS there will be three sources and two questions. Question (a) will be worth 10 marks and Question (b) will be worth 20 marks. For the A Level there will be four sources and one question, which will be worth 30 marks.

In Section B there will be two essay questions, both worth 20 marks and you will have to answer one of them. Each essay will be drawn from a different Key Topic, although the questions could be drawn from more than one Key Topic.

AS Section A questions on the Enquiry

The first Section A questions on the Enquiry will be worded as follows for AS:

(a) Use your knowledge of X to assess how useful Source Y is as evidence of Z.

For example:

Use your knowledge of the problems Britain faced in the 1930s to assess how useful Source A is as evidence about how realistic Churchill's view of appeasement was. [10]

In this type of question the key term is 'useful' – this requires you to consider the provenance of the source. It will involve you discussing issues such as who wrote it, when and why it was written and whether the tone or language suggests it might be exaggerated.

The second Section A questions on the Enquiry will be worded as follows for AS:

(b) Using these three sources in their historical context, assess how far they support the view that X was due mainly to Y.

For example:

Using these three sources in their historical context, assess how far they support the view that Churchill was out of office in the 1930s mainly because of his views about India. [20]

This type of question refers to the sources 'in their historical context'. This requires you to explain how events at the time the sources were written might have influenced the author's views. You will also have to consider the provenance of the sources and apply your own knowledge to the sources to test their reliability as evidence when assessing how far they support the view given in the statement.

A Level Section A questions on the Enquiry

Section A questions on the Enquiry will be worded as follows for A Level:

Using these four sources in their historical context, assess how far they support the view that X was due mainly to Y.

For example:

Using these four sources in their historical context, assess how far they support the view that Churchill offered unrealistic criticisms of foreign and defence policies in the 1930s. [30]

As with the second question for AS, this type of question refers to the sources 'in their historical context' (see above for guidance on this).

Section B questions on the Period Study

For AS and A Level Section B questions on the Period Studies the types of questions set will be the same. Examples of questions using some of the more common command terms and specific requirements for each can be found at the end of Period Study chapters. The command terms are important and a key to success is understanding what these terms mean and what you have to do.

Command term	Description	Example in the book
Assess	Weigh up the relative importance of a range of factors and reach a **supported judgement** as to which is the most important.	Page 109
To what extent	Consider the relative importance of the named issue by comparing it with other issues and **reach a balanced judgement** as to its relative importance.	Page 165
How far	Consider the relative importance of the named issue and weigh up its role by comparing it with other issues to **reach a balanced judgement** as to its relative importance.	Page 166
How successful	Consider a range of issues and make a judgement as to how successful each was before **reaching an overall judgement** about success.	Page 140

Answering the questions

Both the AS and A Level examination are one and a half hours in length. Section A carries slightly more marks than Section B and therefore, particularly as you will need time to read the sources, it would sensible to spend about 50 minutes on Section A and 40 minutes on Section B. Before you start any of the questions, make a brief plan. Advice on planning essays is given on pages 109–10.

The answers you write will be marked against the relevant mark scheme. It would be useful to familiarise yourself with these before the examination so that you are aware of the criteria against which your work will be marked. Mark schemes offer guidance, but they cannot cover everything and if you write something that is relevant and accurate, but not in the mark scheme, you will gain credit for it. You will be rewarded for well-argued and supported responses. Marks will not be deducted for information that is incorrect, but you should remember that incorrect knowledge may undermine your argument.

What will the examination paper look like?

The cover of the examination paper will tell you the level for which you have been entered, either AS or A Level. It will tell you the unit number, which for the AS is Y143 and for the A Level Y113. It will also tell you the title of the unit, the date of the examination and the time allowed for the examination. The cover will also give you instructions about the answer booklet and the marks available.

3 About this book

At the start of the Period Study and the Enquiry covered in this book there is a section called 'Gateway'. This provides a one-page summary of background material to the period you are about to study.

Each chapter in the book then covers one of the Key Topics listed in the OCR specification for the unit.

Chapters start with a brief introduction and a series of key questions. An overview of the period or theme of the chapter provides a brief introductory narrative along with a timeline which outlines the key events.

Key questions

The chapters are divided into sections, each addressing one of the key questions listed in the chapter introduction. The key questions may be broken down into sub-questions to help your understanding of the topic. By the end of the section you should be able to answer the key questions.

Key terms

The key terms that you need to understand in order to grasp the important concepts surrounding the topic are emboldened in the chapter the first time they are used and defined in the glossary on page 200.

Sources

As the Enquiry Topics are source-led those chapters will contain a significant number of sources, often with questions to enable you to develop and practise the skills you will need for the examination. There will also be other visual sources within the book.

Activities

In both the Period Study and Enquiry chapters there are activities
to help you develop the key skills needed for the examination. In the
Period Study chapters they will focus on developing analytical skills and
making judgements, whereas in the Enquiry chapters they will focus on
understanding and evaluating sources.

AS Level

There are some elements of the AS examination in Unit 1 that are different
from the A Level, particularly in the Enquiries where two questions are set
and there are fewer sources used. The types of question for AS Level are
identified by an icon and the skills needed for these questions are explained
in AS textboxes which appear throughout Chapters 1–3.

Historical debates

As historians often disagree about the causes or significance of historical
events or personalities, each chapter of the Period Study units has contrasting
extracts from the writings of two historians. Not only will this introduce
you to some of the key historical debates about the period you are studying,
but by using your historical knowledge and the information in the chapter
you will be able to test the views of the historians in order to determine
which view you find more convincing. There will also be a list of books for
further reading on the issue. Knowledge of the debate is not necessary for the
examination in Unit 1, but it will enrich your knowledge and help to develop
a valuable skill, which is further tested in Unit 3 of the A Level.

Summary of the chapter

At the end of each chapter there is a bullet-point list of the key points covered
which will help with revision.

Study Skills

Each chapter has a Study Skills section. These gradually help you to build
up the skills you need for the Period Studies and Enquiries examination
papers, providing examples of parts of strong and weak responses and further
questions and activities in which you can practise the skills.

Revise, reflect, review

At the end of each study topic there is a section which helps you to
consolidate your understanding of the whole topic. It encourages you to
think about the period as a whole and question many of your earlier views.
There will also be further activities to help you prepare for the examination.

Gateway into Churchill, 1929–51

Churchill's career before 1929

- He was from an aristocratic family. His grandfather was the Duke of Marlborough. His father, Lord Randolph Churchill, was a leading Conservative politician.
- He had been a professional soldier serving in India and the Sudan before entering politics as a Conservative MP in 1900, though he joined the Liberals in 1904.
- He rose rapidly and quickly became a minister in 1905. He was in the cabinet by 1908 as president of the board of trade, and then home secretary and first lord of the Admiralty.
- He played a leading role in introducing social reforms before 1914 and then was influential in the First World War before a failed attack on Turkey in 1915 led to his resignation.
- After a brief spell in the army in France, he was back in government in 1917 as minister for munitions.
- He served in Lloyd George's coalition government from 1918 to 1922 and then re-joined the Conservatives and was chancellor of the exchequer 1924–29.

A controversial figure

- Many Conservatives saw him as someone who had betrayed his party by joining the Liberals.
- His support for the use of troops against striking miners in south Wales in 1910 made him unpopular with many in the Labour movement.
- His support for the poorly planned attack on Constantinople in the Gallipoli Landings in 1915 made him widely distrusted.
- He was seen as an extreme opponent of communism because of his support for a war against the new communist regime in Russia after 1917.
- His decision to return Britain to the **Gold Standard** in 1925 was criticised by many economic experts as it made exports dearer.
- He was seen as an extreme opponent of trade unions because of his opposition to the General Strike in 1926.

Churchill's political ideas

- He had supported social reforms and believed government had a duty to help poorer people.
- He opposed any threat to Britain including rebellion in Ireland, both from the Protestant population in Ulster before 1914 who opposed Home Rule and from the Irish who wanted independence.
- He was a strong believer in the British Empire and was determined to defend it.
- He supported the First World War, first by wanting to knock out Turkey by a daring attack; then by building up British arms production as minister of munitions 1917–18. He even served on the western front in person in 1916.
- He bitterly opposed communism, especially after the killing of the Russian Tsar in 1918 and urged Britain, France and the US to send forces against the Russian Revolution.
- He opposed any threat to the monarchy or to the British constitution, urging a very strong line against the 1926 General Strike because he thought it tried to use union power in a political way.

Winston Churchill

Churchill's personality

- He was outspoken, outwardly self-confident and often controversial.
- He was very ambitious and enjoyed being in control.
- He was admired for his writings and for his speeches.
- He loved the House of Commons and relished debates.
- He had a gift for encouraging strong friendships, but also had bitter enemies.
- He had a wide variety of interests and enthusiasms.

Gateway into Britain, 1929

The world of 1929 was very different from the one Churchill knew as a young man and many thought that he had not come to terms with it, a theme which will be considered in this chapter.

The British Empire

- Britain was the head of an empire of 240 million people.
- The Empire was very important and many British people lived and worked in it either in administration, education or in farming, business or church activities.
- Some areas were self-governing: Australia, New Zealand, Canada and South Africa.
- India had limited self-government only.
- Britain's African possessions and its other colonies in Asia were ruled directly.
- Britain also controlled the Suez Canal and dominated Egypt.
- The Empire had helped Britain to win the First World War, but was very costly and difficult to defend.

Society

- Britain had been deeply affected by the loss of over 750,000 men in the First World War. There was a loss of faith in old values of patriotism and a deep reluctance to go to war again.
- There was a rise in the relative wealth and influence of the middle classes as the suburbs grew and the importance of banking and financial services to the economy began to outstrip that of industry.
- The war had confirmed social change with regard to the role of women who had the vote on equal terms with men after 1928 and had much more freedom of movement, dress and way of life than had been true in the previous century.
- The rise of radio, cinema, the popular press, the telephone and the use of motor transport increased awareness of the wider world and improved communications.

Political life

- The two main parties were Conservative and Labour. The Liberals, who had been the major party of change before 1914; had declined to the third party.
- Labour was a relatively new party, representing working people, and had increased its support during and after the First World War to become a national party. It did not form a government until 1924, which lasted under a year, but it did win the election of 1929.
- The Conservatives had lost the 1906 election badly and were out of power until they joined a wartime coalition with Labour and the Liberals in 1915. They were the major party in the continuing coalition from 1916 to 1922 under the Liberal, Lloyd George, but ended the coalition agreement in 1922. They were in power 1922–23 and 1924–29.
- The Liberals had been the great party of reform since 1859 and introduced many important changes, including the beginnings of the modern welfare state. However, the party split during the First World War and were overtaken by Labour. They did not hold office in their own right after 1915.

Britain in 1929

The economy

- Britain had been a great industrial power in the nineteenth century with textiles, iron and steel, engineering, coal and chemical industries leading the world.
- However, by 1929 its older industries were in decline. There was much less demand for its heavy industry products.
- Unemployment had not fallen below a million in the 1920s and trade had been hindered by the high price of the pound after the return to gold.
- In October 1929 the collapse of the US stock market saw the beginning of the Wall Street Crash and a long period of world economic depression which lasted into the 1930s.

Chapter 1

Churchill's view of events, 1929–40

This chapter deals with the period that Churchill spent out of government from 1929 to 1940, his return to the cabinet in 1939 and his appointment as prime minister in 1940. It considers why he was in 'the political wilderness' for so long and whether this should be seen as his own fault. The major areas of disagreement he had with the Conservative-dominated National Governments were over India, rearmament, the abdication and foreign policy. The reasons for these quarrels are analysed. The chapter also examines how realistic his views were about these issues. The main issues of the period 1929–40 to be considered are:

- Why was Churchill out of office for so long, 1929–39?
- What were Churchill's views on India?
- What were Churchill's views on the abdication of Edward VIII?
- What were Churchill's views on rearmament and appeasement?
- Why did Churchill become prime minister in 1940?

The skills needed in answering questions about Churchill are those of using, analysing and assessing historical sources. This chapter introduces the key skill of interpreting sources – that is, understanding their relevance to a historical issue. It also discusses how to assess the value of sources in relation to their provenance. The nature of the evidence and the context in which it was produced is considered in order to assess how far it can be used to confirm an historical view.

Timeline

1929	May	Labour is the largest party after the general election. Churchill goes into opposition
1930	November	The first of three Round Table Conferences on India. Churchill opposes concessions
1931	August	National Government formed under Ramsay MacDonald. Churchill is not included
1933	January	Hitler comes to power
1935	March	Germany reintroduces conscription
	June	Baldwin becomes prime minister. Anglo-German Naval treaty
	August	The Government of India Act
1936	March	Germany remilitarises the Rhineland
		Abdication crisis
1937	May	Neville Chamberlain becomes prime minister
1938	March	Germany annexes Austria
	September	Crisis over Czechoslovakia
		Munich Agreement
	October	Munich debate in the House of Commons
1939	March	Germany invades Bohemia and Moravia (Czechoslovakia)
	September	Britain declares war on Germany and Churchill re-enters government as first lord of the admiralty
1940	April	Norway campaign
	May	German forces invade Low Countries
		Churchill becomes prime minister

Overview

The 1929 general election led to Labour forming a government. Winston Churchill, who had been the Conservative chancellor of the exchequer since 1924, left office. He was not in government again until September 1939, even though he was one of the most experienced and best known political figures of his day. He had been a major figure in governments, both Liberal and Conservative, since 1905 and was to go on to be prime minister from 1940 to 1945 and 1951–55.

The 1930s were an unusual period in his life. They were also an unusual period for Britain. In 1929 the country began to experience the worst economic depression in its history as a result of the Wall Street Crash, a major economic collapse in the USA, which spread to most countries of the world. Politically this led to the creation of a coalition government in 1931 made up of Labour, Liberal and predominantly Conservative political leaders and called the National Government. The economic crisis also brought Hitler and the Nazis to power in Germany. Hitler's policy of rearming Germany and overthrowing the peace treaty of Versailles led to a dangerous period of instability in Europe, which culminated in the outbreak of the Second World War in 1939.

As well as concerns over economic problems and the possible threat from Germany, Britain faced problems in its empire. There had been considerable unrest in India and the rise of opposition to British rule. A campaign of non-violent protest led by Gandhi had disrupted India and British leaders faced the task of making enough concessions to reduce protests while not losing control of the 'jewel in the crown' of the empire. The role of the crown as the head of the empire was thought to be highly important, so a crisis involving the new king, Edward VIII, caused considerable concern. Unable to marry the woman he loved because his intended wife, Mrs Simpson, was a divorced woman, he abdicated in 1936.

There was a great deal of general political agreement about the need to avoid war, the need to reform India, the need to maintain respect for the monarchy and the need to focus on helping economic recovery. In contrast, Churchill found himself isolated politically. His ideas were highly controversial and unpopular:

- He advocated rearming rapidly, whatever the cost, and taking action to prevent German expansion at a time when public opinion was against war and money was short.
- At a time when most people favoured reform, he opposed any weakening of British control in India by giving concessions to Indian opinion.
- He supported Edward VIII even when public opinion was against him.
- His political style and ideas were thought to be old fashioned and out of touch with the realities of dealing with the depression.

However, when war in 1939 came, his experience and determination were more valued and, in May 1940, he became prime minister.

Why was Churchill out of office for so long, 1929–39?

The 1930s were a threatening period for Britain. Led by a ruthless and extreme dictator, Germany had emerged as a threat to European peace. Japan was intent on creating a new empire in the Far East and was threatening China. Italy was ruled by an expansionist dictator. There was civil war in Spain and the Communist regime in Russia was imprisoning and killing large numbers of its own people. Europe and the USA were suffering from the worst economic depression in history.

In this type of dangerous situation, it might have been expected that Churchill would thrive and be needed as a daring and imaginative political leader with massive experience of government. However, this was not the case. He did not hold office again until 1939. He was in conflict with the bulk of his own party and its leaders. He took up a series of unpopular causes and spoke about them in an increasingly reckless way. He became a more isolated figure in British political life, relying on a group of loyal advisers who were seen as outsiders and eccentrics. In the age of radio and cinema, when more people voted than ever before in British history and politicians no longer addressed great public meetings as the major way of communicating with their audiences, Churchill's style of speaking came to seem old-fashioned and out of touch. By the mid-1930s, though mentally and physically vigorous, he was in his 60s and seemed to many to be part of a long-gone imperial age, described so vividly in his autobiography *My Early Life*.

By 1931 the key issues were economic. International investors and markets needed a calm, confident and united government. Even within the Conservative party many saw Churchill as unhelpful in establishing that. In any case, for many people, Churchill was a renegade. They remembered his pre-war speeches attacking Conservative views on the House of Lords and on Ireland. During the First World War his Gallipoli campaign was condemned as reckless. It achieved almost nothing at great human cost. The economists of the 1930s argued that Churchill had made the wrong decision in returning Britain to the gold standard when he was chancellor of the exchequer in 1925; indeed, Britain had to leave it in September 1931. When the Conservatives joined with the Labour leader MacDonald and some of the Liberals in 1931 to form a National Government to deal with the perceived national financial and economic crisis, there was no room for Churchill.

The Wall Street Crash affected him personally, wiping out his investments and savings and compelling him to write for a living. He wrote both journalistic pieces and historical studies, including a book on his ancestor Marlborough, in order to maintain his beloved home Chartwell, in Kent.

There were several issues that set him aside from mainstream Conservative thinking:

- **India**
  The bulk of political opinion held that negotiating with the Indian nationalists and their high-profile leader Gandhi was necessary and wise. Churchill believed in uncompromising opposition to any move to make India more independent.
- **The abdication of King Edward VIII**
  The behaviour of David, Prince of Wales, who became king in 1936 as Edward VIII, did not command the respect of many Conservative politicians and voters. His desire to marry a twice-divorced American woman was widely unpopular, but it was supported by Churchill out of loyalty to the throne.
- **Rearmament**
  When public opinion was clearly against war and the economy was weak Churchill urged rearmament and won little support.
- **Concessions to Hitler**
  Churchill made it clear that Britain should resist Germany's expansion. He opposed the appeasement policy of the government which allowed Germany to take over the German-speaking areas of the state of Czechoslovakia in 1938 after threats of war. As the horrors of the First World War were still a vivid memory, the idea of Britain going to war to prevent Germany ruling over German-speakers was unpopular among many British people and politicians.

What were Churchill's views on India?

Churchill had served in India as a young officer. He took the late-Victorian view that India was 'the jewel in the crown' of the whole British Empire and that it had to be protected, no matter what, in order to maintain the empire. He took it for granted that Britain's greatness was bound up with its imperial status. He also took the view, common among those who had served and worked in India, that British rule alone prevented the domination of the Hindu elites over the large Muslim Indian population. British rule had ensured the end of what he saw as barbaric practices and meant economic and social progress. He thought that it had ensured good government, prevented endemic corruption and protected the weak. He also had a strong belief in the racial superiority of the Anglo-Saxons and in their destiny to rule over and develop 'lesser' peoples.

Source A Churchill is shown as the 'lone ex-minister' obsessed with preventing change in India.

HIS MORNING EXERCISE.
THE LONE EX-MINISTER UPON HIS ELEPHANT.

[Mr. WINSTON CHURCHILL—not without a large body of Conservative support in the country—continues to demonstrate his opposition to the policy of the National Government.]

Cartoon from 1931.

Source B Churchill gives his views about Indian people living in East Africa to the minister responsible for India.

The Indians in East Africa are mainly of a very low class of coolies (labourers) and the idea that they should be put on an equality with the Europeans is revolting to every white man throughout British Africa. Montagu in his reply said that this view 'might have been written by a European settler of a most fanatical type'.

Conversation with Edward Montagu, 1921.

Activity

1 How do Sources A and B show that Churchill was seen as an old-fashioned figure?
2 In what ways could they help to explain why he was out of office in the 1930s?
3 Using your knowledge of the situation in India and British policy towards it, how useful is Source B in explaining why Churchill was thought to be extreme. (AS)

British rule in India

British rule in India was coming under increasing pressure in the 1920s and 30s from an Indian population who wanted self-governance and representation. This pressure came from both the educated elite and increasingly from the mass populace led by Mohandas 'Mahatma' Gandhi. Dressing like a poor farmer, he developed *satyagraha*, literally 'holding onto truth'. This led him to the pursuit of freedom by non-violent protest. Britain responded to the unrest which these protesters caused with a mixture of repression and reform. The Rowlatt Acts of 1919 increased police powers by allowing imprisonment without trial but the 1919 Montagu–Chelmsford measures gave locally elected councils a measure of control over some internal matters. In April 1919 Gandhi led a mass campaign against the Rowlatt Acts and troops fired on a protesting crowd at Amritsar, killing 400 and wounding 1200. This brutality gave Indian nationalism huge numbers of new supporters.

There followed a mass civil disobedience campaign. In the late 1920s the British government faced calls for independence, and in 1930 Gandhi led a mass march to the sea to protest about the salt tax by gathering natural sea salt. Numerous arrests followed, including Gandhi, who was released from jail to attend conferences in London in 1930 and 1931 to get agreement on ending the conflict. However, these had limited success and he was arrested on his return. Nevertheless, in 1933 Britain announced its intentions of allowing India greater self-government. This paved the way for the Government of India Act of 1935, which took effect in 1937. The electorate expanded to 35 million (out of a population of 338 million) and there were elected legislatures set up to deal with local affairs.

Churchill's reaction to the independence movement

Churchill was bitterly opposed to the movement for greater independence for India, which gathered pace after 1918. More hard-headed analysts looked at the increasing costs of maintaining the status quo; the existence of Indian educated elites; and the changes in public and international opinion. Before 1918 only one person in seven was entitled to vote in Britain; British women and many male workers had little more say in the democratic process than Indian people. However, after 1918 Britain had become more democratic. Australia, New Zealand, Canada and South Africa had been utterly loyal to Britain during the First World War despite enjoying self-government within the Empire. To oppose any change in India did not seem to be motivated by anything except prejudice. More self-government, carefully guided, did not seem a danger, and it was essential to separate moderate Indian people from the more radical movement led by Gandhi. Churchill saw it as his duty to launch a personal crusade to defend Britain's interests as he saw them and he found himself allied with the most reactionary elements in Britain.

Source C Churchill, speaking to the India Empire Society. This Society was supported by many ex-officers and was strongly opposed to any change in India.

No agreement reached at the round table conference will be binding. The British nation has no intention whatever of relinquishing effectual control of Indian life and progress. The bold experiment of the Montagu reforms and Lord Irwin's efforts at compromise have failed. It is time for Parliament to reclaim its right to restrict Indian constitutional liberties. Gandhi-ism and all it stands for will have to be grappled with and crushed. It is no use trying to satisfy a tiger by feeding it cat's meat.

Speech by Churchill, December 1930.

Mohandas Gandhi, 1869–1948

Gandhi was a London-trained barrister who worked in South Africa between 1893 and 1914 and improved the rights of Indians there. He became a leading figure in protesting about British rule by non-violent means. Though he resigned from the nationalist Congress Party in 1934 he remained a major influence. He contributed much to Indian independence in 1947. He was assassinated in 1948.

▲ A statue of Mohandas Gandhi in San Francisco, USA

Source D Churchill speaks to the West Essex Conservative Association about India.

It is alarming and even nauseating to see Mr Gandhi, a seditious [treasonous] Middle Temple lawyer now posing as a *fakir* [holy man] of a type well-known in the East, striding half naked up the steps of the Viceroy's palace, while he is organising and conducting a campaign of civil disobedience, to negotiate on equal terms with the representative of the King-Emperor [King George V]. Such a spectacle can only increase the unrest in India and the danger to which white people there are exposed.

Speech by Churchill, February 1931.

Activity

Read Sources C (on page 12) and D and answer these questions:
1 What do they show us about what Churchill thought of Gandhi and his campaign? (Think of the implications of the comparison with a tiger!)
2 Do the extracts contain similar views about Churchill's attitudes and personality?
3 Who was Churchill talking to and would that have affected his language?
4 What was happening to affect how Churchill thought and spoke about India?
5 Does the information in this chapter help you to see these statements as typical of Churchill, or not?

Churchill's increasingly extreme public statements and his support of eccentric and racist organisations that were opposed to negotiations and change isolated him from the more moderate Conservatives. Stanley Baldwin, the Conservative leader, undermined Churchill's position through calm and moderate speeches and by mocking references to Churchill's views.

In 1934 Churchill was bitter in his attacks on government ministers over India reform proposals. Even his former supporter Leo Amery MP said that it was Churchill's 'unique achievement to stir up a hornets' nest where there were no hornets'. In aiming to make Sir Samuel Hoare, the Secretary for India, resign he threatened to shatter the Conservative party. This won him only ridicule from Conservative MPs and the deep distrust of the Conservative leadership. Yet when the Government of India Act was finally passed, Churchill stopped agitating and even invited a close friend and political supporter of Gandhi to lunch, saying he wished India well: *'India, I fear, is a burden to us. If India could look after herself, we would be delighted. Make the reforms a success!'* (Arthur Herman, *Churchill and Gandhi*, 2009, page 401.)

Churchill has strong opinions or just likes to be outspoken?

To consider

How important was Churchill's stance on India in contributing to the decision not to include him in the National Government in September 1931?

What were Churchill's views on the abdication of Edward VIII?

Despite the crises that Britain had faced since 1910 both at home and abroad – war, social unrest, discontent in the Empire and economic problems – the monarchy had been a stable element in British life. George V, who reigned from 1910 to 1936, was in many ways the first of the modern monarchs. His respectable lifestyle, in contrast to the mistresses and visits to Parisian houses of ill-repute of his father, was in accord with the desire for respectability of middle-class Britain. George V had been a solid supporter of the war effort. His bearing was dignified and suitably naval. He broadcast directly to the nation, but both he and Queen Mary kept an appropriate degree of reserve and aloofness. David, his eldest son, has been seen as neurotic and unstable. He had a reputation as a playboy and, despite doing his duty by serving in the armed forces during the First World War and by carrying out imperial tours and official openings, his private life was less respectable. He had a predilection for older women, regardless of whether they were already married, and for parties more typical of the 'roaring twenties' than the more staid formal gatherings of his parents. He also had a tendency to make off-the-cuff remarks which could be seen as political interference. Some believed that he was an admirer of Nazi Germany.

However, there had been erratic heirs in the past who had knuckled down to do their royal duties. The main problem was his attachment to Wallis Simpson, an American woman who had previously been divorced before marrying Mr Simpson, who may have encouraged her liaison with the Prince. Whether Wallis liked adventure or was driven by the Prince of Wales's rather obsessive devotion into actions which went beyond her control is debated. However, following her second divorce, David, now King Edward VIII, was determined to marry her. This raised a considerable constitutional issue. The King was officially the head of the Church of England and as such committed to defending its values, which included opposition to divorce. In November 1936, Prime Minister Stanley Baldwin told the King that public opinion would not accept Wallis Simpson as Queen. Edward proposed a morganatic marriage in which she would merely be Consort, not Queen. However, this would have required parliament's approval both in Britain and in the self-governing dominions. The cabinet did not give its approval. If the King married Wallis, then it would have meant the resignation of the government and the possible break-away of the dominions. Thus there were very serious constitutional and imperial issues at stake at a time of dangers from abroad and continuing economic difficulties.

In December 1936 Edward broadcast his speech of abdication.

The first studio portrait of Edward VIII (then Prince of Wales) and Mrs Simpson, 1935.

Churchill and the abdication

Churchill took up a minority position. He was a member of a limited and informal group called 'The King's Friends' who undertook to support the monarch for reasons of personal loyalty and chivalry. The bulk of parliament, despite any personal sympathy, did not take that view. In one of the worst days of his career Churchill misjudged the mood in the House of Commons and made a speech in favour of the King that was shouted down. Once again, Churchill seemed rooted in the past. In Edwardian Britain, for instance, King Edward VII (1901–10) had been well-known for his mistresses and raucous behaviour, but the Britain of the 1930s had a different moral outlook.

Source E Churchill, speaking to the House of Commons on the day Edward VIII abdicated.

It was my duty as Home Secretary, more than a quarter of a century ago, to stand beside his present Majesty and proclaim his style and titles at his investiture as Prince of Wales amid the sunlit battlements of Carnarvon Castle, and ever since then he has honoured me here, and also in wartime, with his personal kindness and, I may even say, friendship. I should have been ashamed if, in my independent and unofficial position, I had not cast about for every lawful means, even the most forlorn, to keep him on the throne of his fathers.

Speech by Churchill, 10 December 1936.

To consider

How important was Churchill's attitude to the abdication in keeping him out of office compared to his views on India? Are these attitudes linked? Did they all make him seem outdated and out of touch with the public mood?

Activity

1 What does the speech in Source E show about Churchill's attitude to the monarchy?
2 What do you think about its style?

What were Churchill's views on rearmament and appeasement?

What were Churchill's views on rearmament?

What linked India and Churchill's next major concern was the defence of British power and influence. In January 1933 Hitler became chancellor of Germany. His views about the need to rearm and end the restrictions of the **Treaty of Versailles** were well known. Churchill did not object to the concept of a nationalist dictatorship, as his praise for Mussolini's rule in Italy in the 1920s had shown.

However, when German rearmament started, Churchill became alarmed and wrote and spoke about the dangers. Why did he object so much?

- Churchill saw the new regime in Germany as brutal. He disliked its racism and the violence it displayed, for example, in the murder of opponents.
- Churchill feared a repeat of the situation prior to 1914 when Germany had been a threat to the peace of Europe and had challenged Britain by building a new naval fleet. Churchill had written about this in his history of the First World War, *The World Crisis*.
- Unlike the other leaders, Churchill had been a member of the government which had agreed the Treaty of Versailles which Hitler now wanted to break.
- Churchill was especially worried about air power and Hitler building up a new German air force. He understood the dangers of air warfare and feared that Britain would be defenceless. As colonial secretary he had approved air attacks on Iraqi rebels in 1920 and knew the effects of aerial bombing.

Churchill used his position as a backbench MP and his journalism to utter warnings about the need to rearm. In his history of the Second World War, *The Gathering Storm*, Churchill quoted a speech to the Commons he made in 1934:

Mussolini

Benito Mussolini (1883–1945) led the Italian fascist movement and established a one-party dictatorship in Italy after taking office as premier in 1922. He believed in the expansion of Italy's influence and territory and in creating a new type of state which would unite all classes behind a powerful leader. He waged a war of conquest in Abyssinia (now Ethiopia) in 1935, participated in the Spanish Civil War 1936–39 and allied with Hitler from 1936. He entered the Second World War in 1940 and this led to Italy being invaded by Britain and the USA and Mussolini being overthrown.

▲ Benito Mussolini

In 1936 Germany will be definitely and substantially stronger in the air than Great Britain. There is cause for anxiety because of the physical strength of the German air force [and] the character of the present German dictatorship. If the Government have to admit at any time in the next few years that the German air forces are stronger than our own, then they will ... have failed in their prime duty to the country.

(Winston Churchill, *The Gathering Storm*, 1948, page 101.)

↗ Contradiction

However, there were problems. First, his critics pointed out that he himself had been deeply responsible for disarming in the 1920s and for maintaining the 10 Year Rule. (This was a rule that defence planning should not consider a war likely for the next ten years and justified cut-backs in defence. It lasted from 1919 to 1932.) Second, the financial crisis had necessitated, at least in the view of the governments and their advisers, deep cuts in government expenditure. When poorer people were suffering, and when the 1934 **means tests** imposed stringent conditions on any public help for the unemployed or those in poverty, there would need to be a very compelling reason to begin an arms race with Germany.

Many felt that the First World War had originated in such an arms race, which was seen as dangerous. It was also seen as unnecessary: the idea that Germany could be restricted to a small army, no air force and a weak navy for ever on the basis of a peace treaty which even at the time had seemed harsh and unrealistic was challenged. Hitler may have been a violent and unsavoury character, but it was not unreasonable to many that Germany should build up its defences, especially as the French had very large forces and there was a possible threat from the Soviet Union. It seemed to many that Churchill was too much part of a pre-1914 mentality of opposition to Germany. Also, his tendency to exaggerate the figures and to speak in alarmist terms reduced his credibility. With support for the League of Nations strong, many felt that international disputes should be left to negotiations organised on a worldwide scale and not to individual countries and their armed forces. When circumstances changed after Hitler's policies and utterances became more aggressive, the government did rearm on a very extensive scale. So after 1938 rearmament was not an issue and it seemed to many that the government had acted at the right time.

Source F Prime Minister Stanley Baldwin speaks on the problems of rearming Britain. He is referring to a Labour victory at the by-election at Fulham East in October 1933, when a Labour candidate defeated a Conservative who was campaigning on the need to rearm.

From 1933 I was very worried about what was happening in Europe. There was probably a stronger pacifist feeling running through the country than at any time since the War. You will remember the election of Fulham in 1933. I asked myself: what chance there was within the next year or two of public feeling being changed enough to give the government any support for rearmament? Supposing I had gone to the country and said that Germany was rearming and we must rearm. Does anyone think that this pacific democracy would have rallied to that cry at that moment? I cannot think of anything that would have made the loss of the election from my point of view more certain.

Speech by Stanley Baldwin in the House of Commons, 12 November 1936.

League of Nations

Established in 1920, this association of world nations to maintain peace was the inspiration of the US President Wilson, although the USA was never a member. It was remarkable that such an organisation was created at all and it did have minor successes. However, Germany was only a member between 1926 and 1933 and Russia between 1934 and 1939. Dependent on France and Britain, the League could not deal effectively with aggression by Japan, Italy and Germany after 1931.

To consider

Which was more important in keeping Churchill out of office, his views on India or pressing the government to rearm? Does Source F help you decide?

What were Churchill's views on Germany and appeasement after 1933?

Churchill's concern about the growing power of Germany under a new and very determined leader led him to oppose the government's policy of trying to deal with Hitler's grievances by negotiation, rather than building up a strong alliance and increasing Britain's defences.

Central to Churchill's career in the 1930s was his view about the **appeasement** policy the government followed towards Germany.

Ironically, Churchill himself used the term, urging the 'appeasement of European hatreds' in the 1920s. Britain was a net gainer from the First World War. The threat from Germany and its fleet and the dangerous possibility of German domination of Europe and control of the coastline of Belgium and northern France had been ended. Britain had shown itself a major European military power. The British navy was formidable and, after 1918, the British Empire had grown to include some key oil-rich possessions in the Middle East. All Britain had to do was to maintain the status quo. However, the war did not seem like a victory given the huge casualties and the on-going disturbances in Europe. It would be only a matter of time before Germany and Russia would want to recover their lands.

British policy could have been to maintain enough force to keep the gains and meet any threats. But neither public opinion nor Britain's economic strength permitted this. Instead British statesmen disarmed and put their faith in a mixture of international agreements like the Locarno Pact and in membership of the new League of Nations.

The British leaders of the 1930s thus inherited a dangerous situation, created partly by Churchill himself who had insisted on reducing arms in the 1920s. Developments in military technology – especially aircraft and tanks – meant that existing weaponry was in any case outdated. There was little money for upgrading. The nation was deeply hostile to another war and to the type of military mobilisation that it had endured between 1914 and 1918.

When the first aggression appeared in the Far East in 1931, with the Japanese invasion of Chinese Manchuria, the tone was set for the decade. There was no suggestion of military action or effective alliance with the USA, France or other Pacific powers to support China. Priorities were domestic, not foreign, disputes. Electoral popularity drove policy: the Conservative leader Stanley Baldwin openly admitted that rearmament would have meant the loss of the 1935 general election (see Source F on page 16).

German rearmament in the 1930s

Hitler reintroduced conscription in 1935, breaking the Treaty of Versailles. His numerically small forces remilitarised the Rhineland in March 1936, again breaking Versailles. The British were more anxious to stop French action against Germany that could lead to a war, rather than taking any action themselves. As Germany had left the League of Nations in 1933, this body could not act – and in any case had little reason to. Italy had aligned itself with Britain and France against German expansion into Austria in the Stresa Front in April 1935. However, Mussolini was no longer a possible ally because Britain had been reluctantly forced by public opinion to condemn Mussolini's invasion of the African state of Ethiopia in 1935, although it had done nothing to stop it.

The Locarno Pact, 1925

An agreement between France, Britain, Italy and Germany guaranteeing Germany's western frontiers as established by the Treaty of Versailles in 1919.

Mussolini and Ethiopia

Mussolini used border incidents with Italian Somaliland to justify an invasion of Ethiopia in 1935. Ethiopia appealed to the League of Nations. Britain and France felt they must support the League but needed to keep Italian friendship against Hitler, so Sir Samuel Hoare, the British Foreign Secretary, and Pierre Laval for France made an agreement (the Hoare–Laval Pact) to allow Mussolini to keep most of Ethiopia as a possible compromise. This caused a storm of protest in both France and Britain and had to be dropped. Sanctions were imposed, but weakly, on Italy. As a result, Italy was not stopped from taking Ethiopia, was angered by Britain and France and drew closer to Hitler.

Unable and unwilling to stop German rearmament, the government decided to try and limit it by agreement. The Anglo-German Naval Treaty of 1935 had given British approval to Germany developing its fleet, provided that it was limited to only 35 per cent of the British fleet. This broke the treaties of Versailles and Locarno. The argument was that Germany might develop its fleet even more without restriction and negotiation. Churchill was horrified.

Chamberlain and appeasement

The incoming prime minister, Neville Chamberlain (who took office in 1937) did not approve of British policy either, but for different reasons. He saw the policy of reacting to events and piecemeal negotiation as dangerous; it seemed to him that foreign policy was drifting. However, his solution was to accept that Germany did have legitimate grievances and to negotiate rationally about them. Chamberlain had little faith in international bodies like the League of Nations or vague agreements for peace like the Kellogg–Briand Pact of 1928. Chamberlain believed that coming to a negotiated agreement with Germany would reduce the danger of Britain being drawn into war and allow time to build up defences and recover economically. Public opinion in Britain and the Empire would not support any decisive action unless everything possible had been done to negotiate with Germany over legitimate grievances. There was a widespread belief that, if more negotiations had taken place in 1914 and the British position had been clear, then the First World War might have been avoided.

Chamberlain looked at the situation as it was: the chiefs of the armed forces had told the government that, if peace policies failed, Britain could not fight a war against Germany in Europe, Italy in the Mediterranean and Japan in the Far East at the same time because of a lack of resources. There was a small regular army with massive commitments in the Empire; the navy could not ensure both home defence and commitment to worldwide war and the air force needed building up before it could both defend Britain and support any actions overseas.

Chamberlain's solution was to negotiate proactively with Germany to prevent war and build up defences in case appeasement failed. This had the support of most of his party. The Labour opposition had not supported rearmament. The difference between the parties was not about taking action but over the type of negotiation needed to prevent war, with Labour supporting **collective security**. Those who opposed appeasement were a minority. Again Churchill found himself in an unrepresentative minority group.

German expansion

The news that Germany had recommenced conscription in 1935 and had exceeded the limits in aircraft production established by the Treaty of Versailles in 1919 was greeted with dismay by Churchill. For him the priority was defence against what he perceived as a German threat. This argument was made less credible to the public and government by Hitler's well-thought-out indifference to regaining the German colonies in Africa and the Pacific lost to Britain and other Allied powers after the First World War. If Hitler demanded the European lands Germany had lost, then Britain would not be directly threatened, and many people felt that it was not Britain's concern as these lands contained German speakers. The restoration of lands lost at Versailles or ending restrictions on Germans being in the same country did not pose an obvious threat to Britain.

Kellogg–Briand Pact

The work of the US Secretary of State, Frank B. Kellogg, and the French Foreign Minister, Aristide Briand, this pact outlawed war as a means of settling international disputes. Originally signed by 15 nations in August 1928, another 47 subsequently signed. In 1928 a major war seemed a long way off and no mechanism for actually enforcing the pact was set up. Although Japan, Italy and Germany had all signed the pact, it was routinely ignored in the 1930s.

Nevertheless, the long-standing British interest in not seeing any one power dominate Europe remained, but to engage the public in matters of balance of power was difficult. Nazi Germany was an unpleasant regime, but had not yet launched its later policy of murdering millions of Jewish people or put itself outside normal relations with Britain. The Olympic Games of 1936 held in Berlin after the remilitarisation of the Rhineland was seen as a sign that Germany was a 'normal' European country.

The abdication crisis (see pages 13–15) proved a distraction in 1936, and it was not until March 1938 when Neville Chamberlain was prime minister that the next European crisis – the annexation by Germany of Austria took place. Hitherto prevented by opposition from Mussolini, the annexation went directly against the Treaty of Versailles, but appeared to be popular in both Germany and Austria. There were limited grounds for any action and, despite French protests, British reactions were mild. The greater problem came when a now confident Hitler stirred up unrest among the German speakers in the border areas of Czechoslovakia (see the map below) and complained about their supposed ill-treatment in provocative speeches and protests to the Czech government.

The so-called 'Sudetenland' (see the map below) had never been part of Germany. There were German speakers in many areas of Europe – including northern Italy – which had not been in the German Reich created in 1871. Czechoslovakia was a democracy, albeit one which had substantial ethnic minorities. It had alliances with both the Soviet Union and France. Moving the border would remove vital fortifications and make her defenceless. Britain was not obliged to act, but the French were. If France supported the Czechs, who had a large army of 35 divisions, then there would be a European war which Britain could not have ignored. Chamberlain's government put pressure on the Czechs to make concessions and, as agitation grew among

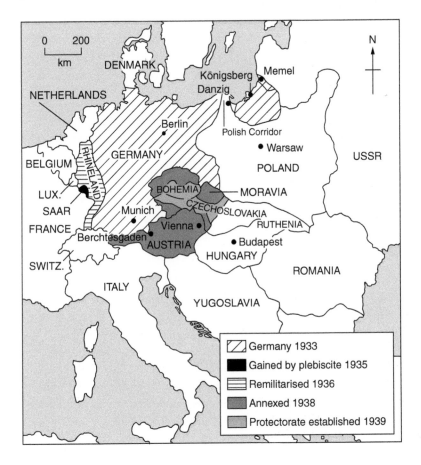

◀ Central Europe in September 1938.

the German speakers in Czechoslovakia, and Hitler's speeches became more war-like, Chamberlain took a bold decision in flying to see Hitler to negotiate an agreement. However, given that Britain was not directly involved and an agreement involved another independent country – Czechoslovakia – this action was dubious on grounds of both validity and morality.

There was no attempt to involve the League of Nations and very little discussion with what would now be called the international community. Chamberlain acted virtually alone in an attempt to avoid having to take a decision about whether to join a war. Having negotiated an agreement for self-government in the Sudetenland at a meeting with Hitler in Germany, Chamberlain was outmanoeuvred by Hitler who, sensing that Britain would do nothing, repudiated it and insisted on full union of German-speaking areas with Germany.

In the face of this humiliation, Britain made some preparations for war, though not very fully. There was much relief when Mussolini offered mediation and a four-power conference met at Munich in September 1938. There was little attempt to resist Hitler's demands. The conference had been the suggestion of Hitler's fellow dictator with whom he was allied in the grand-sounding, but not very binding, Pact of Steel. The French government was anxious not to fulfil its obligations to the Czechs. Chamberlain pursued personal diplomacy and, without consultation, asked Hitler to sign a pact guaranteeing future consultation. He regarded this as somehow a diplomatic triumph. He waved it to cheering crowds on his return and claimed that he had gained 'peace for our time'. There was tremendous admiration for Chamberlain's efforts to keep peace, and leading military figures were relieved. Chamberlain was given large numbers of gifts by admiring members of the public and songs were composed in his honour. However, when the immediate relief had subsided there was growing concern. Churchill memorably expressed it when he said in a debate on Munich that Britain had suffered a defeat.

Source G Churchill, speaking in the debate in the House of Commons on the Munich Agreement.

....

I find unendurable the sense of our country falling into the power, into the orbit and influence of Nazi Germany and of our existence being dependent on their goodwill and **pleasure** …

There has been gross neglect and deficiency of our defences … we have sustained a defeat without a war … this is only the beginning of **the reckoning**. This is only the first sip of a bitter cup which will be **proffered** to us year by year, unless by a **supreme recovery of our moral health and martial vigour**, we rise again and stand for freedom as in the olden time.

Speech by Churchill, October 1938.

Rationally, Chamberlain had been justified in buying time for rearmament and avoiding a war for which Britain was clearly unprepared in every way. However, Hitler had been greatly encouraged by a bloodless victory and had gained almost everything he wanted. Britain had been seen as weak and willing to betray one of eastern Europe's few flourishing democracies. There had been no recourse to the League of Nations, and there was a considerable danger that Germany would now go on to dominate Europe, something that Britain had been unable to accept in 1914 and could not accept in 1939.

Activity

1 The style of Source G is very dramatic and is not in everyday language. Try to rewrite it in a simpler way to ensure that the meaning is clear. Find alternatives for the words in bold.

2 What did Churchill mean by 'the first sip of a bitter cup'?

3 Why do you think Churchill spoke in this way?

4 How would you decide whether his following statements were justified?

There has been … neglect and deficiency of our defences …
… we have sustained a defeat …
… this is only the beginning of the reckoning

5 What do you think the supporters of Chamberlain might have said about this speech?

Britain's rearmament now was accelerated and a growing number of people began to lose faith in any attempt to negotiate with Hitler. The German occupation of Bohemia and Moravia and the dismemberment of the defenceless Czech state in March 1939 was a sign of things to come. Chamberlain was now forced into exactly the sort of 'gesture politics' that he had hoped to avoid and offered a number of guarantees to European states including Poland. Britain could not possibly defend Poland from German attempts to regain the lands lost at Versailles. The guarantee was virtually meaningless and it may have been unwise of the Poles to accept it, as it annoyed Hitler but did not give Poland any meaningful military support against him. By now Churchill had stopped his criticisms of the government and was doing his best to build bridges. His prestige was rising as the man who had stood firm against Hitler, even though his alternative policies were not especially realistic.

Munich – was Churchill's reaction realistic?

When Hitler began backing the demands of the German people in the Sudetenland and there was the danger of a major European crisis, there were a number of options open to Britain. The first was to remain uninvolved. Churchill was strongly against this attitude: Britain was a major European power, a signatory to the treaties which ended the First World War and which would be broken by any territorial change in Czechoslovakia. However, Germans merely gaining more local self-government would not have been a reason to intervene, and there was a case for doing nothing. Britain was not committed to Czechoslovakia formally. The danger was that France and the Soviet Union might act, which could have precipitated a general European war and Britain would then have had to decide whether to stay out or take part, in much the same way as in 1914.

Churchill, unlike some Conservative MPs, did not favour staying out of European affairs. But he rejected the second option – of taking steps to prevent war by persuading Czechoslovakia to make concessions and to persuade Hitler to accept those concessions which were short of outright annexation. There were considerable objections to this. It assumed that it was possible to negotiate meaningfully with Hitler; that what was at stake was really revision of the Treaty of Versailles with Hitler's pronouncements about dominating Europe and the destruction of communism and the Jewish population in Europe dismissed as crowd-pleasing rhetoric. It ruled out collective security and indicated that Britain thought the League of Nations was now irrelevant. It also ruled out joint action with France and the Soviet Union and a possible **Grand Alliance** of countries ready to stop German aggression. The morality of handing over virtual control of part of another country's territory, endangering the anti-Hitler Germans who lived in Czechoslovakia and giving in to obvious aggressive agitation was also a problem.

It was the latter points that moved Churchill. His view was that it was moral cowardice to give in to aggression; that a firm stand with both the League and a widespread alliance of other nations was necessary; and that Britain had shown weakness which would encourage further German expansion. Oddly, the idea that Poland might be next on the list was not discussed as Churchill did not foresee an end to the friendly relations established between Germany and Poland in 1934. The implication in Churchill's view was that, if necessary, Britain should have gone to war, though this was not very clearly and directly stated. At the very least he thought there should have been a forceful response which opposed Germany, made in conjunction with an alliance of other nations.

The Polish Guarantee, 31 March 1939

The guarantee said that 'In the event of any action which clearly threatened Polish independence and which the Polish government accordingly considered it vital to resist with their national forces, His Majesty's government would feel themselves bound at once to lend the Polish government all support in their power.' The British guaranteed Poland's independence but not its existing territorial borders. In the event, when Poland was invaded by Germany in September 1939, Britain decided that it was not within its power to do very much.

▲ General Francisco Franco

The Spanish Civil War, 1936–39

The Spanish Civil War broke out when a military rebellion led by General Francisco Franco, among others, tried to overthrow the left-wing Republican government. The nation was bitterly divided. Nazi Germany and fascist Italy helped the army and the right. The USSR helped the Republic, though Russian-supported communists clashed with other left-wing groups and weakened resistance against Franco's supporters who were victorious in 1939. Britain remained neutral, but Conservative leaders were concerned about the prospect of a communist victory in Spain.

Activity

Look at Source H.

1 What is the source saying about one of Churchill's main ideas – the need for a Grand Alliance?

2 Do you think Chamberlain was right?

Arguments against Churchill's view

The idea that Britain should have gone to war in 1938 is where Churchill's analysis began to break down.

■ If opposition to Hitler had led to war, who would Britain's allies be? There had been no discussions with France or any other country of any joint action in case of war.

■ Britain did not have an expeditionary force ready for war. Its troops were tied down in peace-keeping activities in the Empire, particularly in Palestine.

■ Any move to war had to take into account that either or both of Italy and Japan would take advantage of war in Europe to threaten Britain's vital interests – Egypt and the Suez Canal and India, South East Asia and even Australia – which could not be easily defended. Churchill had very little understanding of the vulnerability of Britain in the Far East and his speeches and writings barely considered that in 1938 Japan was fighting a bitter expansionist war in China and needed the raw materials of western colonies in South East Asia – rubber, ores and oil.

■ Churchill had been relentlessly hostile to the communist Soviet Union which was undergoing massive internal change in the 1930s. It was unlikely that any meaningful alliance could be made with Stalin, given the concerns about Russian activities in the Spanish Civil War and the distrust in France of communism, let alone the hostility of conservative opinion in Britain.

■ France had looked consistently to Britain to provide excuses for not acting. There were no plans for a 1914-style French attack on Germany and little hope of linking up with Czech resistance. Opinion in France was profoundly opposed to any action which risked a repeat of the heavy losses of 1914–18 and the vast defensive Maginot Line was a defensive measure, not a means of attacking Germany and saving the Czech people.

■ The smaller nations of eastern Europe would not have been militarily effective, even if they had decided to join Britain in war against Germany; many of them were more concerned about the threat from the Soviet Union.

■ The majority of public opinion in the USA favoured isolationism; the Neutrality Acts passed by Congress prevented even supplying other countries engaged in war, let alone joining them. US concern was focused not on Europe but on the Pacific where the threat of Japan was more pressing.

■ Churchill expressed enthusiasm for the League of Nations, but that had proved consistently ineffective in preventing aggression since 1931.

Source H Chamberlain gives his view on a possible Grand Alliance.

The plan of the Grand Alliance, as Winston calls it, had occurred to me long before he mentioned it. I talked about it to Lord Halifax, and we submitted it to the Chiefs of Staff and Foreign Office experts. There is everything to be said for it until you come to examine its practicability. From that moment, its attraction vanishes. You only have to look at the map to see that nothing that France or Britain could do could possibly save Czechoslovakia from being overrun by the Germans if they wanted to do so.

Chamberlain in a letter to his sister, 20 March 1938.

In many ways Churchill could propose no real alternative to appeasement. His critics in the House of Commons were quick to point out the flaws in his logic, but really that was to miss the point. His rhetoric hit the mark when he spoke of moral defeat as it summed up a lot of the concerns about the future that critics of Chamberlain felt.

The situation after Munich

Public and political opinion in Britain changed after 1938. If Munich were repeated then European democracy had no real future and neither did Britain's position as a great power. Public opinion began to swing after Munich and the events of March 1939 and the end of Czechoslovakia confirmed the change of mood. Churchill's position had become less unrealistic because opinion both in Britain and in the Empire – vital if Britain were to survive a war – did not find by 1939 the prospect of war as unthinkable as it had earlier. By 1939 conscription, planning for air raids, the formation of an expeditionary force and a much enlarged air force had made war more of a possible option than it had been at any time since 1919.

The British government's guarantee to Poland did not make war inevitable, but it would be hard for any invasion of Poland not to lead to British intervention. Hitler made a non-aggression pact with the USSR in August 1939 which meant that he could be sure of being able to defeat Poland without Russian intervention, and he gambled that an invasion of Poland would not be met with immediate military action by either Britain or France. Indeed, there was the possibility that they would not go to war. The lands gained by Poland in 1919 were the ones closest to German hearts and their recovery would complete the destruction of the Treaty of Versailles and open the way to eastward expansion.

German forces invaded Poland on 1 September 1939 and Chamberlain asked Churchill to become a member of an inner war cabinet. But on 2 September there was still no British declaration of war. In Churchill's own words: 'I thought it probable that a last-minute effort was being made to preserve peace.'

However, the House of Commons made it clear that any last-minute concession by Britain was unacceptable and an ultimatum was issued for Germany to withdraw. On 11 a.m. on 3 September the ultimatum expired, and Britain declared war.

Source I Churchill writing about his reaction to the Munich Settlement in his post-war history of the war.

Once again defence of the rights of a weak State, outraged and invaded by unprovoked aggression, forced us to draw the sword. Once again we must fight for life and honour against the might and fury of the valiant, disciplined, and ruthless German race. Once again! So be it.

Churchill, *The Gathering Storm*, 1948.

With that change, Churchill ceased to be an outsider and he re-entered government in September 1939 as first lord of the admiralty. For all his opposition to the government, Churchill was a practical politician and he worked with Chamberlain and his former enemies. It was truly extraordinary that he was in the same job in 1939 as he had been in 1914 and once again urged the navy into action against Germany.

> **Further research**
>
> Read the parliamentary debate about Munich on 3 October 1938 by searching Hansard, the report of debates in parliament, which can be found online (hansard.millbanksystems. com). What arguments against Churchill's criticisms were made?

> **Activity**
>
> How would you explain the tone of Source I?

Why did Churchill become prime minister in 1940?

Churchill remained a somewhat isolated figure. Old criticisms and resentments remained, but he did his utmost to remain loyal to Chamberlain. He also wanted to wage war vigorously. In the event, British forces were able to do nothing to save Poland, in whose name Britain had gone to war. The small British expeditionary force sent to France could not take initiatives and France did not launch the sort of daring offensive that characterised the start of the war in 1914. Bolstered by the unexpected Nazi–Soviet pact with Stalin in 1939, German forces took western Poland while the Soviet Union occupied the east. The Soviet Union also waged a winter war against Finland after taking back the Baltic States. Britain seriously considered sending help to Finland and engaging in a war against Germany and the Soviet Union at the same time. Unable or unwilling to open a western front, Britain instead looked at Norway. The Norway campaign was a disaster for Britain and revived memories of Gallipoli in 1915.

Norway, 1940

Churchill had pressed for action in Norway, as its waters in the North Sea were a vital routeway for Germany to obtain Swedish iron ore. He had proposed laying mines in Norwegian waters and action to prevent a possible German invasion of Norway. Chamberlain agreed to mining on 28 March 1940, but on 1 March Hitler had approved a German invasion as a pre-emptive measure. This began in April. The Germans invaded Denmark and landed forces in Norway, capturing the capital, Oslo, but losing twelve large ships in naval actions against Britain. British army landings did not meet with success and there were disputes about methods and objectives. Forces landed at Namsos and Andalsnes were forced to withdraw in early May. Forces landed at Narvik achieved little and it finally fell to Germany on 28 May. The campaign was poorly managed and its purpose was questionable. Hitler succeeded in taking Denmark and Norway.

To consider

Since Churchill bore substantial responsibility for the failed Norway campaign, why did it lead to his becoming prime minister?

The debate in the House of Commons about Norway led to major political change. Since September 1939, Britain's achievements had been limited and the war had been called 'the phoney war' by a US commentator. The Norwegian campaign was the first real initiative and it had clearly failed. However, the debate was not focussed entirely on the Norwegian campaign but on the whole record of the government since the war began. It was obvious that the war effort was not being well co-ordinated. There was an ineffective Minister for the Co-ordination of Defence; a Military Co-ordination Committee had not proved effective; the economic planning had not been synchronised or effective. Churchill apart, the government did not have dynamic ministers with much war experience.

The first day of the debate saw a powerful intervention by Sir Roger Keyes, in his admiral's uniform. Over two days on 7 and 8 May 1940, Chamberlain came under some unexpected attacks from his own side, especially from Leo

Amery, a former ally. He quoted Oliver Cromwell's words to the so-called Rump Parliament in 1653: 'You have sat too long for any good you have been doing. Depart, I say, and let us have done with you, In the name of God, go!' However, there was little indication that the debate would lead to Chamberlain's resigning. Labour took advantage of the unexpected amount of criticism by Conservative MPs to force a vote. This made it much more a vote of confidence in Chamberlain than simply a vote on an unsuccessful expedition. Churchill took responsibility for this failure, and defended the government, oddly increasing his own standing despite the reverses in Norway by appearing to be loyal to Chamberlain. The vote about the conduct of the war in Norway was 281 to 200 for the government instead of its usual 200-strong majority. Over forty Conservative MPs had voted against the government and another 40 had abstained.

Chamberlain had not been defeated but the vote had exposed a lot of hostility to him among his own MPs. By May 1940, he was unwell and, though he retained the admiration and respect of most of his party, there now seemed to be a feeling that a new leader was needed. Those who spoke against the government were not voting for Churchill to become prime minister. Only a minority of Conservative MPs wanted that. For most, it was Lord Halifax, the former Foreign Secretary and friend of George VI. Lord Halifax was a peer, and as such he sat in the House of Lords and would not have been able to lead the country from the House of Commons without renouncing his title. In any case, he was reluctant to take on a job he knew he was not fit for. So Chamberlain could not stay and Halifax would not step up; there were no other figures of sufficient confidence or stature, making Churchill the only alternative. As well as backing from a group within his own party, support from Labour and its leader, Clement Attlee (despite previous disagreements over domestic policies), ensured Churchill's promotion. Chamberlain might still have carried on, but Labour would not serve under him. Churchill was not a popular figure with Labour, but he was seen as a leader who would bring a new determination to the war against Hitler.

On 10 May the news came that Germany had invaded Holland and Belgium. Chamberlain initially thought it his duty to stay on, but it was clear that the war cabinet was not in favour, especially the influential Kingsley Wood.

- There was a substantial show of no confidence among backbench Conservatives.
- Labour would not serve under Chamberlain.
- Halifax would not take office.
- There was an obvious need for a leader who was decisive.

The King, against his judgement, appointed Churchill Prime Minister on 10 May 1940. This had not been expected, he did not have solid support in his party and he was plunged into the most serious crisis Britain has faced in modern times.

Activity

1 What impression does this cartoon give of the support for Churchill in 1940?
2 Was this image more myth than reality?

ALL BEHIND YOU, WINSTON

This cartoon appeared in the *London Evening Standard* newspaper on 14 May 1940. The artist, David Low, had been a consistent critic of appeasement. Churchill is shown at the front with Attlee behind him on the right and Chamberlain on the left. Halifax and the Liberal leader, Sinclair, are also shown. ▶

Chapter takeaways

- Churchill was one of the most experienced and eminent politicians of his day. However, at the very time when dangerous situations at home and abroad needed men of experience he was out of office because of his views about some key issues: India, rearmament and foreign policy and the abdication.
- He was distrusted by many in his own party and was seen as old fashioned and out of touch with modern thinking.
- Through the 1930s he drew attention to the dangers of German rearmament and urged greater spending on air defences and more efforts to gain international co-operation against a German threat.
- He opposed the Munich Settlement of 1938 on the grounds that Britain had suffered a moral defeat, while he himself admitted that British war preparations were poor.
- Not until 1939 did his warnings about Hitler and his criticism of appeasement gain him more support and he re-entered government. Despite his mishandling of the Norway campaign, his confidence and knowledge of war made him a candidate for the premiership and, as Lord Halifax did not promote himself, Churchill was chosen as prime minister at a time of grave national crisis.

Study Skills: Understanding sources and how they relate to an issue

In the examination, you need to show key skills in approaching evidence.

- You have to interpret evidence. You need to link it to the issue in the question and decide what the evidence is saying about that issue. In the example below the issue in the question is whether Churchill became prime minister because his contemporaries believed that he had the necessary abilities to lead.
- You will need to consider how useful the evidence is. This involves thinking carefully about who wrote it, why it was written and how typical it might be.
- This really involves knowledge of the whole situation in 1940 but it is also important to look at the type of evidence. The use of knowledge is a skill that will be developed in the next two chapters. Here, it is helpful to ask 'Was the person who produced this evidence in a position to know? Is there a reason why he or she might hold a certain view?'

Example

Look at the sources below about how Churchill became prime minister in 1940.

Using these sources in their historical context, assess how far they support the view that Churchill became prime minister in 1940 because he was thought to be the best person for the job.

Source A An officer in the Admiralty has an unfavourable view of Churchill.

I dread any more influence from that arch-idiot Winston. I'm quite certain that he has played the whole war of the last eight months to become prime minister, often at the expense of helping to win the war. Witness his refusal to back the demands of the Navy against the Air Force. The high ups still insist on going on with the mad Narvik campaign in Norway.

Acting Director of Naval Operations, diary, 9 May 1940.

Source B A former Conservative cabinet minister who resigned in 1938 over Munich gives a view of why Churchill became prime minister.

On 10 May 1940 the Germans invaded Holland and Belgium. Chamberlain's first reaction was that this terrible event gave him an excuse to remain as prime minister. This shows how men in very high office can acquire the belief that they cannot be replaced. He was persuaded that the events only meant he should depart urgently. The choice lay between Churchill and Lord Halifax. Churchill's reputation had risen sharply since 1939. He had shown himself a highly competent First Lord of the Admiralty. His speeches in the Commons had been better than any of his colleagues. Everything that he had prophesied in the past had come disastrously true. Halifax had merely remained the foreign minister of Munich. The choice was obvious.

Duff Cooper, *Old Men Forget*, 1953.

Source C A prominent Conservative politician recalls his reaction to the events preceding Churchill's appointment as prime minister.

The news of Chamberlain's intentions to stay was given out. The Labour leaders, Attlee and Greenwood, said they were willing to serve in a new national government but not under Chamberlain. The Cabinet was left in doubt what their attitude would be and Churchill knew that the task of forming a government would certainly fall on him.

Leo Amery, *My Political Life*, 1955.

Source D Chamberlain's secretary who went on to be Churchill's secretary recalls in his diary the King's decision on 10 May. He added comments when the diaries were published.

Friday 10 May The King has sent for Winston (fortunately because Halifax, true to form, had gone off to the dentist!). Mr Chamberlain would have liked Halifax to be prime minister. The King certainly disliked the change to Churchill and would have preferred Halifax. The feeling in Conservative circles was represented by a letter sent by Queen Mary to my mother hoping I would not go on to work with Mr Churchill. Winston told me that when he met with Chamberlain and Halifax, Chamberlain said to Halifax 'if the King asks me I should suggest sending for you to be prime minister'. Halifax said if asked he would propose Mr Churchill.

Sir John Colville, *The Fringes of Power: Downing Street Diaries, 1939–1955*, 1987.

Focus on AS

If you are studying this unit for AS you will have to answer two questions, unlike the A Level where there is only one question. The first question is worth 10 marks and will ask you to:

Use your knowledge of British policy since the outbreak of war to assess how useful Source B is as evidence that Chamberlain clung to power for as long as possible.

In order to do well answering this type of question you should evaluate the source, using both its provenance (see page 29) and your own relevant knowledge of the historical context (see page 57) specified in the question. This will allow you to engage with the source and reach a supported analysis of its usefulness as evidence for the issue in the question. You should reach a judgement about its value. Remember it might be useful for some issues but not others.

At AS the second question is worth 20 marks. The second question you have to answer will be of a similar style to the A Level, but you will have only three sources, whereas the A Level has four. The question will be worded as follows:

Using Sources A, B and C in their historical context, assess how far they support the view that Churchill became prime minister in 1940 because he was thought to be the best man for the job.

In order to do well answering this type of question you must ensure that your answer is focused on the question. You need to evaluate the sources, using both their provenance and relevant knowledge of their historical context. This is in order to engage with the sources and reach a supported analysis of them in relation to the issue in the question. The balance between using provenance and your own knowledge to evaluate the sources does not have to be a 50:50 split, but you must both consider the provenance and use your knowledge.

The guidance given in the Study Skills section for the A Level Enquiries should also be consulted as the skills that it explains are exactly the same for this type of question.

Activity

1 This table will help you establish the basic relevance of the four sources.
One example – for Source A – has been done for you. Make a copy and fill
it in for Sources B–D. You would not necessarily do this in the examination;
this is to help you to develop the skill of interpreting the sources.

Source	View of key issue	Evidence from the source
A	This source does not think that Churchill was the best man for the job and has a low view of his ability. It thinks Churchill has low intellectual ability and is an ambitious schemer who has put his own interests first.	'arch-idiot' He has 'played the whole war' to become PM The Norway campaign is 'mad' and his own ambitions have come 'at the expense of winning the war'
B		
C		
D		

2 You will need to consider how useful the evidence is.
This involves thinking carefully of who wrote it, why
it was written and how typical it might be. This really
involves knowledge of the whole situation in 1940 but
it is also important to look at the type of evidence.
Was the person in a position to know? Is there a
reason why he or she might hold a certain view?

To help you it might be a good idea to question
the sources. The idea is to test the evidence. For
example, here are some questions you could ask
about Source B:

- Was Duff Cooper in a position to know what was
going on?
- What is the significance of his being a former
Cabinet minister, out of office since October 1938?
- Would he know more or less than the author of
Source D?
- Would he be a 'neutral' observer or might he be
favourable to Churchill?

- Do any of the other sources here suggest anything
different from Duff Cooper's view?
- Is there anything that might make Duff Cooper's
view more or less credible?
- Do you think this view is typical of Conservative
political opinion?

What questions would you ask about Sources A, C
and D?

3 To get further you need to apply your own
knowledge of the historical context. This is
the next skill and will be developed in the
following chapter (page 55). However, to test
these sources, discuss what sorts of knowledge
might be used. For example, what knowledge
might confirm or challenge the reasons given
in Source B for Churchill being chosen? What
knowledge might confirm the views about his
abilities and ambition?

Chapter 2

Churchill as wartime prime minister

This chapter considers the situation in the summer of 1940 and how Churchill maintained the war effort. It describes Churchill's style of leadership, the impact of his speeches and his policies. His relations with his generals and his impact on key decisions taken during the war, particularly the strategy of waging war in the Mediterranean, are analysed. Churchill's role in the decision to bomb Germany and the conduct of the war from June 1944 to May 1945 are covered. There is an explanation of the outcome of the general election of 1945, which saw the Conservatives, led by Churchill, lose office to Labour. The main issues of this period to be considered are as follows:

- What was Churchill's stance towards the war in 1940?
- What was special about his leadership style during the war?
- What characterised his relations with his generals?
- How effective were his strategic decisions during the war in the Mediterranean?
- How justified was the bombing of Germany?
- How important was his role in the war, 1944–45?
- How important were the reconstruction policies of his government and what role did he play?
- Why did he lose office in 1945?

In this chapter there will be continued practice in interpreting evidence, linking it to key issues, but there will be more consideration of evaluating pieces of evidence by considering their provenance, weighing their usefulness and using knowledge to test them.

Timeline

1940	May	Dunkirk evacuation
	June	France surrenders
	July–September	Battle of Britain
1941	June	Nazi invasion of USSR
	December	US enters war
1942	February	Singapore falls to Japan
	October	Battle of El Alamein
	November	Operation Torch – US landings in North Africa
		Beveridge Report
1943	February	German defeat at Stalingrad
	July	Allies invade Sicily
1944	June	D-Day landings in Normandy
1945	February	Yalta Conference
	May	War in Europe ends
	July	Churchill loses election in Britain

Overview

Churchill was invited by King George VI to become prime minister on 10 May 1940. The whole style of government changed. Churchill was determined to continue the war, even though the British people faced a greater crisis than at any time since the invasion fears in the Napoleonic period. Churchill made mighty speeches to rally them behind the war. It has been said that he made the English language a weapon of war, so powerful were the words he used. Though there is a debate about how much these speeches actually influenced opinion, they have passed into legend. Churchill rejected a compromise peace and hoped that the USA would eventually join in.

British military leaders now faced direction from a powerful and opinionated leader. Churchill was unusual in having direct experience of war and thought that war was too important to be left to the generals, as it had been in most previous wars. He took a very active part in military matters and his relations with leading figures of Britain's army, navy and air force was often stormy. By 1944, though, Britain had really lost control of the war to allies with much larger forces and resources. Churchill had much less control over generals like Eisenhower. British forces came under an American commander for the invasion of France in 1944 and their role was far less significant than that of the Russian armies fighting in the east.

One of Churchill's most important strategic decisions came early in his premiership in his reinforcement of British forces in North Africa. The British had won their first victories in the air and at sea. British forces were also victorious in North Africa in a struggle against Italian forces. A major decision was taken to commit forces to the Mediterranean sector which would be where British and German land forces fought until the invasion of northern France in 1944. This involved a lengthy struggle in North Africa and then in Sicily and Italy, which some US commanders thought was unsound and merely postponed the inevitable clash with the main German forces in northern Europe.

Britain preferred to fight in the Mediterranean and to try to defeat Germany by bombing campaigns of increasing violence and intensity. The bulk of the German army was fighting against Russia from 1941 and the Russian leaders were critical of British policy. When Japan successfully attacked British colonies in South Asia from December 1941, British forces fell back to India. The war effort was conducted outside Europe for much of the war.

Most of Churchill's time was taken up with diplomacy with the other members of the alliance against Hitler and by military matters. Churchill played a major role in a series of conferences, but from 1943 he found himself increasingly isolated, with the major decisions being taken by the USA and the USSR. He tried to divide up eastern Europe with Stalin in 1945 but could not prevent the Russians taking over much of eastern Poland, even though Britain had gone to war in 1939 to protect Poland. Despite the warm personal relationship he had with President Roosevelt, there were considerable differences between Britain and the USA, especially about trade policy and the future of the European empires after the war.

Churchill's government made extensive plans for post-war Britain from as early as 1942. Labour played a major role in these and Labour ministers were well-known and important members of the wartime government. By 1945 the public mood in Britain was for major domestic reform and change and, for all his immense popularity as a war leader, Churchill did not have the chance to lead Britain after 1945. Labour gained a large majority of seats in the general election of 1945, and Churchill left office.

What was Churchill's stance towards the war in 1940?

Churchill felt that he was destined to lead Britain; he had first-hand experience of war and confidence in the ability of Britain and its considerable empire to wage war successfully.

Source A Churchill recalling his feelings on the night of his appointment as prime minister.

• •

As I went to bed at about 3 am I was conscious of a profound sense of relief. At last I had the ability to give directions over the whole scene. I felt as if I were walking with destiny, and that all my past life had been but a preparation for this hour and for this trial.

Winston Churchill, *The Gathering Storm*, 1948.

Activity

1 What do Sources A and B suggest about the confidence Churchill had in his leadership?

2 Why do you think that in Source B the order is first 'sea', then 'land' and then 'air'?

3 Do you think that there were alternatives to Churchill's view that 'without victory, there is no survival' for Britain and her empire? Could Britain have negotiated a peace? (See below for more information on this.)

4 Use your knowledge of the situation in 1940 to assess how useful Source B is as evidence of Churchill's abilities as prime minister. (AS)

Source B Churchill speaks to the House of Commons about Britain's war aims.

• •

You ask what is our policy? I will say: it is to wage war by sea, land and air, with all our might and with the strength that God can give us.

You ask, what is our aim? I can answer that in one word: victory – victory at all costs, victory in spite of all terror, victory, however long and hard the road may be; for without victory, there is no survival. Let that be realised: no survival for the British Empire.

Speech by Churchill, 13 May 1940.

By 13 May, the situation was dangerous but the British army was intact; the French had large forces; Italy had not joined Germany; the British were fighting on only one front and Churchill had put together a Cabinet with some of his own supporters. He was highly determined to wage war energetically, but his past record was not especially encouraging. The Norway campaign had not been a success; he did not have a good record in the First World War (see page 24); there was little enthusiasm from US President Roosevelt for his appointment; and both the House of Commons and the government contained many who liked and admired Chamberlain.

The war moved quickly and on 14 May Germany broke the French defences. The prospect of a rapid defeat of France was suddenly a reality. If France were defeated, Britain's army would be isolated. Hitler had already defeated Poland, and his treaty of friendship with Russia meant that all his forces could be directed against Britain.

By 28 May 1940 Churchill was facing a profound challenge:

■ The British army had been cut off from the French forces and had fallen back on Dunkirk, hoping to be evacuated. The chances of rescuing 300,000 troops seemed low given German air superiority and the possibility of a German assault.

■ There was the danger of Italian entry into the war, which would threaten Egypt and the Suez Canal. This would cut off Britain's quickest sea route to India, and its colonies in the Far East and make them more difficult to defend against Japan.

■ Japan was a possible threat to British possessions in South Asia.

■ Gold reserves were running out and it was not clear whether Britain could afford to go on fighting.

■ Germany had bombed Poland and the Low Countries. There was considerable fear of large-scale bombing of Britain and very heavy casualties were expected.

■ Lord Halifax, who had been a major supporter of appeasement, was still in the cabinet as foreign secretary, and was making discreet approaches to discover what German terms for peace with Britain might be.

Churchill and Edward Wood,
◀ Lord Halifax, circa 1940.

Halifax's position was not cowardly nor defeatist, but simply a way of making a rational decision. As Italy was still neutral, it was a possibility that Italy could be asked to find out what Hitler would offer and then Britain could make a decision as to whether it was indeed necessary for national survival to continue fighting.

On 28 May the Cabinet discussed a French proposal to approach Mussolini to find out what peace terms Hitler might accept. As foreign secretary, Halifax needed to know what Britain's options were, but it would have been dangerous to suggest by approaching Italy that Britain was considering a negotiated peace, as this would have shown Hitler that Britain was weakening in her resolve to carry on the war.

Look at these sources below. C, D and E are from the official cabinet minutes of 28 May 1940.

Source C Churchill makes his view clear to the cabinet.
....

We should find the terms offered us touched our confidence and integrity. When at this point we got up to leave the Conference table, we should find that all the forces of resolution which were now at our disposal would have vanished.

Churchill's speech to the cabinet, 28 May 1940.

Source D Chamberlain, then lord president of the council, puts his considerable influence behind Churchill.
....

Mediation at this stage, in the presence of a great disaster, and at a time when many people might think we had no more resources left, could only have the most unfortunate results. The present was not the time at which advances should be made to Mussolini.

Chamberlain's speech to the cabinet, 28 May 1940.

> ### Cabinet minutes from 28 May 1940
>
> The official cabinet minutes for the crucial period of May 1940 are available online and make gripping reading. They are accessible through www.ukwarcabinet.org.uk. It is particularly exciting to see the discussion develop and 'eavesdrop' on some of the most critical meetings in British history.

Halifax's proposals both for an approach to Mussolini and an appeal to the USA were rejected.

Source E Churchill speaks to the cabinet.

••

An appeal to the United States at the present time would be altogether premature. If we made a bold stand against Germany, that would command their admiration and respect; but a grovelling appeal, if made now, would have the worst possible effect.

Churchill's speech to the cabinet, 28 May 1940.

Source F In speaking to the junior members of the cabinet, Churchill later in the day on 28 May was even more direct about not negotiating. A Labour minister, Hugh Dalton, wrote in his memoirs what Churchill said.

••

It is idle to think that if we tried to make peace now we should get any better terms from Germany than if we went on and fought it out. The Germans would demand our fleet. We should become a slave state through a British government which would be Hitler's puppet.

On the other hand, we had immense resources and advantages. Therefore he said 'We shall go on and we shall fight it out, here or elsewhere and if at last the long story is to end, it were better it should end not through surrender but only when we are rolling senseless on the ground when each of us lies choking on his own blood.'

Hugh Dalton, Memoirs: The Fateful Years, 1931–1945, 1957.

Activity

1 What do Sources C–F tell you about Churchill's leadership qualities in May 1940?

2 Consider their provenance (i.e. their nature, who said them, when, why and under what circumstances). How important is it to know this when assessing how useful they are as evidence? Three of these sources come from official cabinet minutes and the fourth from the memoirs of a minister. How useful does this make them as evidence?

Halifax had argued that it might be better to consider terms before France was defeated and before German bombing destroyed Britain's aircraft factories. The Australian High Commissioner pleaded for an appeal to Roosevelt for a peace conference but his memorandum was firmly rejected by Churchill with the word 'rot'.

The situation had improved by 4 June with the evacuation of 224,318 British troops and 111,172 of their allies from Dunkirk. The cabinet had resisted French demands for more aircraft and an air defence of Britain was possible. Belgium had surrendered and relations with France were very poor. The cabinet members who favoured any negotiation had been silenced and Churchill made his most famous speech to the Commons:

We shall not flag or fail. We shall go on to the end ... We shall fight on the beaches, we shall fight on the landing grounds, we shall fight in the fields and in the streets, we shall fight in the hills; we shall never surrender.

There was a direct appeal to the USA when, after saying the Empire would continue the fight if Britain were invaded, he went on to say until 'the New World, with all its power and might, steps forth to the rescue and the liberation of the old'.

The speech was broadcast with the actor Norman Shelley impersonating Churchill, who was too busy to speak on the radio himself.

Events moved quickly and even an offer of union, which would have seen France and Britain becoming one country and pooling their forces, could not prevent the French surrender. Once again, there was talk of peace terms but by now these were not considered a serious possibility. The remarkable achievement of Churchill was to maintain a war with no allies against what was perceived to be one of the greatest military powers the world had ever seen. On 3 July 1940 a massive gesture of defiance was made by the attack on

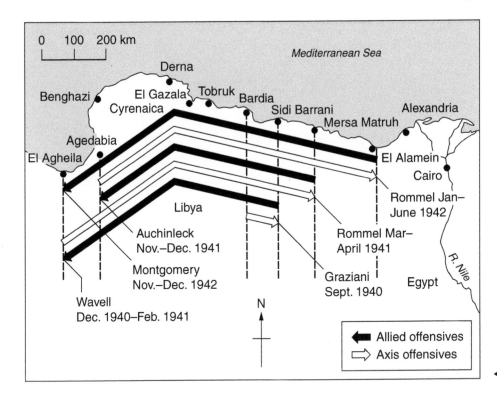

Western Desert campaign, ◀ 1941–42.

the French fleet to prevent it falling into German hands. The RAF had been bombing Germany since its invasion of the Low Countries and continued to do so, despite inevitable German reprisals. A very bold decision was taken to send British armoured forces to Egypt even when there was a real threat of German invasion. The British achieved rapid victories against Italy, Hitler's ally, which had colonies in North Africa adjacent to Egypt.

The brunt of the war fell on Britain with the German decision to launch an air offensive in August 1940, which had the aim of destroying the RAF. Churchill spoke on 20 August:

Never in the field of human conflict was so much owed by so many to so few. All hearts go out to the fighter pilots, whose brilliant actions we see with our own eyes day after day; but we must never forget that all the time, night after night, month after month, our bomber squadrons travel far into Germany.

Hitler and Göring, the head of the German air force, thought that bombing cities was more important than destroying the RAF. They believed that civilian populations would not withstand bombing, that morale would crack and that this would make a continuation of the British war effort impossible. In September Germany diverted its attention from the RAF airfields to the bombing of British cities, which had the unintended effect of enabling the RAF to recover. The strategies of Sir Hugh Dowding in mobilising small groups of fighters and preserving the strength of the RAF by not pursuing German bombers over the Channel with the suggested 'big wing' or massed groups of aircraft of his rival strategists proved effective. But Dowding had enemies who thought that a larger-scale strategy would have worked better and Churchill, despite Dowding's success, did not back him. Dowding's dour personality did not help. He was removed from command in November 1940 with Churchill's blessing. This was a poor reward for his services.

By the end of 1940 Britain had enjoyed some victories in North Africa and had defeated the German air offensive. Churchill had established his position over his rivals and his oratory had become a weapon of war. His determination had prevented any negotiations with Germany and the nation had steeled itself for a long struggle. Given the situation – Britain standing alone against Germany, Italy and possibly Japan with no allies, with no commitment to help from the USA and with a population who had suffered the terrible losses of the First World War – this was a considerable achievement.

What was special about Churchill's leadership style during the war?

'The prime minister expects all His Majesty's servants in high places to set an example of steadiness and resolution.' This memo of July 1940 sums up the very high levels of dedication and energy demanded by Churchill. He was a hard taskmaster because of his determination to supervise details.

He was fascinated by what he saw as imaginative ideas, particularly the ideas of one of his special advisers and close associates, Frederick 'the Prof' Lindemann, even when scientific experts showed that many of the ideas, such as germ warfare, were impractical.

Constantly restless and energetic, Churchill worked irregular hours and exhausted his staff. He revolutionised methods, and often insisted on very precise and concise paperwork. He insisted that queries and ideas were presented only on 'one sheet of paper', and would fire off demands in a mass of written instructions. He was happy to dictate from his bed and even, to the dismay of new secretaries (male), from his bath.

Officials who could not keep up or who displeased him were dismissed, but there are many instances of Churchill being able to take advice and respecting those who stood up to him.

Source G The first sea lord, in a letter to Admiral Cunningham, sums up working with Churchill.

The PM is very difficult these days, not that he has not always been. One has, however, to take a broad view, because one has to deal with a man who is proving to be a magnificent leader; and one just has to put up with his childishness, as long as it isn't vital or dangerous.

Sir Dudley Pound, letter, 1 December 1940.

There were a number of key elements in Churchill's leadership style that marked him out from his twentieth-century predecessors:

- His belief in establishing strong personal relations with his allies. His personal diplomacy was of considerable importance and played an important part, for example, in his relations with both Stalin and Roosevelt. He also relied on strong personal friendships with informal advisers and friends.
- His mastery of both written and spoken expression, seen at its finest in 1940 and in many speeches in the House of Commons, which he never neglected throughout the war.
- A personal flamboyance. No other British prime minister appeared in such an array of uniforms and costume – from the famous one-piece 'siren suit' to the various naval and military uniforms he wore to emphasise that he was a war leader.
- He was the most travelled of all prime ministers before him. His wartime journeys undertaken at considerable hazard and lack of comfort for a man of his age were remarkable and showed his astonishing energy.

Activity

Read Source G.

Use your knowledge of relations between Churchill and military leaders to assess how useful Source G is as evidence of how well he managed relations with them. (AS)

- His daring and ruthlessness marked him out from his predecessors. This included his determination to fight on in 1940; his decision to destroy the French fleet even at the cost of thousands of lives of former allies in 1940; his support of civilian bombing of Germany; his plans to destroy the German invaders by poison gas; his impatience with any signs of delay or weakness in pursuing campaigns; and his support for covert operations by spies and saboteurs in occupied Europe, regardless of the cost to either the agents or the civilian populations.

Source H Churchill's private secretary writes about Churchill's way of working in his diary, 9 January 1945.

The PM has a cold and so saw the King of Yugoslavia in bed.

About midnight while Lord Beaverbrook and Brendan Bracken were closeted in the PM's bedroom having come, no doubt on some intrigue against Ernest Bevin whom the PM cherishes more than any of the other Labour ministers, Anthony Eden [the Foreign Secretary] rang up in a storm of rage.

It was about a memo that Lord Cherwell [Frederick Lindemann] had sent which the PM had forwarded to the Foreign Office. In it Eden's view that Europe was on the brink of starvation had been contradicted. He ranted in a way which neither I nor the PM had heard before. The PM handled the storm in a very adept and paternal way, protested at Anthony vexing himself at the end of a long and tiring day. He said there was one thing he would not allow: the feeding of Europe at the expense of an already hard-rationed England.

Sir John Colville, *The Fringes of Power: Downing Street Diaries, 1939–1955*, 1987.

Activity

Read Source H about Churchill's working methods.
1 What does Source H show about how Churchill did business?
2 What does it tell you about the role of his special friends and advisers?
3 What does it tell you about his ability to deal with colleagues?

What characterised Churchill's relations with his generals?

Though Churchill wanted to influence the way the war was fought, his military chiefs were all too aware that Churchill's own military career had not been very distinguished. As a young man he had seen action in the Sudan, the North West Frontier of India, Cuba as an observer, and South Africa as a war correspondent. He had little experience of command, planning or overall strategy and no naval experience. This did not stop him giving direct orders to the navy when he was first lord of the Admiralty, a political post, or offering opinionated strategic views when the First World War broke out in 1914. The attempt to avoid large-scale war in France against the main enemy Germany by invading Germany's ally Turkey was a disaster. The Gallipoli campaign of 1915, which involved the navy landing armed forces, mainly from Australia and New Zealand, to take the Turkish capital Constantinople, resulted in heavy losses and total failure to get beyond the beaches. Only the evacuation by the navy was a success. Churchill was forced to resign and went to the western front as a colonel. He saw little action, left his regiment to pursue political intrigues in London and quickly went back into government. When he was once more in charge of the navy in 1939–40 he again supported a large-scale and unsuccessful military campaign in Norway.

What dominated his view of the generals was, first, the experience of the First World War and the heavy losses in the fighting in France, which he attributed to politicians letting generals like Haig pursue their costly plans without proper supervision. Second, he had been frustrated by the caution of the leading military commanders during the appeasement of the 1930s in advising against decisive action because of their fears of under-preparedness and having to deal with a possible war on three fronts – against Germany, Italy and Japan. What influenced the generals' view was Churchill's unpredictability, lack of what they viewed as realism and his amateur strategy. They were all too aware of his previous failures.

His first months as prime minister saw him making criticisms of military leaders and issuing unrealistic orders from London. When the German forces broke through the French lines at Sedan and their fast-moving attack proved too much for the French, the British commander, Lord Gort, was forced to ignore Churchill's orders in order to preserve the British forces – a key decision that allowed Britain to continue the war. Churchill's insistence that the port of Calais be defended to the last was pointless in military terms and lost valuable men. Churchill's desire to send another British force even when France was on the brink of defeat was thwarted only by firm and tireless argument by the Chief of the Imperial General Staff, Sir John Dill. Churchill got rid of Dill as soon as possible.

Brooke

Throughout the war Churchill constantly interfered with operational matters, sacked able and thoughtful commanders and preferred military leaders with often doubtful abilities but with the 'right attitude'. The main burden of Churchill's interference fell on the head of the army, Field Marshal Sir Alan Brooke. Brooke was a highly competent organiser and a thorough professional. However, in temperament he was very different from Churchill. He was conscious of the need to deploy British forces carefully and avoid heavy casualties. He was often annoyed by Churchill 'thinking aloud' and coming up with all sorts of different military ideas. His wartime diaries, often written up after long and exhausting meetings, give a sense of frustration with political interference. They are supported by many other recollections by senior officers.

Personal dealings with Churchill, a highly opinionated and charismatic leader, tended to be tricky but when it came to major decisions there were fewer disagreements between Brooke and Churchill.

Churchill took a bold decision in 1940. It was not clear whether, after the fall of France, Hitler would invade Britain. But Churchill decided to send a substantial amount of Britain's military equipment to the Middle East to deal with any potential Italian threat to Egypt, the Suez Canal and the route to India. The need to maintain Britain's empire was not challenged by the military leaders as it was seen as the role of the navy and the RAF to defend the homeland. Brooke and other generals supported Churchill's decision to send troops and equipment to North Africa. They, too, had little enthusiasm for a renewal of fighting in northern Europe.

◀ Sir Alan Brooke in 1943.

Wavell

The rapid British victories in North Africa in 1940 justified the decision to concentrate on fighting in North Africa, but Churchill gave little credit to the commander, Sir Archibald Wavell, whom he personally disliked. Churchill took forces away from him when Italy invaded Greece in 1940 and the cabinet made a decision to send troops to defend it and establish a new Balkan front. Wavell was not given time to prepare properly without him in command in Greece. His troops were taken off to a deeply flawed campaign. Without proper planning and resources, this was another expedition that failed when German forces invaded. The British had to be evacuated to Crete and then were defeated there by a German attack and forced out again. The early successes in North Africa were thrown away, and Wavell did not have the resources to meet German forces under Rommel who were sent to Africa. He took the blame and was demoted.

Auchinleck and Montgomery

Wavell's successor, Sir Claude Auchinleck, was not prepared for a premature attack on the German forces and, to Churchill's annoyance, he insisted on delaying until he was well prepared. Despite an effective defence against German attacks and making thorough preparations for a counter attack, he too was sacked for his delays and not being sufficiently daring and aggressive.

His replacement, Bernard Montgomery, won over Churchill by his self-confidence but insisted on very thorough preparations involving accumulating more than twice the men that Rommel had before attacking at El Alamein in October 1942. Much of the credit for the first major British victory in the war should have gone to Auchinleck because of the efficient preparations he had made, even though he did not actually lead the attack. However, Churchill disliked him and favoured 'Monty'. Montgomery was very slow in following up his victory after El Alamein, which allowed Germany to retreat to Tunisia. But Churchill continued to favour him.

The war in 1943–44

The defeat of the German forces after a protracted struggle in Tunisia led to more British army expeditions. American and British forces first invaded and captured Sicily and then landed in southern Italy. This led to a long campaign of slow progress right through Italy which distracted the allies from the major task of defeating the main German armies and invading Germany. It kept more British and American troops occupied than it did German troops and forced Russia to take on the main task of moving towards Germany. The British commander, Sir Harold Alexander, merely showed persistence in maintaining a slow advance, but Churchill admired him for his gentlemanly and unruffled style of leadership.

There is little evidence that Brooke or the generals were eager for the invasion of France that Russia was urging. Churchill and his generals did not clash about the overall strategy of the war. Brooke thought that an invasion of France might well not succeed and might lead to such heavy casualties that the war would be lengthened, not shortened. However, the invasion of France could not be delayed indefinitely and Churchill planned it for the summer of 1944.

Brooke was not put in charge – that honour went to the US general Eisenhower and Churchill did not appear sympathetic to his leading general's disappointment. The planning under General Morgan was one of the most important achievements of the war for which Morgan received limited credit. Churchill showed little appreciation for the detailed and meticulous planning, only for 'bright ideas' such as deceiving Germany about the invasion site. Monty remained Churchill's favourite, giving the impression of confidence and energy that was not altogether borne out by his actions. Compared to US forces, the British forces faced relatively limited resistance at D-Day on 6 June 1944 but were slow to break through from the beachhead and take the key port of Caen. Thereafter a dogged and costly campaign against more flexible and experienced German forces characterised the rest of the war.

There was one exception to the predominantly cautious advance and that was another expedition – airborne landings to outflank the German forces by taking the bridges at Nijmegen, Eindhaven and Arnhem, leading to a possible invasion of the Ruhr. Despite Montgomery's confidence in it and US doubts, the operation went ahead and failed. Flawed in planning, execution and aim, 'Operation Market Garden' in 1944 was the last hope for a bold stroke to end the war. Churchill had not managed to control the bad and costly ideas of his general any more than had been the case during the First World War. Like Gallipoli in 1915, the Arnhem attack was a bold idea which was over-ambitious.

From 1940 to 1944, Churchill and his generals had occupied Germany in what was really a minor military action in North Africa while the German army was engaged and defeated with massive losses by the Russian forces. The war in North Africa was characterised by the Prime Minister's obvious loss of confidence in his major commanders. It was dominated by his belief that somehow the war could be won in the Mediterranean without the British army destroying the German forces in the west. Churchill exerted a major influence on the joint strategy of the British and American alliance and his outlook influenced the reckless final adventure of the war at Arnhem. He did, however, provide constant energy and determination, forcing his generals to examine their practice, their attitudes and their plans and backing new and imaginative ideas; for instance, the very effective campaigns to deceive the Germans about the landing place for the invasion of France in 1944.

Source I Field Marshal Wavell expressing his view of Churchill's military outlook.

The Prime Minister thought that because a comparatively small number of mounted Boers had held up a British division in 1899 or 1900 during the Boer war in South Africa, it was unnecessary for the South African brigade under my command to have more equipment than rifles before taking the field in 1940. Winston's tactical ideas had to some extent crystallised at the South African War of 1899.

Quoted in Gordon Corrigan, *Blood, Sweat, Tears and Arrogance*, 2007.

Source J Churchill's Chief of Staff writes to Sir Claude Auchinleck after his appointment to command in the Middle East in July 1941.

The idea that Churchill is rude, arrogant and self-seeking is entirely wrong. He is certainly frank in speech and writing, but he expects others to be equally frank with him. A 'child of nature', he does not appreciate the changes that have taken place in modern armies, with their heavy and complicated logistic needs. Do not be irritated with telegrams on every kind of topic, many of which may be irrelevant and superfluous.

General Sir Hastings, letter, 1919.

Source K Churchill writes to his son, Randolph, from Cairo, where he was awaiting an offensive against the Germans in North Africa.

The admirals, generals and Air Marshals chant their stately hymn of 'Safety First'. In the midst of all this I have to restrain my natural pugnacity by sitting on my own head! HOW BLOODY!!

Churchill, letter, October 1941.

Source L Britain's most senior soldier records an encounter with Churchill during the El Alamein campaign in North Africa.

29 October 1942

I was presented with a telegram which the Prime Minister wanted to send to Alexander! Not a pleasant one and brought about purely by the fact that Anthony Eden had come round late last night to have a drink with him and had shaken his confidence in Montgomery and Alexander (the British commanders in North Africa) and had given him the impression that the campaign in the Middle East was petering out! When I went to see Winston I was met with a flow of abuse about Monty. What was my Monty doing now, allowing the battle to peter out? Had we not got a single general who could win one battle? My temper was on edge. I felt very angry and asked Winston why he consulted his foreign secretary when he wanted advice on strategic and tactical matters. He flared up and asked why he was not entitled to consult whoever he wished!

Sir Alan Brooke, diary, October 1942.

Activity

1 What do each of these sources, I–L on page 41, say about Churchill's relations with his generals?
2 How do Sources I and J corroborate each other in showing Churchill might have been out of touch with the needs of modern war?
3 How do Sources K and L give differing evidence about Churchill's dealing with the generals?
4 Does a knowledge of the circumstances in which Source L was written (i.e. the situation of the war at that time) help to explain Churchill's anger?
5 To what extent do Sources I–L show that Churchill's dealings with his generals was unsuccessful?
6 Use your knowledge of Churchill as a wartime leader to assess how useful Source L is as evidence of his ability to work well with his generals. **(AS)**

How effective were Churchill's strategic decisions during the war in the Mediterranean?

The importance of North Africa

The Suez Canal

The Suez Canal was opened in 1869. It created a waterway from the Mediterranean to the Red Sea. Britain acquired a major shareholding interest in the canal in 1876 and from the 1880s dominated Egypt.

Britain had a long history of concern with the Mediterranean as a vital trade route. This had increased with the building of the Suez Canal, which became a major link with India. Mediterranean strategy should be seen as part of this long tradition of British policy.

Before 1939 British military leaders were intensely concerned about the Mediterranean and the danger that Italy might pose if it allied with Germany against Britain in a war. Italy actually joined the war in 1940 and invaded southern France. Italy had troops in her North African colonies, modern-day Libya, bordering on Egypt. She had a major naval base at Taranto. Britain controlled the entrance to the Mediterranean at Gibraltar, but there was a danger that Franco, the Spanish dictator, might threaten that control by joining Hitler. Britain had possession of the Suez Canal, unofficial control of Egypt, controlled Palestine, dominated Iraq and Transjordan and had a colony in Somalia. As well as Mediterranean territories, the Suez Canal was the major link to Britain's Asian colonies, especially India. The Mediterranean was also the key to the defence of oil supplies from the Middle East.

In 1940 it was the defence of Empire and the routeway to Empire that dominated military thinking. An important part of that was the Suez Canal and the route to India. From 1942 another dimension was added. Germany had gone to war with Russia in 1941 and by 1942 had driven the Russian forces back considerably in the south. If a North African attack by Germany broke through into Egypt, then German forces might link up with forces in Russia and secure the vital oil fields of southern Russia and the Middle East. The outcome of the entire war was thus at stake in the war in the Mediterranean.

British forces were highly successful against the Italians in North Africa but faced a more serious enemy in the form of the German Afrika Korps and its commander, General Erwin Rommel. But for Churchill the Mediterranean was more than North Africa. He hoped for a Balkan front consisting of Greece, Yugoslavia and Turkey and to achieve that sent forces into Greece when Italy invaded in 1940. A front in Greece would draw German resources and opened up the prospect of greatly increased British influence in south-east Europe.

Churchill had staked much on an attack in Turkey in 1915 to open 'the soft underbelly of Europe' into the Balkans, and the Mediterranean dominated his thinking. However, in 1940–41, as in 1915, the Balkans proved to be not such a soft underbelly as British forces were defeated in Greece and forced out. North Africa proved to be a difficult battleground when British troops were faced by a well-equipped German force under a strong leader. By 1941 Egypt was under threat.

In the event Rommel was too short of men and supplies to take Egypt and was forced back after the Battle of El Alamein. After December 1941, Britain had to take the USA into account. Churchill was determined to pursue the Mediterranean strategy while the US military favoured a rapid invasion of northern France.

The American general, George Marshall, saw little point in wasting resources in the Mediterranean and argued for taking the pressure off Russia and establishing a western front. There was a case for this view – some military historians have argued that:

- The great German Atlantic fortifications were not yet built in 1942.
- The success of the war depended on the survival of Russia and also in engaging with and defeating the main German forces.
- The Mediterranean was a distraction and of limited strategic importance, especially once Rommel's advance on Egypt had been halted.

Churchill and the war in Italy

In 1943 considerable resources were devoted to an invasion of Sicily by British and US forces, which failed to prevent the Germans retreating to the mainland. With North Africa, Gibraltar, Malta, Cyprus and Sicily in Allied hands, the Mediterranean was secure. By 1943, also, Italy had been weakened by defeats and was no longer a serious threat. The German forces were established in Italy but the British had naval supremacy and considerable air power. What was the point of an extended campaign to take Italy? This seems one of the most puzzling decisions of the war. Sixteen Allied divisions were occupied in heavy fighting in Italy. As Germany had roughly the same number of forces, there was no question of a smaller Allied force holding down large numbers of German troops which could have been used against Russia or the Allied invasion of France. It was rather the Allies who were tied down. Finally, if Italy had fallen, it is difficult to see how this would have led to the defeat of Germany. This required a decisive defeat of the German forces in France, rather than in Italy, and an invasion of Germany itself.

It was not until June 1944 that Britain and the US launched the long-awaited D-Day invasion of occupied France. Thus the bulk of the war in Europe had been centred on the Mediterranean. Why was there such a delay?

- Such high casualties were expected that an invasion of France was put off as long as possible. The more Russia was weakening Germany and the more the Allied bombing campaign was hitting German cities, the fewer losses there might be from invading northern Europe.
- The long struggle in Italy was not anticipated and the Allies hoped that bold landings might speed the process, such as the failed landings at Anzio, south of Rome, in 1944.
- British policy was to maintain British dominance over the Mediterranean to preserve the links with Empire and to extend British interests in south east Europe. This was vividly shown by the so-called 'percentages

agreement' that Churchill made with Stalin in 1944, virtually dividing eastern Europe into Russian and British spheres of influence.

■ The invasion of Sicily and Italy seemed the logical next steps from the long pursuit of German forces after the Battle of El Alamein in 1942.

Source M The senior US commander advocates an assault on occupied France.

A British–American attack through Western Europe provides the only feasible method for employing the bulk of the compact power of the USA, the United Kingdom and Russia in a concerted effort against a single enemy.

General Marshall, memorandum, 1 April 1942.

Source N In his post-war history of the war Churchill recalls a visit by US envoys, General Marshall and Harry Hopkins, to urge a 'second front' in April 1942. This phrase was used to describe a major new front in northern Europe to take pressure from the main European front in the east where Russia and Germany were fighting.

I had to place this point of view before the American envoys:

It was not possible for us to lay aside our other duties. Our first imperial obligation was to defend India against the Japanese. To allow Germany and Japan to join hands in India or the Middle East involved a measureless disaster. I had faith in the power of the Russian armies and nation fighting in defence of their native soil. Without British aid, India might be conquered in a few months. Hitler's subjugation of Soviet Russia would be a much longer task. Before it was accomplished, Anglo-American command of the air would have been established beyond challenge. Even if all else failed, this would be decisive.

Churchill, *The Hinge of Fate*, Volume 4 of *The Second World War*, 1951.

Source O Report of a meeting between Stimson and Roosevelt about wartime strategy.

Secretary of State Stimson warned the President that the indirect British approach which he labelled 'pinprick warfare' not only would not work but would violate pledges given to the Soviet Union and would create serious problems with Stalin in the post-war world. If left in British hands, the cross-channel invasion would never take place, for the shadows of World War I trenches 'still hang too heavily over the imagination' of Churchill and other British leaders. The time had come for the President to assume responsibility for leadership of the 1944 cross-channel attack.

Report of a conversation, August 1943.

Source P The overall head of the army expresses doubts about D-Day in his diary entry for 5 June 1944.

It is very hard to believe that in a few hours the cross channel invasion starts. I am very uneasy about the whole operation. At best it will fall so very far short of the expectation of the bulk of the people, namely all those who know nothing of its difficulties. At the worst it may be the most ghastly disaster of the whole war.

[He added later]
A sudden storm might wreck it all; confusion may degenerate into chaos at any time. The difficulty of controlling the operation once launched, the danger of leakage of information, knowledge of the commanders engaged. Too good a

knowledge of their weaknesses makes one wonder whether in moments of crisis they may shatter one's hopes.

From the *Diaries of Sir Alan Brooke*, edited by Alex Danchev and Don Todman, 2001.

Activity

Read Sources M–P.

1 Explain what evidence each source provides about the opening of a 'Second Front' in Europe. How useful is this evidence for explaining why there were disagreements over this strategy?

2 How useful are Sources N and P for explaining why there was no invasion of northern France until 1944?

3 Use your knowledge of strategy in the Second World War to assess how useful Source N is as evidence of the wisdom of Churchill's Mediterranean strategy. (AS)

How justified was the bombing of Germany?

If waging war against Germany in North Africa was one alternative to invading France, the other was to destroy German morale and its capacity to provide for its extensive armed forces by relentless bombing. Germany had used civilian bombing to create terror in Poland in 1939 and in the Low Countries, Belgium and France in 1940. British cities had been the subject of a 'blitz' after the focus of the Battle of Britain had switched from attacking the RAF to the major cities. There was considerable public pressure to take the war in the same way to Germany. The RAF Bomber Command had been created with a bomber offensive in mind and was eager to show that it could hasten the end of the war by destroying both morale and war capacity. There were some problems, however:

■ A specialist report in 1942 had indicated that bombing was not effective or precise enough to substantially damage German industrial production.

■ The Blitz had not destroyed civilian morale in Britain. There was little chance that it would destroy German morale either, as so many had supported the Führer before 1939. This did not weaken, as from 1943, many German people saw Hitler's supposed genius as the only way to stop Russia invading and taking terrible revenge once it was clear that Germany could not defeat the USSR.

■ There were also ethical objections to killing large numbers of civilians, including women and children. These were voiced by brave objectors such as Bishop Bell of Chichester when heavy bombing raids initiated by Sir Arthur Harris began in 1942 and continued throughout the war with the enthusiastic support of the USA.

Harris deliberately aimed at as much destruction of German cities as possible by assembling large forces of bombers with incendiary bombs to deliberately create fire storms. There was considerable loss of life in major cities like Hamburg, the industrial cities of the Ruhr, Berlin and, in February 1945, Dresden. The death toll for this raid on one of Germany's most famous and historic cities was probably 40,000. Total casualties for the bombing of Britain from 1939 to 1945 were 60,595. In all, between 400,000 and 600,000 German civilians died in bombing raids.

Ruins of a church in Dresden after Allied bombing, 1945. ▶

Dresden was not an obvious military target. Bombing a city which was sheltering thousands of refugees led to criticisms at the time. It remains one of the most controversial acts of the war. Despite the heroism of the bomber crews and the heavy losses they endured, the effectiveness and morality of their work have both been questioned. Churchill himself had doubts about a policy he had enthusiastically supported.

Source Q Churchill writes to the Head of Bomber Command, Arthur Harris, after the 1000-strong bomber raid on Cologne.
....

I congratulate you and the whole of Bomber Command upon the remarkable feat of organization which enabled you to despatch over a thousand bombers to Cologne in a single night. The proof of the growing power of the British Bomber force is also the herald of what Germany will receive city by city from now on.

Churchill, letter, 1 June 1942.

Source R Churchill writes to senior RAF commanders expressing concerns about the bombing of Germany.
....

It seems to me that the moment has come when the question of bombing German cities simply for the sake of increasing the terror though under other pretexts should be reviewed. Otherwise we shall come under control of an utterly ruined land – the destruction of Dresden remains a serious query against the conduct of allied bombing. I feel the need for more concentration upon military objectives rather than more acts of terror and wanton destruction.

Churchill, letter, March 1945.

Source S Bishop George Bell speaks in the House of Lords about the bombing.
....

I turn to the situation in February, 1944, and the terrific devastation by Bomber Command of German towns. Hitler is a barbarian. It is clear enough that large-scale bombing of enemy towns was begun by the Nazis. There is no decent person on the Allied side who is likely to suggest that we should make him our pattern or attempt to be competitors in that market. The question with which I am concerned is this. Do the Government understand the full force of what area bombardment is doing and is destroying now? Are they alive not only to the

Activity

1 How do Sources Q and R differ in their view of the bombing strategy? Why do you think they differ?
2 Consider Sources S and T. How and why do these views of the morality of air attacks differ?

vastness of the material damage, much of which is irreparable, but also to the harvest they are laying up for the future relationships of the peoples of Europe as well as to its moral implications? I fully realize that in attacks on centres of war industry and transport the killing of civilians when it is the result of bona-fide military activity is inevitable. But there must be a fair balance between the means employed and the purpose achieved. To obliterate a whole town because certain portions contain military and industrial establishments is to reject the balance.

Bishop George Bell of Chichester, speech, 9 February 1944.

Source T Churchill discusses bombing and possible gas attacks on the Germans.

It is absurd to consider morality on this topic when everybody used gas in the last war with no complaints from the moralists or the church. On the other hand in the last war the bombing of open cities was forbidden. Now everybody does it as a matter of course. It is simply a matter of fashion changing. I want a cold-blooded calculation of how it would pay us to use poison gas. We could drench the cities of the Ruhr and many other cities in Germany in such a way that most of the population would be requiring medical attention.

Churchill, memorandum to the Chiefs of Staff, 6 July 1944.

Source U A modern historian considers the value of the bombing.

The British Bombing Survey Unit produced an Overall Report in 1945. Its study came to the conclusion that it was not, in fact, area bombing (of cities) that had smoothed the path to victory. In the final analysis it had not decisively weakened German armaments production. Bomber command only acquired decisive strategic importance in the final phase of the war when the raids were concentrating on German transport and communications networks. Doubts had been raised in many quarters whether German morale could be broken.

Dietmar Suss, *Death From the Skies*, 2014.

Source V A senior scientific adviser and close associate of Churchill advises the British government on bombing.

In 1938 over 22 million Germans lived in 58 towns of over 100,000 inhabitants. If even half our bombs were dropped on ... these 58 towns the great majority of these inhabitants [about one-third of the German population] would be turned out of house and home. Investigation seems to show that having one's home demolished is most damaging to morale ... there seems little doubt that this would break the spirit of the people.

Lord Cherwell, memorandum, 1942.

Activity

1 How far do you think the view given in Source U is justified? The alternative view is given in Source V by Churchill's personal scientific adviser.
2 Use your knowledge of bombing policy by Britain to assess how useful Source R is as evidence for whether the bombing campaign was appropriate. (AS)
3 Use your own knowledge of the British bombing strategy in the Second World War to assess how useful Source V is in explaining why Churchill supported it. (AS)

How important was Churchill's role in the war, 1944–45?

Churchill had severe anxieties and doubts about the invasion of France, but was eager to be with his forces as soon as possible. However, by this stage of the war the nature of the conflict had changed and, after standing alone in 1940, Britain found itself dominated by a richer and more powerful USA with whom strategy had to be agreed. Britain was also conscious that the USSR had made victory possible by the enormous sacrifice of its people and forces in wearing the German war machine down. After the Normandy landings British forces began to take much heavier losses and Britain, now a junior partner in the Grand Alliance, lost its freedom of action. The British tried one last great imaginative campaign but 'Operation Market Garden' fell foul of some poor planning, the unexpected presence of a German SS division and some muddled thinking about possible outcomes. After the Arnhem disaster (see 'Market Garden Operation' section, page 41) there was no alternative but to go forward at a pace directed by US Commander Eisenhower in a dogged fight against determined German units until Germany itself was invaded.

Churchill found himself sidelined in meetings of the '**Big Three**' leaders (the name given to Churchill, Roosevelt and Stalin), and he had to accept at the Yalta Conference in February 1945 some very unpalatable decisions. Instead of defending the integrity of Poland, a British aim in 1939, Churchill had to accept that its frontiers were moved westwards and that Stalin took back eastern Poland. Russian prisoners of war who had fought on the German side – one historian has called them 'victims of Yalta' – were handed back to Stalin for punishment. Churchill was forced to watch Stalin ignore the crushing of a rebellion in Warsaw by the Poles against German rule until the Germans had crushed the rising and killed off those who were spirited enough to provide any opposition to future Russian domination. He was also frustrated that Roosevelt paid limited attention to his warnings of a Russian-dominated post-war eastern Europe.

Even with the importance of the main European campaign being established after 1944, Churchill still saw the Mediterranean as key and sent troops against a communist rising in Greece. Stalin, true to his agreement with Churchill, did not intervene. British forces, already stretched by the advance into Germany, the defence of India and the Middle East and a bitter war in Burma against the Japanese, now entered into a campaign in Greece to defend the monarchy.

Source W Churchill speaks to the House of Commons.

During these last three winter months, the human race all over the world has undergone more physical agony than in any other period. I must admit that I never felt so grave a sense of responsibility as I did at Yalta. In 1940 and 1941 when we were all alone and invasion was so near, the actual steps one ought to take seemed plain and simple. Now we are entering in a world of imponderables, and at every stage self-questioning arises. It is a mistake to look too far ahead.

Churchill, speech, 7 February 1945.

Activity

Read Source W and answer the questions that follow.

1 How would you describe the mood of the statement?
2 What were the 'imponderables' that Churchill refers to and why had the situation changed since 1941?
3 Do you think that Source W shows that Churchill felt he was losing control of the war by February 1945?
4 What information in this chapter would confirm his worries?

How important were the reconstruction policies of Churchill's government and what role did he play?

It was not entirely clear quite what the war was being fought for by 1944.
- Initially the war had been for Poland, but Poland's wishes were being ignored and there was every prospect of Russian domination and control.
- Britain had seemed to be a defender of 'civilised values', but had subjected German cities to heavy bombing and caused civilian casualties on a large scale.
- Britain was in alliance with the communist USSR, but a campaign in Greece against communism was going on at the same time.
- A war to preserve British independence of action was ending with the United States controlling military strategy and large numbers of US soldiers based in Britain.
- A war to preserve the territorial integrity of the British Empire had seen much of the 'Empire in the East' lost to the Japanese in 1942; no diminution in powerful pressure for Indian independence; and the USA hostile to British imperialism.

Given these problems, it is not surprising that attention was increasingly given to ensuring that post-war Britain should be a better place by radical social reforms. There were hopes that the massive national effort which had gone into war would go into post-war reconstruction. This had failed after the First World War and there was a determination among many British people that this failure would not be repeated. Churchill, though a well-known social reformer before 1914, saw discussion of what would happen after victory as a distraction to achieving that victory. Nevertheless, the wartime coalition which Churchill headed made substantial progress in planning the post-war period and paved the way for important reforms after 1945.

Table 1 Some of the social changes made during the Second World War.

Rest centres and meal service centres	To help those who had suffered in air raids.
Committee for the Homeless	A million homes were made habitable. Prefabricated homes were created to meet the housing shortages.
National Assistance	The old 'means test' was abolished in 1941 and help was given to the needy.
Emergency Hospital Service	By 1941 eight out of ten hospitals were brought under a national scheme for the first time.
National Fire Service	Over 1500 different fire services were brought together.
Mothers and children	Diphtheria immunisation; free milk to school children; extension of free school meals; orange juice and cod-liver oil provided. There were reductions in infant mortality.
Railways	In 1942 British railways united and nationalised the rail network.
Factory Acts	The 1940 Factory Acts were the responsibility of the Minister of Labour: improved welfare for 6 million workers introduced; improved conditions of work for younger workers; Catering Wages Act 1942 and Wages Councils Act of 1945 improved wages for the low-paid.

Table 2 Wartime reports, committees and measures which made plans for reconstruction after the war and an improvement in living standards.

1941 Post-War Problems Committee	Chaired by the Tory, R. A. Butler, this began to consider post-war reform and reconstruction.
1942 Beveridge Report	Influential report which aimed to deal with poverty, ill-health and unemployment after the war.
1940 Barlow Report 1942 Uthwatt Report 1942 Scott Report 1944 White Paper on Land Use	These reports paved the way for the purchase of land after the war for development of housing; for the location of industries to be controlled; and for planning of new towns, conservation areas and control of smoke.
1944 Full Employment in a Free Society	Beveridge published another report advocating an end to unemployment.
1944 Ministry of National Insurance	This brought health and unemployment insurance under one ministry. They had previously been divided between Health and Labour.
1944 Town and Country Planning Act	A ministry of town and country planning had been set up in 1943 and this act dealt with reconstruction of badly bombed or 'blighted' areas.
1944 Education Act	• Each area in Britain was to provide 'a varied and comprehensive education service'. • The school leaving age was to be raised to 15 by 1947 and then after that to 16. • Education to be divided into primary (5–11) and secondary (11–16) and tertiary 16+. • School fees in state schools ended and milk and meals were provided. • An exam at the age of 11 was introduced to decide on the type of school to be attended.

The Beveridge Report, 1942

The Beveridge Report proposed a far-reaching series of changes designed to achieve 'freedom from want' after the war. Everyone of working age would be expected to pay a weekly National Insurance contribution. In return benefits would be paid to people who were sick, widowed, retired and unemployed and there would also be an allowance for families. It was the basis of the post-war Welfare State.

Thus the war had forced the state to extend medical services, care for the poor and homeless, plan for future extension of the **Welfare State**, make provision for more town and country planning and reform education. There was a determination not to return to the disappointments which followed the First World War and the poverty and unemployment in many areas in the 1930s.

The key document was the report by William Beveridge in late 1942. However, though the Conservatives as a whole supported this, many feared the growth of the state. The report was debated in February 1943. Churchill expressed concerns about the costs but the Conservatives and Liberals accepted the principles of what Beveridge called 'a social service state', with citizens paying contributions for health and welfare benefits, and Labour thought it did not go far enough.

Source X Churchill gives a private view about social reform.

Churchill said that the government had gone further with Beveridge than he would have gone himself. He said that Beveridge was an awful windbag and a dreamer.

Diary of Churchill's secretary after the debate on the Beveridge Report, February 1943.

Source Y The Prime Minister speaks about social reforms.

Here is a real opportunity. You must rank me and my colleagues as strong partisans [supporters] of national compulsory insurance from the cradle to the grave. There is no finer investment for any community than putting milk into babies. There is a broadening field for state ownership and enterprise.

Churchill, speech to the nation, March 1943

Source Z The Prime Minister speaks about more government intervention in social and economic life.

Control for control's sake is senseless. Controls under the pretext of war or its aftermath which are designed to favour the accomplishment of quasi-totalitarian systems, however innocently designed or whatever slogans they mouth, are a fraud which should be exposed.

Churchill, speech to the Conservative conference, March 1945.

Source AA Following Churchill's denunciation of 'socialism' in his election campaign, his daughter writes to him.

Socialism as practised in the war never did anyone any harm and quite a lot of people good. The children of the country have never been so well-fed or healthy; what milk there was was shared equally; the rich didn't die because their meat ration was no larger than the poor; this common sharing and sacrifice was one of the strongest bonds that united us. So why cannot this continue into peace?

Sarah Churchill, letter to her father, April 1945.

Activity

1 How and why do Sources X–AA give a different impression of Churchill's attitude to post-war social reform?
2 What do you think is the significance of whom Churchill was speaking to in each source?
3 What does Source AA suggest about why both parties, Labour and Conservative, supported the need for more social reform?
4 Use your knowledge of the election of 1945 to assess how useful Source AA is as evidence of Churchill's responsibility for the outcome (AS)

Why did Churchill lose office in 1945?

This considerable interest in post-war change may have been the main reason for Churchill losing office in the election of 1945. Many voters were sceptical that the Conservatives would actually deliver key reforms. The seeming indifference of the Conservatives to high unemployment in the 1930s was a major criticism levelled at the party. Churchill had been out of office at that time, but the voters of 1945 were voting for a different kind of Britain and it was Labour and not their wartime leader that was more likely to deliver it.

- The wartime reports offered much better prospects for the working classes. By far the most significant was the Beveridge Report of 1942. Though written by a Liberal, supported by the Conservatives and criticised by Labour, it was generally thought that Labour would be most likely to implement it.
- The Conservatives were blamed for the 'hungry decade' of the 1930s and also for appeasement, while Labour offered a progressive manifesto for change and were seen as proponents of collective security and supporters of Churchill in 1940.
- Churchill, for all his popularity and reputation, was seen as a person somewhat apart from the Conservatives. He did not help their campaign by aggressive campaigning and making ridiculous associations between Labour and the Nazi Gestapo. The Labour leaders by 1945 were known to

have served loyally in the war and were well known in their own right. For example, Herbert Morrison was a household name after the domestic air raid shelter which was called after him.

■ The great achievements of the USSR pointed the way to greater economic control and social reform by the state, something that Labour with its socialist origins promised to deliver.

■ The war had produced more social mobility, as men of ability were promoted in the forces. Many wanted to ensure that there was greater opportunity for ordinary people. During the war, women had once again taken on key roles in previously male-dominated occupations. Many saw a vote for Labour as a vote for more social change and a less class-ridden Britain.

Table 3 Votes cast in the 1945 election.

Labour	47.7%
Conservative	36.2%
Liberal	9%
Liberal National	2.9%
Others	4.2%

Table 4 Seats won in the 1945 election.

Labour	61.4%
Conservative	30.8%
Liberal	1.9%
Liberal National	1.2%
Others	4.7%

Britain's electoral system meant that the popular vote was not as great as the number of seats won by Labour. However, the result was still a resounding victory for change. It reflected a widespread desire to ensure that costly and grinding years of war would result in a better Britain.

Source BB Churchill's private secretary gives a view about the election in June 1945.

• •

The weekend was devoted to the preparation of the first political broadcast before the general election of 5 July 1945. The PM's speech was a fighting and provocative effort, mentioning the necessity of a political police to a really socialist state. His gestures to the microphone were as emphatic as those he uses to a large audience. The speech aroused widespread criticism and did not really go down well with the educated classes. Labour propaganda is better and it links to the popular mood. I think the Service vote will be for Labour and the housing shortage has left many people disgruntled.

Sir John Colville, *The Fringes of Power: Downing Street Diaries, 1939–1955*, 1987.

Source CC This pro-Churchill election poster refers to the wartime coalition. Churchill was strictly a National Government candidate, though in practice a Conservative.

▲ Election poster from 1945

Source DD This poster depicts ordinary servicemen and is a reference to a speech by Churchill in which he said 'Give us the tools and we will finish the job'. Both Labour and the Conservatives used this idea.

▲ Labour election poster from 1945

Source EE A friend of the Conservative MP Harold Nicolson writes about the election. The author was a left-wing writer and editor.

I think that Churchill more than anyone else was responsible for the squalid lies in these elections. He started the rot with his talk of Mr Attlee's Gestapo. The result is to make sensitive people keep out of politics. I should like to see Churchill retire. I think him quite the wrong man for directing the reconstruction of England. Our debt to him is probably greater than to any other politician in our history. But I could not feel on any account any obligation to vote for him.

Raymond Mortimer, letter, 10 July 1945.

Activity

Applying knowledge to sources

Using your own knowledge and sources AA–EE, do you think that Labour won the election mainly because of Churchill's misjudgements?

Try to link your knowledge to the explanation you take from the sources. For example, one reason may be found in Source BB – the reference to the political police by Churchill. He had said that Labour's programme would need 'some form of a Gestapo'. This had upset many voters and was blatantly unfair. From what you know of Labour and their contribution in the war, does this seem likely to be seen as unfair?

Chapter takeaways

- Churchill's larger-than-life political style was important in keeping Britain in the war and giving confidence to the British people.
- His speeches 'put the English language to war' and he was able to create a heroic picture of Britain's war effort.
- His leadership style was distinctive but often erratic and his relations with his military leaders were stormy.
- Both key elements of his war strategy were controversial:
  - The first, to wage war in North Africa and the Mediterranean rather than to launch an invasion of Europe, was heavily criticised by the American generals and has been seen as possibly delaying the end of the war; but he was anxious to avoid the heavy land casualties of the First World War.
- The second, the bombing offensive, has been seen as both immoral and ineffective; but at the time may have seemed the only way to strike decisively at the ability of Germany to wage war.
- During the war, Churchill left post-war reconstruction to his ministers, particularly Labour colleagues, but his government deserves the credit for accepting the key Beveridge Report which laid the basis for the modernisation of post-war Britain's health and social welfare.
- Despite his massive personal efforts on Britain's behalf and his reputation as a great war leader, Churchill did not win the election of 1945 because it was Labour and not the Conservatives who were seen as the better hope for a fairer society and a new Britain.

Study Skills: Evaluating a series of sources

Look at the following sources about Churchill as a war leader.

Source A Churchill's Chief of Staff recalls working with him during the Second World War.

....

Churchill was certainly frank in his speech and writing and expected others to be equally frank with him. No commander who engaged the enemy need ever fear that he would not be supported. His knowledge of military history was encyclopaedic, and his grasp of the broad sweep of strategy was unrivalled. He had a considerable respect for the military mind, but refused to subscribe to the idea that generals were infallible.

Lord Ismay, *Memoirs*, 1960.

Source B A left-wing Labour critic of Churchill and later post-war Minister of Health offers a view of his war-time leadership.

....

Churchill's greatest contributions were to persuade people not to look at facts. When the people of this country might have been depressed by the brute facts of Dunkirk, he was persuading them to think about Queen Elizabeth and the defeat of the Armada in 1588. He flung a Union Jack over five tanks and got people to behave as if they had been fifteen. He put the case of Britain to the world and the destiny of Britain to the British.

Aneurin Bevan, *Churchill By His Contemporaries*, 1965.

Source C The Military Assistant Secretary to the War Cabinet reflects on the strengths and weaknesses of Churchill's view of military affairs during the Second World War.

Churchill tended to think in terms of 'sabre and bayonets'. He did not seem to understand that infantry had little power unless properly organised in battle formations with good communications and a real command structure, backed by artillery and anti-tank weapons. He did not fully realise the change that had taken place since the First World War in large-scale warfare. He also, though, had an interest in new inventions. He kept fully abreast of developments in radar, in aerial navigation. He encouraged the development of new weapons. Nothing fell outside his enquiring mind.

General Sir Ian Jacob, *Action This Day*, 1968.

Source D The Chief of the Imperial General Staff records a conference with Churchill.

Another poisonous day! The Prime Minister behaved like a spoilt child that wants a toy in a shop irrespective of the fact that its parents tell him that it is no good! Got nowhere with him and settled nothing. I feel unable to face another day of conferences such as the present one with the Prime Minister. He shook his fist in my face, saying 'I do not want any of your long-term plans, they stifle initiative!' All this made arguing impossible.

Sir Alan Brooke, *Diary*, 19 August 1943.

1 Think of the adjectives about Churchill that you might use after reading each one. Copy and complete the following tables:

A	For example: *supportive, knowledgeable, balanced*
B	
C	
D	

2 Now think which parts of the source support this adjective:

A	*Supportive because ... no commander who went into battle against the enemy would ever fail to be supported.* *Knowledgeable because ...* *Balanced because ...*
B	
C	
D	

3 Now think if there is any knowledge that you have after reading the chapter that might either support or challenge the view:

A	*Supportive because ... no commander who went into battle against the enemy would ever fail to be supported.*	*+* *Gave resources and encouragement to Montgomery 1942.*	*−* *Did not support Wavell 1941.*
B			
C			
D			

4 Is there anything in the provenance that you need to take into account
   when assessing these pieces of evidence which do give different views of
   Churchill?

Source	What is it?	When was it written?	Why was it written?	Is the author in a position to know?	Might the author be prejudiced either for or against Churchill?
A					
B					
C					
D	Diary	Just after stormy meeting. Brooke has had no time to reflect and he may be 'letting off steam'.	To record important events as they happened.	Brooke worked closely with Churchill.	They had many disagreements but he knew Churchill well.

5 Which do you think is the most useful source here for understanding
   Churchill as a war leader? Compare your view with the views of others in
   the class.

Focus on AS   (AS)

Look at Sources A, C and D on pages 55 and 56 and answer the question below. (This is an indication of the type of skill needed when considering three sources at AS.) In order to do well answering this type of question you must ensure that your answer is focused on the question. You need to evaluate the sources, using both provenance and relevant knowledge of their historical context. This is in order to engage with the sources and reach a supported analysis of them in relation to the issue in the question. The balance between using provenance and your own knowledge to evaluate the sources does not have to be a 50:50 split, but you must both consider the provenance and use your knowledge.

Using these three sources in their historical context, assess the view that Churchill had bad relations with his generals during the Second World War.

Chapter 3

Churchill and international diplomacy, 1939–51

This chapter deals with Churchill's diplomatic aims and his views of Britain and its empire as a major world power. It outlines the relations that Churchill had with President Roosevelt both before and after the US entered the war. It looks at Churchill's policy towards Stalin, and the series of international conferences which determined both wartime policy and the planning for the post-war world, as well as his stormy relationship with Charles de Gaulle. Churchill's reactions to the spread of Soviet control over eastern Europe in and after 1945 and his views on Europe when he was in opposition from 1945 to 1951 are assessed. The main issues to be considered are as follows:

- What were Churchill's views on Britain's world and imperial roles?
- How did he manage his relations with other wartime leaders?
- What contribution did he make to the wartime international conferences?
- What were his plans for post-war Europe and his attitude to Europe and the Empire?
- What was the significance of the 'iron curtain' speech, 1946?

This chapter offers practice in looking at sets of sources. They should be used to make a judgement about an issue. Their value as evidence should be assessed by looking at what they are and why and in what circumstances they were produced. Knowledge should be used to assess the value and reliability of the evidence.

Timeline

1940	September	'Destroyers for Bases' agreement with USA
1941	March	Lend-Lease Act
	June	German forces invade Russia
	August	Meeting of Churchill and Roosevelt at Placentia Bay; the Atlantic Charter
	December	Japan attacks US base at Pearl Harbor
		Germany declares war on USA
1942	June	Churchill and Roosevelt agree on a Mediterranean strategy
	August	Churchill meets Stalin in Moscow
1943	November	Tehran Conference
1944	June	D-Day landings open 'second front' in northern Europe
	October	Stalin and Churchill make 'Percentages Agreement'
1945	February	Yalta Conference
	April	Roosevelt dies
	July–August	Potsdam Conference
1946	March	Churchill's 'iron curtain' speech
	September	Churchill's speech on Europe at Zürich
1951	October	Churchill returns to office

Overview

Churchill had never been responsible for foreign affairs but in 1940 found himself having to deal with other countries in order to ensure Britain's survival. He tried desperately to keep France fighting after the invasion by Germany in 1940, even offering a union with Britain. The destruction of the French fleet (see Chapter 2) alienated France's new Vichy government and Churchill dealt with France through the self-appointed leader of the 'Free French', Charles de Gaulle. Relations were stormy throughout the war. However, Churchill knew that the key to British victory, and even survival, lay with the USA. He believed that the US could not allow Germany to dominate Europe and set about building a strong relationship with US President Franklin Roosevelt. The view that a 'special relationship' was built up has been challenged and, despite the warm feelings between the two men, there were strains in the alliance between Britain and the USA that came about when Hitler declared war on the USA in 1941. Churchill put great stress on the shared democratic values of the two countries. That could hardly be said of Churchill's other major ally, communist Russia. Churchill had denounced communism in bitter terms since 1917, but as soon as Hitler invaded, he offered friendship to Stalin.

The war was won by the Grand Alliance led by the USSR, USA and Britain. However, there were considerable disagreements during the war and, as Russian forces advanced into eastern Europe in 1944, these became worse. Stalin was very conscious that Britain and the USA had avoided a large-scale invasion of France until mid-1944 and that the brunt of the casualties was being taken by the USSR. Even when the so-called 'second front' (see page 40) was opened by the landings in Normandy in June 1944, there was mistrust. Churchill tried to persuade the US of the threat from Russia, but Roosevelt did not share Churchill's anxieties and became increasingly suspicious of British policy.

Churchill turned to negotiating a division of Europe with Stalin in 1944 on one hand and resisting communism in Greece on the other. There were major decisions taken about post-war Europe, especially at conferences held at Yalta and subsequently at Potsdam in 1945, though by the time of Potsdam Churchill was no longer in office. Churchill was deeply suspicious about Russian intentions and his fears seemed to be confirmed by Russian take-overs in occupied eastern European countries. Having gone to war to protect Poland, Britain had to watch that country lose territory to the USSR and then be dominated by pro-Soviet leaders protected by the occupying Red Army. In 1946 Churchill, by then in opposition, made one of the most influential speeches of his career and warned of an **'iron curtain'** stretching across Europe.

Free to express his views, he spoke about the future of Europe and encouraged European unity. By 1951 though, when he returned to power, Britain's place in both Europe and the world had changed considerably. The war to preserve the Empire had led to a severe weakening of Britain's imperial power. The strains of war had made Britain's ability to sustain itself as a great world power considerably less than the two 'superpowers' that had emerged by 1945.

What were Churchill's views on Britain's world and imperial roles?

Enquiry Units are all about sources so this chapter begins with a source activity.

Source A Churchill speaks to the House of Commons at the beginning of the last year of the war.

I am clear that nothing should induce us to abandon the principle of unconditional surrender but the President of the United States and I have repeatedly declared that the enforcement of this surrender on the enemy in no way relieves us of obligations to humanity, or our duties as civilised and

Christian nations. We declared war not for any ambition or material advantage, but for the sake of our obligation for Poland against German aggression, in which aggression, there or elsewhere, it must in fairness be stated, our own self-preservation was involved. After the defeat of France in June 1940, for more than a year we were alone. We stood alone; we kept nothing back in blood, effort or treasure from what has now become the cause of more than thirty nations. We seek no territory; we covet no oilfields; we demand no bases for the forces of the air or the seas. We are an ancient Commonwealth, dwelling, and wishing to dwell at peace within our own habitations. We do not set ourself up in rivalry of bigness or might with any other community in the world. Our motives are disinterested, lofty and true. I repulse those calumnies that the British Empire is a selfish, power-greedy, land-hungry, designing nation.

Speech by Churchill, January 1945.

Source B Early in his premiership, Churchill speaks to the House of Commons.

Upon this battle depends the survival of Christian civilisation. Upon it depends our own British life and the long continuity of our institutions and our Empire. If we fail, then the whole world, including the United States, including all we have known and cared for, will sink in the abyss of a new Dark Age.

Speech by Churchill, 18 June 1940.

Source C At the Mansion House, addressing business leaders in London, Churchill talks about war aims.

We mean to hold our own. I have not become the King's First Minister in order to preside over the liquidation of the British Empire. For that task, if ever it were prescribed, someone else would have to be found. And under democracy, I suppose the nation would have to be consulted.

Speech by Churchill, 10 November 1942.

Source D Hitler questions the basis of British policy.

I feel a deep distrust for the type of unscrupulous politician who wrecks whole nations and states. Mr Churchill ought for once to believe me when I prophesy that a great Empire will be destroyed – an Empire which it was never my intention to destroy or even harm.

Speech to the Reichstag by Hitler, July 1940.

Source E President Roosevelt gives an American view of empire in a private conversation with his son Elliott.

The British must never get the idea we are in the war just to help them cling on to their archaic mediaeval empire ideas or watch their system stultify the growth of every country of Asia.

Conversation between F.D. Roosevelt and his son, 1943.

Activity

Answer the questions on Sources A–E.

1 Source A sums up a view of Britain's role in the world. Some key ideas are set out below. Explain what Churchill meant by them.

Unconditional surrender
Civilised and Christian nations
We entered war for the sake of our obligation to Poland
We seek no territory
We wish to dwell in peace 'within our own habitations'
Our motives are disinterested (i.e. unselfish)
Our motives are lofty (noble)
The British Empire is not selfish

2 Study Sources A and B. How far do these two speeches show that Churchill's view of Britain's role and responsibility in the world remained the same during the war?

3 Below are two circumstances relating to Source C:
   - The first is the suppression of disturbances in India in August and September 1942. These followed a campaign of opposition to British rule led by the opposition Congress Party. The viceroy, Lord Linlithgow, thought the disturbances were the worst opposition since the Indian Mutiny of 1857, in which thousands rose against Britain and there was heavy loss of life. Churchill approved of the repression in which mobs were machine-gunned from the air. 'Indian show-down v. satisfactory' (Cabinet secretary's notebook, quoted in Richard Toye's *Churchill's Empire*, page 226).
   - The second is the British victory over the German forces in North Africa at El Alamein in October 1942 (see Chapter 2).

   Explain the possible connection between the tone of Source C and these circumstances.

4 How far, if at all, do you think Source D casts effective doubts on Churchill's view of the aims of the war?

5 How does Source E challenge the view of A?

6 How far is Source E supported by the evidence in this section?

Churchill dramatised the war as a conflict between democracy, freedom, civilised and Christian values and the dark forces of Nazism and dictatorship. It was Britain's role to defend its values against these dark forces. However, it was also Britain's role to maintain an Empire which used violent repression to maintain control and did not allow most of its non-white subjects the right to vote.

To defend British values Churchill was a key part of a coalition of, as he said, 30 nations, but in practice dominated by the 'Big Three'. Thus Britain, despite being defeated in 1940 in both Norway and France, was by 1941 playing a very considerable role in the world. Not only did it maintain its links with the Empire, with considerable support from its **dominions** and colonies but it sustained an alliance with the very powerful USSR and USA and played a major role in determining the way the war was fought. Until 1944 it did this without committing large land forces to Europe. In a sense, this was a notable achievement.

- There was no need for Britain's Empire to give its support; and at the time of the appeasement policies of the 1930s it was not at all certain that the self-governing dominions would support a war.
- The USA was persuaded, despite making a much greater contribution to the war effort, not to prioritise the Pacific war – where its main interests lay – but to defeat Germany first and to follow British ideas of waging war in the Mediterranean, not opening up a second front for Germany with an invasion of northern France.
- The very great losses of the USSR were not matched by Britain and yet the Russian alliance was maintained. Estimates of Soviet military casualties vary but there were probably about 9 million dead and an additional 13 million civilian deaths. Total British deaths were 452,000 and US deaths were 420,000. The scale of loss by the USSR was considerably greater. One battle alone, Stalingrad had over 1 million casualties according to official Soviet records.
- Despite agreeing to the Atlantic Charter of 1941 (see page 63), affirming democracy and self-government as a principle, Britain was not forced to make any commitment to ending her empire as the price of US support.

Churchill managed to hold on to Britain's world role as moral leader, champion of civilisation, major influence on war policy and imperial power. However, as the rest of this chapter will show, Britain's position deteriorated as the war went on.

How did Churchill manage his relations with other wartime leaders?

Churchill and Roosevelt

It seemed as if Churchill might be a more natural ally of Roosevelt than of Stalin; both headed English-speaking democracies. However, the US leader was a difficult person to know. On the surface he could be charming and seemed to be sympathetic; but he had a reputation for not committing himself, while giving his listeners the impression he had. As his biographer Conrad Black wrote about the meeting in Canada in August 1941, 'Churchill would not have noticed the conditions and qualifications and nuances with which Roosevelt clouded almost everything he said'. Their correspondence reveals much more affection from Churchill than from Roosevelt and Roosevelt's deliberate snubbing of Churchill at the Tehran Conference of 1943 was more characteristic of the US leader than of the more open Churchill.

On 12 September 1942 Churchill sent Roosevelt this message:

You know how I treasure the friendship with which you have honoured me and how profoundly I feel we might together do something really fine and lasting for our two countries

(Lowenheim, Langley, Jonas Barrie and Jenkins (editors), *Roosevelt and Churchill: Their Secret Correspondence*, page 367.)

Their personal relationship has been seen as 'the partnership that saved the West' and Churchill worked very hard to maintain it.

However, the relationship had started badly. Roosevelt had first met Churchill in 1918 and took a dislike to him. He thought him 'a stinker' and that he had 'lorded it' over him. Churchill had made unfavourable remarks about Roosevelt in 1937 which were quoted by Roosevelt's opponent, Wendell Willkie, during the US election campaign of 1940.

US support but non-intervention

Churchill had hoped for US intervention in the war, but Roosevelt had to be careful, as there was a danger of war with Japan and US public opinion was generally against a war in Europe. Nevertheless, the USA did offer some support:

■ In November 1939 the USA repealed the Neutrality Act which allowed Britain to purchase American arms.
■ In October the USA declared a neutral zone along the entire coast of the USA and South America and the US navy patrolled this to prevent the sinking of merchant shipping by Germans naval forces. This involved Anglo-American naval co-operation.
■ In September 1940, 50 old US destroyers were exchanged with Britain for leases to 8 British naval bases from Newfoundland to British Guiana.
■ In December, Roosevelt used the phrase 'arsenal of democracy' to defend sales of arms to Britain.
■ In March 1941, the Lend-Lease Act was passed permitting the President 'to sell, transfer title to, exchange, lease, lend or otherwise dispose of' defence articles to 'any country whose defence the President deems vital to the defence of the USA'. It led to $31.6 billion of assistance going to Britain by 1945.
■ In April US troops occupied Greenland and, on 1 July 1941, Iceland, in order to stop Germany using either as a military base.

Churchill disliked the way that Roosevelt stressed US isolationism at the time of the presidential election of 1940:

... as the PM says, President Roosevelt is ready to play a dirty trick on the world and risk the ultimate destruction of the Western Democracies in order to secure re-election ...

(Sir Robert Vansittart, Chief Diplomatic Adviser, quoted in Joseph Lash, *Roosevelt and Churchill, 1939–41*, 1977, page 117.)

Their first meeting as national leaders took place in Placentia Bay in Canada in August 1941. Churchill was keen to make a good impression and obtained a joint declaration of 'certain common principles', known as the Atlantic Charter. This was remarkable as the USA had not declared war, yet the document referred to plans 'after the destruction of the Nazi tyranny'.

As Churchill was well aware, the problem was that, though Roosevelt could offer support for Britain, a declaration of war lay in the hands of Congress. The South African, General Smuts wrote to Churchill of 'the growing belief that Roosevelt intends to keep America out of the war, in spite of his brave words'.

Churchill replied, saying: 'He may take action as Chief Executive but only Congress can declare war ... we must have patience and trust to the tide that is turning our way.'

If Churchill had put more pressure on, the result would not have been helpful as the USA was concerned about a number of issues:

The Atlantic Charter

The Atlantic Charter confirmed that neither the US nor Britain wanted territorial gains. The third point said that 'they respect the right of all peoples to choose the form of government under which they will live' and the fourth said that all states should have 'access on equal terms to the trade and raw materials of the world'. The fifth committed both to work for 'improved labour standards, economic advancement and social security'. There was also a commitment to peace and disarmament. Churchill never accepted that it applied to Britain's subject peoples and accepted it only as a sign that the USA had entered into a 'tacit alliance' with Britain.

US Congress

Congress is the collective name for the House of Representatives and the Senate in the USA, the equivalent of the British parliament. But unlike Britain, the legislature (Congress) is separate from the executive branch (the government) and US government ministers are not members of Congress and do not take part in debates. In Britain all government ministers are either members of the House of Commons or the House of Lords. Congress must approve any act of war declared by the president.

US–Japanese relations

The US had been concerned about Japan's war against China which had broken out in 1937 and Japan's expansion in the Far East. Roosevelt blocked Japan's oil supply. To end US interference and to pave the way for taking US and European colonies in Asia, Japan attacked Pearl Harbor, the US naval base in Hawaii, on 7 December 1941. This started a war which Hitler decided to join.

■ US military chiefs were concerned that Britain was dispersing its forces by fighting in North Africa instead of getting ready for an invasion of France.

■ The State Department (the US equivalent of the Foreign Office in Britain) was concerned that Britain would want to gain territories as it had in 1919 when it gained control over German and Turkish colonies.

■ The secretary of state (the US equivalent of the foreign secretary in Britain), Cordell Hull, was concerned that the British Empire stood in the way of world free trade, which was likely to become a US war aim.

■ Roosevelt thought it was morally wrong for Britain to rule over the subjects of the British Empire, and wanted colonial peoples to be free – something that runs through the correspondence of the two leaders.

Though the USA had gone some way to showing support (see page 63), there was no certainty that it would actually declare war on Germany, or even if it did, would put the defeat of Germany as its priority. Also Britain had got less than generous terms:

■ The destroyers provided by the USA were obsolete.

■ The USA took Britain's gold reserves in South Africa as security for Lend-Lease payments.

■ The USA made large profits from supplying arms.

The USA enters the war

By December 1941 it seemed increasingly likely that Japan's war in China would lead to conflict with the USA, as America had imposed embargos on oil and metal ore supplies to Japan. When Japan attacked the US Pacific fleet in **Pearl Harbor**, Hitler made possibly his greatest mistake of the war and declared war on the USA. Churchill had been proved right that 'the tide is turning our way' and had helped to prepare the ground by his meetings; but he could not really have foreseen Hitler's decision and his strategy was based on hope.

What followed was a remarkable turn of events. Though Roosevelt wanted to wait before meeting Churchill, the Prime Minister went to Washington as soon as possible, where he made a very positive impression. America was now more inclined to see Churchill as a heroic figure in a very emotional time rather than as an old-fashioned imperialist warmonger and Churchill's oratory and confidence now were major elements. British policy prevailed. The US General Marshall did not get his way and there was no invasion of northern France until 1944. The USA supported Churchill's strategy of fighting mainly in the Mediterranean. It also supported a policy of 'Europe First', defeating Germany before Japan. From being alone, Britain now was a member of a Grand Alliance of 26 nations.

Source F A British view of the relationship between Churchill and Roosevelt.

SAILORS DO CARE

" The more we get together
The merrier we shall be."

Cartoon from Times & Advertiser, 13 May 1942.

Source G A German cartoon, 'Roosevelt and Churchill struggle for control of Africa'.

Cartoon from 1942.

In June 1942 Churchill met Roosevelt in New York and later that month, again at Washington. He persuaded the USA against the idea of 'Operation Sledgehammer' for an invasion of France to take pressure off the Russians and instead promoted the idea for a joint campaign in North Africa. At the next meeting at Casablanca the British strategy for invading Sicily and then Italy was accepted by Roosevelt.

There were limits, though. Roosevelt disliked Britain's backing of de Gaulle as representing France – the USA preferred to work with the French General Giraud, a higher ranking officer, and did not see de Gaulle as representing French opinion. There was also a build up of US forces in Britain, amounting to one of the most remarkable developments of the war with huge numbers of US forces coming to the country. Beginning in January 1942, over a million US troops came to Britain before being shipped to North Africa and Italy and then taking part in the build up to D-Day.

In Washington, in May 1943, US pressure forced a date for the invasion of northern France – May 1944 (a month earlier than the actual invasion). Roosevelt was also moving to the logical position that, given Russia's immense war effort, the key element in US diplomacy should be to negotiate with Stalin and to sideline Churchill, whose forces were not contributing to the war on the scale of the USA or the USSR. By the time of the meeting at Quebec in August 1943, splits were apparent. The USA favoured an attack on southern France, which Churchill did not. Churchill favoured attacks in the Balkans which the USA did not. Churchill and Roosevelt met at Cairo in November 1943 and then moved on to Tehran to meet Stalin. Here it was clear that relations between Roosevelt and Churchill had changed.

- Roosevelt refused to meet Churchill privately to decide on a joint policy before the conference.
- He met the Chinese leader Jiang Jieshi without Churchill's knowledge.
- He made it clear that he wanted British attacks in Burma at the expense of more attacks in the Mediterranean.
- The USA had now abandoned 'Europe First' and were working for the defeat of Japan.
- There were very bitter exchanges about the invasion of northern France.
- At Tehran, Roosevelt clearly favoured Stalin over Churchill.
- Churchill's plan of bringing Turkey into the war and setting up a Balkan front were rejected.
- The USA would supply the supreme commander of 'Operation Overlord', the D-Day Allied invasion of France in 1944.

At Quebec in September 1944 Churchill got no commitment for post-war financial assistance for Britain. By 1944 it was also clear that America was not as concerned about post-war Soviet expansion as Britain, and that the USA was not prepared to back the idea of an Anglo-American race to occupy Berlin before the Russian army got there.

At the last of the meetings at Yalta in February 1945, Roosevelt and Churchill agreed on the policy that there should be free elections and democracy in post-war Europe; Roosevelt was concerned that this would not apply to the British Empire. When Roosevelt died in April 1945 Churchill paid a fulsome tribute to him in the House of Commons.

▲ Roosevelt and Churchill at the Casablanca Conference, 1943.

Activity

How accurate is Source H as a picture of Churchill's relationship with Roosevelt? (You should consider when and why it was produced; whether what it contains is really what Churchill thought and is backed up by what you know and whether the source misses anything out.)

Source H Extract from Churchill's speech to the House of Commons following Roosevelt's death.

He devised the extraordinary measure of assistance called Lend-Lease, which will stand forth as the most unselfish and unsordid financial act of any country in all history.

Together we drew up the declaration which has been called the Atlantic Charter and which will, I trust, long remain a guide for both our peoples and for other peoples of the world.

Both our countries were in arms, shoulder to shoulder.

In Franklin Roosevelt there died the greatest American friend we have ever known, and the greatest champion of freedom who has ever brought help and comfort from the new World to the Old.

Churchill, speech , April 1945.

Roosevelt had never visited Churchill in Britain; Churchill did not attend Roosevelt's funeral. Churchill was critical of US policy: 'They played a dominating part in the destiny of Europe, but may well have denied us all the lasting peace for which we had fought long and hard' by not taking a firmer line with the USSR.

Churchill and Stalin

With Stalin, Churchill faced a clever and relentless dictator supporting an ideology which Churchill hated. Churchill's mother was American and he had a strong belief in the united interests of Anglo-Saxon peoples. He had no such sympathy for Russian communism and had been a bitter and outspoken critic of the Revolution of 1917, doing his best to overturn the communist regime of Lenin by sending British forces against it. His opposition was expressed in extreme terms in his writings. However, as soon as Hitler invaded the USSR in June 1941, Churchill put ideology aside and famously said, 'If Hitler invaded Hell, I would at least make a favourable reference to the Devil in the House of Commons.'

Like most western observers, Churchill expected that communism had so weakened Russia that Hitler would soon be successful. The resistance of Russia in the winter of 1941–42, however, was one of the great turning points of the war. Stalin was clearly going to be one of the 'Big Three' Allied leaders and Churchill had to do business with him. Russian resistance was also very popular in Britain and seemed to show that state planning and socialism could produce national unity and success. Churchill was determined, though, not to allow sympathy for the huge sacrifices made by Russia in the heroic sieges of Leningrad and Stalingrad, and then in the counter attacks of 1943, to lead Britain towards an early invasion of northern Europe.

At their first meeting in 1942 Churchill was annoyed by Stalin's scornful criticisms of the failure of Britain to invade Europe.

◄ Churchill and Stalin in the Kremlin, Moscow, in good humour after dinner, August 1942.

By 1943 the sheer scale of the Russian war effort convinced the US that Stalin, rather than Churchill, was the key figure in the alliance. Churchill was much more concerned about the consequences of Russian advances into eastern Europe and by 1944 feared that in defeating Hitler, a dictator who threatened to dominate Europe, Britain had opened the way for another, Stalin, to do the same with an equally repugnant ideology.

This led Churchill to revert in 1944 to old-style diplomacy and the type of agreement about 'spheres of influence' that had been more common in Victorian diplomacy than in the period after 1918. The infamous 'percentages agreement' (see Source L on page 71) challenged the idealistic vision of Britain as a fighter for freedom and was more typical of cynical power politics. There was no question of consulting the people of the countries that were to be dominated by the USSR and the West. It was the sort of deal that Stalin understood and oddly he respected it, not offering help to the Greek communists in a civil war in which Britain supported the royalist side.

Spheres of influence

'Spheres of influence' meant that a region or country would be dominated by a greater power who would not necessarily rule it directly. For example, Britain and imperial Russia made an agreement in 1907 about Persia, Tibet and Afghanistan along these lines.

Greek Civil War

When Germany occupied Greece in 1941 the Greek King George II set up a government in exile backed by Britain in Egypt. Resistance to the Nazis was led by left-wing groups. In 1944 a civil war broke out between the communists and the royalist forces. Britain backed the royalists.

However, whatever Churchill's fears, whatever his warnings and whatever deals he tried to do to stop it, the successes of the Red Army led to the domination of eastern Europe by communist Russia. At Yalta in 1945 Churchill had to accept that Poland would lose her eastern territories to Russia and be dominated by a pro-Russian government. He had to accept the loss of Polish territory and independence in the same way that Chamberlain had had to accept the German gains in Czechoslovakia: neither had the force to prevent it or the support of the USA. The fact is that Churchill needed Stalin far more than Stalin needed Churchill or British forces. Russia protested against the failure to open a second front but may have regarded this as more of a bargaining point than a deeply-held grievance, especially after the German defeat at Stalingrad in February 1943.

Churchill found relations with Stalin surprisingly good and shared the dictator's capacity for drink as well as his unwavering support for the interests of his own country. They also were both anxious to maintain their empires and had limited sympathy for the view that the people they ruled outside their homelands should be allowed to govern themselves. The relationship was less problematic in a sense because British forces were not fighting alongside Russian forces in the same way that the British were fighting alongside US troops. Russian troops did not flood into Britain in the same way as the American and certainly British forces were not under Russian command, though they were led by an overall US commander from 1944 to 1945.

Source I Churchill broadcasts to the British people after the German invasion of Russia in June 1941.

No one has been a more consistent opponent of Communism than I have, and I will unsay no word that I have spoken about it. But now the past, with its crimes, its follies, and its tragedies, flashes away. I see Russian soldiers guarding their homes. I see advancing upon them in hideous onslaught the Nazi war machine. I have to declare the decision of His Majesty's Government that any man or state who fights on against Nazidom will have our aid. The Russian danger is therefore our danger, the cause of any Russian fighting for his hearth and home is the cause of free men and free people in every quarter of the globe.

Churchill's radio broadcast, 1941.

Source J Alexander Cadogan describes Churchill's meeting with Stalin in August 1942. Cadogan was a senior and experienced diplomat and he is here recording his experiences in his diary.

I found Winston and Stalin, sitting with a heavily-laden board between them: food of all kinds crowned by a sucking pig, and innumerable bottles. Everyone seemed to be as merry as a marriage bell. I think the two great men really made contact and got on terms. Certainly, Winston was impressed and I think that feeling was reciprocated ... Anyhow, conditions have been established in which messages exchanged between the two will mean twice as much, or more, than they did before.

Sir Alexander Cadogan, diary, August 1942.

Source K The official record of the discussion between Stalin and Churchill about opening a second front, August 1942. Churchill described this as 'a most unpleasant discussion'.

•••

M. STALIN suggested that higher sacrifices were called for. Ten thousand men a day were being sacrificed on the Russian front.

MR. CHURCHILL said that he envied the Russians their glory, and he hoped that we very soon would show by our deeds that the Democracies were neither sluggish nor cowardly and were just as ready as the Russians to shed blood ... He earnestly desired to hear the ring of comradeship in the discussions. He well knew what the Russians were going through: we ourselves had fought alone for a year ... He had come a long way in the hope that he would receive the hand of comradeship and that he would be believed in a spirit of loyalty and friendship ... It grieved his heart that the Russians did not think we were doing our utmost in the common cause.

M. STALIN said that it was not a case of mistrust, but only of a divergence of view ... He felt that if the British army had been fighting the Germans as much as the Russian army, it would not be so frightened of them. The Russians, and indeed the RAF, had shown that it was possible to beat the Germans. The British infantry could do the same provided they acted at the same time as the Russians.

MR. CHURCHILL said that he pardoned the remark which M. Stalin had made on account of the bravery of the Russian army.

Minutes of meeting at Kremlin, 11.15p.m., 13 August 1942.

Source L Churchill's account of a discussion with Stalin, 1944. The paper mentioned in the source is given as a table below.

•••

The moment was apt for business, so I said to Stalin 'let us settle about our affairs in the Balkans. Your armies are in Romania and Bulgaria. We have interests, missions and agents there. Don't let us get at cross-purposes in small ways. So far as Britain is concerned, how would it do for you to have ninety percent predominance in Romania, for us to have ninety percent of the say in Greece, and go fifty-fifty about Yugoslavia?' While this was being translated I wrote out on a half sheet of paper. I pushed this across to Stalin, who had by then heard the translation. There was a slight pause. Then he took his blue pencil and made a large tick upon it, and passed it back to us. It was all settled in no more time than it takes to set down. After this there was a long silence. At length, I said 'Might it not be thought rather cynical if it seemed we have disposed of these issues so fateful to millions of people in such an offhand manner, let us burn the paper.' 'No, you keep it', said Stalin.

Winston Churchill, *Memoirs of the Second World War*, 1954.

Romania	%
Russia	90
The others	10
Greece	
Great Britain (in accord with USA)	90
Russia	10
Yugoslavia	50–50

Hungary	50–50
Bulgaria	%
Russia	75
The others	25

Source M Churchill to General Scobie, the commander of the British forces in Athens, December 1944.

Do not hesitate to act as if you were in a conquered country where a local rebellion is in progress. We have to hold and dominate Athens. It would be a great thing for you to succeed in this without bloodshed if possible, but with bloodshed if necessary.

Churchill's memorandum to General Scobie, December 1944.

Activity

1 Look at Sources I–M on pages 70–72 about Churchill's dealings with Stalin. How far do they support the view that Churchill was skilful and realistic in his dealings with the USSR during the war?

  (i) As a guide, think about what each of the sources is showing about Churchill's skill in dealing with Stalin.

  (ii) Then think about the extent to which each of the sources shows that Stalin is being realistic.

2 Use your knowledge of the events of 1941 to assess how useful Source J is as evidence of Churchill's attitude towards the USSR. (AS)

Churchill and de Gaulle

Churchill loved France and spoke fluent if heavily accented French. He had been in close contact with France as soon as he took power and was devastated by the French surrender, being willing to send further forces even after Dunkirk and to commit air resources to France against the advice of the RAF commanders. He even offered a union between Britain and France as a desperate attempt to keep

General de Gaulle and Churchill during a parade of troops in Marrakech, January 1944. There are fewer smiles in the photographs of de Gaulle and Churchill than in the photographs of Stalin and Churchill. Perhaps Churchill did not feel the need to try to be affable. ▶

France in the war. Hitler occupied northern France, but allowed a reduced, pro-Nazi French state considerable independence after the peace treaty in 1940.

This pro-Nazi state was known as Vichy France as its capital was the southern town of Vichy. Churchill was shocked at the French surrender and concerned about the French fleet falling into German hands. The actions taken against the French navy by Britain were brutal and, some thought, unnecessary: 1297 French servicepeople were killed when five ships were sunk. These actions ensured that future relations with Vichy France were impossible.

France saw the British retreat as a betrayal. The symbol of continuing French resistance came to be seen as a tall, proud Colonel Charles de Gaulle who saw himself as the spirit of a free France and led the forces known as the Free French (exiles from occupied France who were based in Britain). Churchill admired de Gaulle but found him very difficult to deal with. De Gaulle was uncompromising and often unco-operative and was also disliked by the Americans. De Gaulle was not a political leader or a high-ranking officer; as well as being the self-proclaimed champion of France, he also saw himself as the natural leader of post-war France – something that Churchill and Roosevelt did not accept. De Gaulle would not work closely with former Vichy leaders in North Africa which annoyed Roosevelt and embarrassed Churchill. Churchill had to work hard and restrain his temper and impatience. De Gaulle, despite being totally dependent on British goodwill, felt no obligation and relations between himself and Churchill were stormy throughout the war.

Source N A cartoon in a British magazine shows de Gaulle saluting the Free French flag being raised by a French soldier. Over the Channel (in France) a Frenchman is waving.

REVEILLE !

Cartoon from *Punch*, 1942.

Activity

What does Source N tell you about attitudes in Britain towards de Gaulle?

What contribution did Churchill make to the wartime international conferences?

The Second World War saw a series of conferences on the Allied side which took key decisions about the conduct of the war and the shape of the post-war world. The major conferences which Churchill attended are summarised below.

Table 1 The major conferences Churchill attended during the Second World War.

Name	Location	Dates	Major participants	What was discussed
Atlantic Conference	Argentia, Newfoundland	8–11 August, 1941	Churchill, Roosevelt	Atlantic Charter
First Washington Conference	Washington, DC	22 December, 1941 – 14 January, 1942	Churchill, Roosevelt	'Europe first' policy for fighting war; establishing a United Nations organisation after the war
Second Washington Conference	Washington, DC	20–25 June, 1942	Churchill, Roosevelt	Opening another front in North African campaign
Second Moscow Conference	Moscow, USSR	12–17 August, 1942	Churchill, Stalin, Harriman	Second front; the Mediterranean strategy
Casablanca Conference	Casablanca, Morocco	14–24 January, 1943	Churchill, Roosevelt, Charles de Gaulle, Henri Giraud (de Gaulle was the French leader favoured by Britain and Giraud was the French leader with US support)	Italian campaign; plan for cross-channel invasion in 1944; declaration of 'unconditional surrender' of Axis; plan to unify French leadership in London (de Gaulle) and Algiers (Giraud)
Third Washington Conference	Washington, DC	12–27 May, 1943	Churchill, Roosevelt, Marshall (the leading US general)	Italian campaign; air attacks on Germany; war in Pacific
Quebec Conference	Quebec, Canada	17–24 August, 1943	Churchill, Roosevelt, King (Canadian PM)	D-Day set for 1944; war in Far East
Cairo Conference	Cairo, Egypt	23–26 November, 1943	Churchill, Roosevelt, Jiang Jieshi (leader of Nationalist China)	Plans for post-war Asia
Tehran Conference	Tehran, Iran	28 November – 1 December, 1943	Churchill, Roosevelt, Stalin	First meeting of the Big Three: final strategy for the war against Nazi Germany and its allies; date for the invasion of northern France
Second Cairo Conference	Cairo, Egypt	4–6 December, 1943	Churchill, Roosevelt	War in Far East
Second Quebec Conference	Quebec, Canada	12–16 September, 1944	Churchill, Roosevelt	Morgenthau Plan for post-war Germany; progress of war
Fourth Moscow Conference	Moscow, USSR	9–19 October, 1944	Churchill, Stalin, Molotov, Eden	Establishing post-war spheres of influence in eastern Europe
Malta Conference	Malta	30 January – 2 February, 1945	Churchill, Roosevelt	Preparation for Yalta
Yalta Conference	Yalta, USSR	4–11 February, 1945	Churchill, Roosevelt, Stalin	Final plans for defeat of Germany; post-war Europe; date for United Nations Conference; Soviet Union's entry in war against Japan
Potsdam Conference	Potsdam, Germany	17 July – 2 August, 1945	Churchill, Stalin, Truman, then Attlee (after Churchill lost the election in Britain)	Unconditional surrender of Japan; policy for Germany

In total Churchill attended sixteen meetings, Roosevelt twelve, Stalin seven.

The sheer effort of travelling in often dangerous and uncomfortable conditions shows the energy of the Prime Minister and his determination that Britain should be at the forefront of decision making.

The first priority for Churchill was to establish personal contact with Roosevelt and to put as much pressure as possible on the USA to enter the war. The correspondence that followed their meetings shows that a personal bond was created; but Churchill had to accept the Atlantic Charter which went against Britain's imperial interests and gained no real assurance that the USA would enter the war. When the Japanese attack on Pearl Harbor and the German declaration of war on the USA meant that Britain and the USA were allied, Churchill went to the USA twice in 1942. He did achieve key successes in ensuring that America would not prioritise the war in the Pacific and that US ideas about a rapid invasion of northern France did not prevail. When Hitler invaded Russia, Churchill went to Moscow to meet Stalin and forged a personal bond with him. However, though the force of Churchill's personality was an important factor, Britain was clearly the 'junior partner' in comparison with the much greater resources of the USA and the USSR. Also Churchill could not offer much to Stalin, as he was so determined not to open a second front in Europe to take the pressure off Russia.

Churchill's conduct at the conferences reflected the strain they put on a person of his age. In Moscow in 1942 the British ambassador found him difficult: 'I felt like giving him a good kick up the arse. My respect for him and faith in him have suffered badly.' (Archibald Clark Kerr, quoted in Nigel Knight, *Churchill: The Greatest Briton Unmasked*, 2010, page 307.) This is confirmed by the diplomat Sir Alexander Cadogan who said that Churchill had behaved 'like a bull in the ring maddened by the pricks of the picadors' (ibid). At Quebec in 1943 Sir Alan Brooke said 'Winston made matters almost impossible, temperamental like a film star and peevish like a spoilt child' (ibid, page 311).

By 1943, Churchill's contribution to the conferences was becoming less important. He had to accept that Stalin and Roosevelt were not easily influenced by his view of the war. Faced with humiliating putdowns by Roosevelt at the Tehran Conference in 1943, he did not hide his displeasure and showed some lack of control. When Roosevelt joked with Stalin at his expense he openly scowled and his face reddened. His judgement was also less sure. His deal with Stalin in Moscow (see page 69) in 1944 was improvised and irresponsible as it threatened the vital friendship of the USA and his description of the proposed agreement – 'I have this naughty document here' – seems less than statesmanlike. By the time of the crucial Yalta Conference which shaped post-war Europe, Churchill had to face decisions which went against his beliefs, particularly with regards to Poland and the return of Soviet prisoners of war to face punishment in Russia.

Against this must be set the very real achievements of maintaining the anti-Hitler alliance and being flexible enough to accept some demands that went against British interests for the sake of unity. Examples of this are the Atlantic Charter of 1941 which was a direct threat to Britain's empire, and the Yalta agreement which undermined the whole moral position of Britain's entry into the war in the first place to protect Poland. Churchill's skill in maintaining Stalin as an ally can be seen in the speeches at the close of the Yalta Conference. However, it was vital that the alliance should remain and that Stalin should join the war against Japan to bring that to an end. Churchill also had to deal with the fact that Roosevelt was much less concerned than he was about a threat from Russia.

Source O Churchill in an after-dinner speech at the Yalta Conference, February 1945.

I walk through the world with greater courage and hope when I find myself in a relation of friendship and intimacy with this great man, whose fame has gone out not only over all Russia, but the world. Before us lies the realisation of the dream of the poor – that they shall live in peace protected from aggression and evil. My hope is in the illustrious president of the United States and in Marshal Stalin, in whom we shall find the champions of peace.

Speech by Churchill at Yalta, February 1945.

Source P Stalin's response to Churchill's after-dinner speech.

[Churchill was] ... the most courageous of all Prime Ministers, embodying political experience with military leadership, who when all Europe was ready to fall flat before Hitler said that Britain would stand and fight alone.

Speech by Stalin at Yalta, February 1945.

Source Q In his post-war account of the Second World War, Churchill establishes his view of the situation by the time of Yalta.

Think of the situation in February 1945. The final fall of Berlin had not taken place and the campaign was to cost a million casualties. Japan was not yet defeated and its armies were largely intact. Assaults on minor islands had cost thousands of lives and an attack on Japan was reckoned to cost up to a million lives. Stalin had not yet entered the war with Japan, something that might be decisive, as the atomic weapons which were being developed might not work. The massive soviet war effort was popular in Britain.

Winston Churchill, *Triumph and Tragedy*, 1953.

Activity

Read sources O–Q and answer the questions below.
1. How can these sources be used to assess Churchill's skill in dealing with Stalin at Yalta?
2. The context for Sources O and P is a formal dinner. How far should this be taken into account when assessing the sources as evidence?
3. What do you know about the situation in February 1945 and the Yalta Conference in Source Q that would help you judge whether the opinions expressed by the leaders about each other in Sources O and P were sincere?

Yalta

The conference at Yalta in February 1945 saw Churchill having to face the realities of Britain's position. The Russian forces had swept into eastern Europe and were on the brink of the final battle with Germany. The Allies would not be able to prevent a Russian occupation of Berlin. Evidence of brutal Russian treatment of Polish leaders when Stalin occupied eastern Poland in 1940 was all too clear. For the sake of their own security, Russia was determined to occupy eastern Poland. The so-called 'London Poles', democrats who had formed a government in exile in Britain, were horrified by Stalin's demands. However, Churchill was not getting any support for opposition to Russian demands from the USA and there was little that Britain could do to stop Stalin merely enforcing his will on Poland. British forces were dispersed in

Greece, Italy and on the western front, and Britain had been weakened by years of war. At the Yalta Conference all Churchill could do was to accept the previously-agreed arrangements for dividing Germany, yield to Russian demands for the return of captured Russian prisoners of war, who faced almost certain death in Russia as traitors, and accept Russian demands for revising the frontiers of Poland. Churchill defended his actions in the House of Commons on 27 February 1945.

What were Churchill's plans for post-war Europe and his attitude to post-war Europe and the Empire?

Churchill had seen the weaknesses of Britain's pre-war foreign policy and had hoped during the war that a solid Anglo-American friendship would be the basis of peace and stability in post-war Europe. He did not see Britain abandoning control of its empire. He also supported a worldwide association of nations to replace the old League of Nations and had done his best to make it feasible for the USSR to be a member by making concessions to Stalin's demands for representation of some of the republics of the USSR. So a great deal of his thinking on maintaining peace depended on relations outside Europe.

Churchill thought that his personal relationship with first Roosevelt and then, after April 1945, with his successor Truman was the strongest element in British foreign policy and the key to maintaining peace. In 1944 he had dealt with Stalin in terms of establishing spheres of influence. He thought it possible that Britain could maintain a considerable influence in the Mediterranean which would be close to Egypt and the Suez Canal and the links to Britain's Asian empire and its Australian allies. Churchill was committed to what has been called an Atlantic policy, that is a close relationship with the USA. He was also committed to opposing communism where practical, for example in Greece, and he hoped that Turkey would be brought in as an ally. Thus the focus remained where it had been in the war:

- A **special relationship** with the USA.
- A defence of the Empire.
- Greater interest in the Balkans and the eastern Mediterranean as spheres of influence than in relations with western Europe.

Initially, Churchill was in favour of harsh measures against Germany. The division of Germany had been agreed on during the war, and there was to be punishment for the Nazi leaders and war criminals. However, old fears of building up resentments, such as had happened after 1919, were also present. Churchill expressed concern at the loss of former German lands to Russia as likely to create resentments which might lead to another war.

The changing circumstances of 1945–46 brought a new vision. It was not clear that the USA would continue involvement in Europe or that the relationship between Britain and the USA was so strong. The hopes that Stalin might stick to his agreement made at Yalta for free elections in Europe were fading as the Soviet hold on occupied territories strengthened. The large votes for the communists in Italy and France were a cause for concern. Churchill offered a rather different policy from that pursued in the war.

Further research

The debate on the Yalta Conference in the House of Commons, 27 February 1945, can be accessed at: http://hansard.millbanksystems.com/commons/1945/feb/27/crimea-conference.

Read the debate and summarise the views expressed about Yalta to understand the controversy that Churchill's role in the conference caused.

The division of Germany

It was agreed to create four zones of occupation run by Britain, France and the USA in the west of the country and the USSR in the east. Berlin was also to be divided into four zones, even though it was located in the Russian zone of Germany.

Little Englander

This was a term of contempt used in the nineteenth century for those people who thought that Britain should play little part in European diplomacy or get involved with European political affairs. The idea has had a long tradition and elements of it can be seen in today's **Eurosceptics**.

Churchill's attitude to post-war Europe

After his defeat in the election of July 1945, Churchill had time to reflect on Europe and made a major speech in Zürich in September 1946 which added to his reputation as a major figure in the European movement. His name has been used by supporters of greater European unity, but also by its opponents. For all his patriotism and love of Empire, Churchill had never been a 'little Englander'. He had warmly supported the French statesman Briand's idea for a European union in 1930. He had offered union with France in 1940, drafting a declaration that 'France and Great Britain shall no longer be two nations but one Franco-British union', and in 1942 during the war had written about 'a united states of Europe with reduced barriers of trade and movement'.

A key position Churchill took in the 1930s was that Europe was central to the defence of the Empire and he despised those who thought that Britain could opt out of European affairs. There were many instances of his support for European unity, some of which are given below. However, his view of Europe must be seen as part of his belief that Britain and her Empire were in a unique position. They were part of three major non-communist groupings in the world – the Anglo-American group; the Commonwealth and Empire group; and western Europe. Greater unity in all these groups would strengthen Britain's position and security. As a concept this was very grand, but there also were problems:

- Being part of these groupings involved obligations as well as benefits.
- In all three groups there were those who did not want Britain to dominate.
- Post-war Britain was struggling economically and the defence costs of being such a key player in the world were very high.
- There were those who were sceptical about the value of all the groups: on the left there was concern that Britain was getting sucked in to American hostility towards Russia; within the Commonwealth there was resentment about British dominance and a desire for independence; in Conservative circles, the whole idea of greater European union was seen as undermining Britain's traditional freedom of action.
- Churchill himself did not really favour much more than a loose association of European nations affirming shared values. His son-in-law Duncan Sandys organised a meeting of 800 influential Europeans in 1947 which led to the formation of the Council of Europe in 1949, but this was a long way from being a real union and was more an arena for sharing ideas and affirming western values.
- In any case, Churchill did much to establish the view that Europe was divided by an 'iron curtain'. European unity was very much in the context of Britain's world role and was confined to western Europe.

Source R Churchill speaks at the University of Zürich about Europe.

I wish to speak to you today about the tragedy of Europe. Yet all the while there is a remedy which, if it were generally and spontaneously adopted by the great majority of people in many lands, would as if by a miracle transform the whole scene, and would in a few years make all Europe, or the greater part of it, as free and as happy as Switzerland is today. What is this sovereign remedy? It is to recreate the European Family, or as much of it as we can, and to provide it with a structure under which it can dwell in peace, in safety and in freedom. We must build a kind of United States of Europe. The first step in the recreation of the European Family must be a partnership between France and Germany. There is no reason why a regional organisation of Europe should in any way conflict with the world organisation of the United Nations. On the contrary, I believe that the larger synthesis can only survive if it is founded upon broad natural groupings. There is already a natural grouping in the Western Hemisphere. We British have our own Commonwealth of Nations. These do not weaken, on the contrary they strengthen, the world organisation. They are in fact its main support. And why should there not be a European group which could give a sense of enlarged patriotism and common citizenship to the distracted peoples of this mighty continent? We must all turn our backs upon the horrors of the past and look to the future.

Speech by Churchill, September 1946.

Source S Churchill sends a memo to members of his cabinet, just after he has become prime minister again.

....

I never thought that Britain or the British Commonwealth should, either individually or collectively, become an integral part of a European Federation and have never given the slightest support to the idea. Our first objective is the unity and consolidation of the Commonwealth and what is left of the former British Empire.

Cabinet paper, 29 November 1951.

Activity

Study sources R and S.

1 How far do the three sources support the view that Churchill saw a united European community as the best way to preserve peace post-war? Before answering, consider these questions:

  (i)   What are the reasons given by Churchill for supporting a 'United States of Europe' in Source R?

  (ii) In March 1946 he delivered another major speech about world affairs (see Source U on page 80). How far you think the fears of communism he expressed in that speech might have influenced his speech about Europe?

  (iii) In what way, if at all, does Source S cast doubt on Churchill's view of Europe in Source R?

  (iv) What had changed between his speech in Source R and his memorandum in Source S?

2 Use your knowledge of Churchill's views of Europe to assess how useful Source S is as evidence for his reputation as a supporter of European unity. (AS)

What was the significance of the 'iron curtain' speech, 1946?

In March 1946 Churchill delivered a speech in Fulton, Missouri, during a visit to America. The speech was called 'The Sinews of Peace' but was seen as initiating the **Cold War**.

This speech had a major impact worldwide. Others had used the phrase 'iron curtain' previously. They included Sir James Gammell, the head of Britain's military mission to Moscow, and Josef Goebbels, Hitler's Minister of Propaganda. Churchill, however, made the phrase famous and enabled the West to label Soviet-dominated eastern Europe as 'the iron curtain countries'. It set up the image in the minds of many in the West of a real and permanent division between West and East and helped to create international tension. It was seen as a very hostile speech by Stalin and increased international tension.

Source T From Churchill's 'The Sinews of Peace' speech.

I have a strong admiration and regard for the valiant Russian people and for my wartime comrade, Marshal Stalin. There is deep sympathy and goodwill in Britain – and, I doubt not, here also – toward the peoples of all the Russias and a resolve to persevere through many differences and rebuffs in establishing lasting friendships. It is my duty, however, to place before you certain facts about the present position in Europe. From Stettin in the Baltic to Trieste in the Adriatic an iron curtain has descended across the Continent. Behind that line lie all the capitals of the ancient states of Central and Eastern Europe. Warsaw, Berlin, Prague, Vienna, Budapest, Belgrade, Bucharest and Sofia; all these famous cities and the populations around them lie in what I must call the Soviet sphere, and all are subject, in one form or another, not only to Soviet influence but to a very high and in some cases increasing measure of control from Moscow.

I do not believe that Soviet Russia desires war. What it desires is the fruits of war and the indefinite expansion of its power and doctrines.

What is needed is a settlement, and the longer this is delayed, the more difficult it will be and the greater our dangers will become. From what I have seen of our Russian friends and allies during the war, I am convinced that there is nothing they admire so much as strength, and there is nothing for which they have less respect than for weakness, especially military weakness. We must not let war happen again. This can only be achieved by reaching now, in 1946, a good understanding on all points with Russia under the general authority of the United Nations Organization and by the maintenance of that good understanding through many peaceful years, supported by the whole strength of the English-speaking world and all its connections.

Speech by Churchill at Fulton, Missouri, March 1946.

Source U Stalin responds to Churchill's 'The Sinews of Peace' speech.

Mr. Churchill now stands in the position of a firebrand of war.

As a result of the German invasion, the Soviet Union has irrevocably lost in battles with the Germans, and also during the German occupation and through the expulsion of Soviet citizens to German slave labour camps, about 7,000,000 people. In other words, the Soviet Union has lost in men several times more than Britain and the United States together.

One must therefore ask, what can be surprising in the fact that the Soviet Union, in a desire to ensure its security for the future, tries to achieve that the countries of eastern Europe should have governments whose relations to the Soviet Union are loyal? How can one, without having lost one's reason, qualify these peaceful aspirations of the Soviet Union as 'expansionist tendencies' of our Government?

An article in the official Soviet newspaper, Pravda, 13 March 1946.

Activity

Look at Sources T and U: Source T is from the speech at Fulton Missouri in March 1946 and Source U is from Stalin's response.

1 Compare these two sources as evidence for the threat posed by the USSR to the West.
   In answering Question 1, it may be helpful to copy and complete the following table.

| Compare what each says about the threat | |
| Compare the provenance – who produced the source and why? | |

2 On the evidence of these two sources and your own knowledge, how appropriate is it to call Churchill 'a firebrand of war'?
   In answering Question 2, look closely at what the speech is saying and find key sentences which show that Churchill seemed eager for war and conflict and key sentences which show that he seemed to want peace.
3 Now use this and your own knowledge of Churchill and the post-war situation to say whether you think the criticism is justified.

The Fulton speech has been much quoted, but largely the underlined part (see Source T on page 80). It has been seen as the beginning of the Cold War, as influencing opinion in the USA towards a policy of containment of communism and of hardening attitudes in both West and East.

■ Though subsequently seen as one of the key speeches that rallied opinion behind opposition to Soviet expansion, it was delivered at a time when there was considerable approval for a return to peace and gratitude for the sacrifices of the USSR. This was to change, but at the time there was criticism of the speech as being irresponsible. The *Chicago Sun* newspaper called it 'poisonous' and there were some protesters outside Churchill's hotel in New York on his way back home. Truman did not immediately state his agreement.

■ The speech did not in itself bring about the Cold War. Anti-communist pressures in the USA had been building up beforehand, and Truman was unsympathetic to communism, as were influential foreign policy experts like George F. Kennan who saw Stalin following a long tradition of Russian expansionism going back to the eighteenth century and called for US action to contain the threat.

■ The speech is often only quoted and referred to in part and Churchill also advocated understanding with the USSR.

Chapter takeaways

- Churchill had to devote considerable energy to maintaining an alliance between two very different major powers.
- He aimed to preserve Britain's empire and to avoid a major land war in northern Europe, hoping instead for a Mediterranean-based campaign.
- He was skilful in establishing good relations with both Roosevelt and Stalin but in the end Britain lost influence as both its allies were more powerful.
- Churchill was concerned about the Soviet invasion of eastern Europe, warned the US against it and played a major part in the Cold War by popularising the phrase and concept of 'iron curtain' in 1946.
- He continued to believe in the Empire and also in greater European unity, but his attitude was that Britain was too linked to the Commonwealth to play a full part in Europe.

Study Skills: Using a set of sources with confidence

You should be able to use a set of sources now with more confidence. To succeed you need to do the following:

■ Keep a good focus on the question and don't drift off into describing everything the sources say.
■ Evaluate the sources – that is, say how valid the evidence they give is. You can do this by looking at their *provenance*: i.e. what they are, who wrote them, under what circumstances, why? You can also do this by looking at what they say about the issue and weighing it against your own knowledge.
■ You have to keep a balance. You should not write an essay on the topic in the question just by using knowledge, but you should not explain only what the sources say about the issue either. You need to apply some knowledge to all the sources to answer the question.

Activity

Study the four sources on page 83 and then answer the questions below.

a) Copy and complete the table below. What is each source saying about relations between Churchill's relations with de Gaulle?

A	What are the key words which show poor relations in this evidence?
B	
C	
D	

b) Copy and complete the table below, looking at what each source is and when and why it might have been written.

A	
B	Look at the date of this source – does it help you assess it?
C	Think about de Gaulle's situation in 1942 – does it help to explain why he was so angry?
D	

c) Copy and complete the table below. What knowledge do you have which might confirm or question the evidence which the source is offering?

A	For example, is there evidence in Chapter 3 that in 1940 Churchill did recognise de Gaulle as representing France?
B	
C	
D	

Using these four sources in their historical context, assess how far they support the view that Churchill's lack of understanding of de Gaulle led to poor relations between the two leaders during the Second World War.

Once you have written your answer, use the checklist below:

● ✓ Have I dealt with all four sources?
● ✓ Have I picked out from each source the key points which relate to the question or have I just described the content?
● ✓ How much have I written about the provenance? (Highlight everything in yellow.)
● ✓ How much knowledge have I used? (Check by outlining it in red.)
● ✓ Have I offered a clear view about the issue?

Use your knowledge of Churchill's relations with de Gaulle to assess how useful Source D is as evidence for how far Churchill regarded him as a great Frenchman. (AS)

Source A De Gaulle recalls a stormy meeting with Churchill in 1942.

Mr Churchill attacked me in a bitter and highly emotional way. When I pointed out that the establishment of a British-controlled administration in Madagascar would constitute an interference with the rights of France, he exclaimed furiously 'You claim to be France! You are not France! I do not recognise you as France!' … I interrupted him. 'If in your eyes, I am not the representative of France, why and with what right are you dealing with me…?' Mr Churchill did not reply.

Charles de Gaulle, *Memoirs*, 1956.

Source B Churchill's personal doctor recalls Churchill's view of de Gaulle at the Casablanca Conference, 1943.

The Prime Minister watched de Gaulle stalk down the garden with his head in the air. Winston turned to us with a smile and said 'His country has given up fighting; he himself is a refugee and if we turn him down he is finished. Look at him! He might be Stalin with two hundred divisions behind him. France without an army is not France; de Gaulle is the spirit of that army, perhaps the last survivor of that warrior race.'

Lord Moran, *Churchill, The Struggle for Survival*, 1966.

Source C De Gaulle sends a telegram to the Free French commanders in Africa and the Middle East, expressing resentment about British and American policy. The Madagascar Invasion is a reference to a British landing and occupation of the island (which had been held by Vichy French forces) in May 1942, to prevent it being taken by Japan. Free French forces were not involved although subsequently a Free French administration was set up.

In agreement with the United States, the British are doing everything possible to take away our territory as in the Madagascar invasion. I am not prepared to remain associated with the Anglo-Saxon powers and I am today sending the British government a warning to that effect. We must form a united front against them and have no relations with the Anglo-Saxons under any circumstances and at whatever cost. We must warn the French people and the whole world by radio of the Anglo-Saxon conspiracy against us.

De Gaulle, telegram, 6 June 1942.

Source D Churchill writes to Eden, the foreign secretary, about his reluctance to allow de Gaulle to visit France in the aftermath of the Allied invasion in June 1944.

I could adduce many reasons against compliments being paid to a man who has shown himself entirely free from any sympathy with us or the Americans or the efforts we are making to liberate his country. He would no doubt like to have a demonstration to show that he is the future President of the French Republic, There is not a scrap of generosity about this man who only wishes to pose as the saviour of France, without a single French soldier at his back.

Letter from Churchill, June 1944.

Focus on AS (AS)

In the first question at AS level you only have three sources to consider:

Study Sources A, B and D. Using these three sources in their historical context, assess how far they support the view that Churchill's lack of understanding of de Gaulle led to poor relations between the two leaders during the Second World War.

Remember to use knowledge of the particular topic in the question to assess the use of a piece of evidence.

You do have to consider provenance and relevant contextual knowledge and you can practise this using the sources given in this chapter. For each source you should try to refer to its nature, origin and why it was written and to assess it by using some knowledge. (See page 27.)

Further research

The following are some good texts to expand your knowledge of Churchill.

Geoffrey Best, *Churchill, A Study in Greatness*, 2002.

Winston Churchill, *Never Give In!, The Best of Churchill's Speeches*, 2004.

Martin Gilbert, *Churchill, A Life*, 2002.

Max Hastings, *Finest Years, Churchill As Warlord 1940–45*, 2009.

Samantha Heywood, *Churchill, Questions and Analysis in History*, 2003.

Roy Jenkins, *Churchill*, 2002.

Nigel Knight, *Churchill: The Greatest Briton Unmasked*, 2009.

David Reynolds, *In Command of History*, 2005.

Churchill, 1929–51

Revision for the Enquiry Topic

As the A level examination is taken at the end of a two year course, you will need to revise what you have studied about Churchill. It may well be that this revision takes place after you have had wider experience of historical study. Thus you may wish to review some of your judgements after reflecting on your earlier work. Revision should not be seen as a chore but rather as a vital process of ensuring that the work done earlier in the course is brought to a similar level to that done later in the course.

Using historical sources in context

Firstly, you need to revisit the skills needed to use historical sources in context. The chapters on Churchill were structured in such a way as to lead you from understanding and interpreting sources, to making use of your understanding of their provenance and then to offering a full assessment of them by using appropriate contextual knowledge.

Consider this source and then assess it as evidence for the strength of Anglo-American relations in 1941.

Source A A broadcast by Churchill after his meeting with Roosevelt at Placentia Bay.

The meeting (with Roosevelt) was therefore symbolic. It symbolises the deep underlying unities which stir and at decisive moments rule the English-speaking peoples throughout the world. Would it be presumptuous of me to say that it symbolises something even more majestic – namely: the marshalling of the good forces of the world against the evil forces which are now so formidable and triumphant and which have cast their cruel spell over the whole of Europe and a large part of Asia?

This is a meeting which marks for ever in the pages of history the taking up by the English-speaking nations, amid all this peril, tumult and confusion, of the guidance of the broad toiling masses in all the continents; and our loyal effort without any clog of selfish interest to lead them forward out of the miseries in which they have been plunged back into the broad highroad of freedom and justice.

A broadcast speech by Churchill, 24 August 1941.

The first task is to understand the source and to decide what it could be saying about Anglo-American relations.

Try underlining the key elements:

> The meeting (with Roosevelt) was therefore symbolic. It symbolises <u>the deep underlying unities which stir and at decisive moments rule the English-speaking peoples throughout the world</u>. Would it be presumptuous of me to say that it symbolises something even more majestic – <u>namely: the marshalling of the good forces of the world against the evil forces</u> which are now so formidable and triumphant and which have cast their cruel spell over the whole of Europe and a large part of Asia?

> This is a meeting which marks for ever in the pages of history the <u>taking up by the English-speaking nations, amid all this peril, tumult and confusion, of the guidance of the broad toiling masses in all the continents; and our loyal effort without any clog of selfish interest to lead them forward out of the miseries in which they have been plunged back into the broad highroad of freedom and justice</u>.

So, focusing on these key elements, the source seems to show:

1 That there was deep underlying unity between the English-speaking peoples – in other words, Britain and the USA.
2 That they represented the good forces in the world and were opposed to the evil forces.
3 That the meeting meant that the US and Britain would work for freedom and justice for the oppressed people of the world.

Taken at face value, the source would be evidence for strong bonds between Britain and the US and strong shared values and a commitment to work together for high ideals.

Why and when was the source written?

The next stage is to consider what the source actually is. It is a radio broadcast after the first major meeting of Churchill with Roosevelt. Why did Churchill make the broadcast and why did he use the words he did?

> He was trying to persuade opinion in both the US and Britain that there were strong bonds. Why? Because he desperately wanted Roosevelt to join the war against Germany. Why was this so important? Because Britain depended on the US for war supplies and credit and it would give Britain the support of the world's greatest economic power with a potentially massive army.
>
> He used this type of language to suggest a high moral tone and purpose. It is highly emotional and rhetorical and stresses 'good' against 'evil'.

Put the source in context

Next you have to apply your knowledge of the historical period to the source. What does knowledge of the context suggest about the source as evidence?

1 The US had not joined the war, but had given help to Britain.
2 Isolationist feeling in the USA was still very strong, so Churchill needed to persuade US opinion of the 'mission' of the 'English-speaking peoples'.
3 Roosevelt had not made any real commitment at the meeting at Placentia Bay, so this was very much Churchill's interpretation of the importance of the meeting.

Activity

Look again at the sources in Chapter 1 and Chapter 2. Where the exercises in the Activities did not specifically require consideration of knowledge of the context, apply your own knowledge to assess them as evidence for the issues stated.

4 The statesmen had agreed on the Atlantic Charter which is evidence for some shared values.

5 However, as Churchill had no intention of abandoning the British Empire, the reference to giving freedom to the 'toiling masses' of all continents must be seen merely as an attempt to get US support rather than as evidence of agreement.

Evaluating usefulness

So how useful is the source?

1 It shows how powerfully Churchill used language to get US support.

2 However, it is not really useful for showing the strength of relations with the USA as it was not until Roosevelt was forced into war by the Japanese attack on Pearl Harbor on 7 December 1941 that Britain and the USA were fully committed in the way this source suggests.

Reviewing initial judgements

In your initial study of Churchill 1929–51 you will have come to conclusions about the key questions in each chapter. For each question, summarise what the possible interpretations are and your own view.

For example, in Chapter 1:

Issue: Was Churchill responsible for being out of office 1929–40?		
Different possible interpretations		Your view and why you decided this
YES	NO	
He refused to see that British opinion was in favour of change in India and that India deserved self-government.	The Conservative Party simply used his views on India as an excuse not to include a former Liberal who seemed old-fashioned.	
He did not take into account the economic and financial problems involved in rearmament and he exaggerated the threat.	He showed foresight in warning about the German threat and never saw Hitler as just another statesman with whom Britain could negotiate.	
He seemed out of touch in his support of Edward VIII.	The abdication was not a political but a personal issue of loyalty.	
He took an unrealistic line to Munich and appeasement.	Churchill was right to see Munich as a defeat and right to have urged Britain to seek more allies. Munich damaged Britain morally and allowed Hitler more time to prepare for war.	

It is possible that now you have finished your course of study you want to reconsider your view:

Issue	Your initial view	Do you want to modify it after reconsidering the evidence?
How far was Churchill responsible for the election defeat in 1945?	Yes – he made ridiculous claims that Labour wanted to introduce a Gestapo and did not take enough interest in post-war reconstruction. There were other reasons such as Labour's strong campaign and the failures of the Conservatives in the 1930s but Churchill did not appear to be a good peacetime leader however much he was admired as a wartime prime minister.	Churchill did not help the Conservatives by some unwise speeches, but these were less important than long-term factors. After a long war, the people wanted to see change and improvement. Labour promised this; they had a strong campaign and their leaders were well-known for offering loyal support during the war. It was much more a vote for domestic change than a vote against Churchill, who was still much admired.

Please note that you may not want to change your initial view at all!

Further practice

Revising should be a matter of reviewing and reflecting on earlier judgements and analysis of evidence, rather than gazing at a textbook or trying to memorise notes. If you want to test yourself, here are another two sources.

How useful are they in assessing the view that Churchill was made prime minister because of his outstanding abilities?

■ What do they say about the issue?
■ Why and when were they written?
■ Why do they use a particular tone or words?
■ How does knowledge of the context in which they were written help you to assess them?

Source B Chamberlain's private secretary Jock Colville reacts to the news that Churchill will be prime minister.
• •

The mere thought of Churchill as prime minister sent a cold chill down the spines of the staff at 10 Downing Street, where I was working as assistant private secretary to Mr Chamberlain. Churchill's impetuosity had, we thought, contributed to the Norwegian fiasco and General Ismay had told us in the most despairing tones of the confusion caused by his enthusiastic irruptions in the deliberations of the Military Co-ordinating committee and the Chiefs of Staff; his verbosity and restlessness made unnecessary work, prevented real planning and caused friction.

Jock Colville, diary, May 1940.

Source C A letter from Robert Boothby MP, a strong supporter of Churchill.
• •

Dear Winston

Opinon is hardening against Halifax. I cannot feel that he is, in any circumstances, the right man.

I find a growing consensus of opinion in all quarters that you are the necessary and inevitable prime minister. God knows it is a terrible prospect for you, but I don't see how you can avoid it.

Yours ever

Bob

Letter from Robert Boothby, 9 May 1940.

Gateway into Britain, 1951

Britain in 1951

Politics

- The Conservatives under Winston Churchill and Labour under Clement Attlee were the main parties. The Liberals under Clement Davies polled only 730,000 votes in the 1951 election.
- There was a great deal of agreement about the need for a Welfare State and also policies to maintain full employment.
- In theory Labour was committed to nationalising industries and in theory the Conservatives believed in free enterprise. However, the Conservatives kept most of the industries which Labour had nationalised under state control and Labour's leaders did not support a fully state-run economy. There was 'consensus politics' by 1951.

Economics

- A long war 1939–45 had been followed by a period of austerity as governments tried to keep the import bill down and to encourage exports, not spending at home. Petrol rationing only ended in 1950 and rationing of sweets and sugar ended in 1953. Food rationing did not officially end until 1954.
- There was still considerable concern about the balance of payments as Britain struggled to boost exports. The physical damage of the war was still evident in British towns and cities and there was a housing shortage as a result of housing loss during the war. The war and the difficult post-war period had resulted in a loss of investment in peacetime industry, utilities, roads and railways as the nation had to build up its armaments. In 1951 Britain was still making the transition.
- There was a determination that full employment would be maintained and that governments should take responsibility for ensuring that Britain did not go back to the 'bad years' of the 1930s. The ideas of the economist John Maynard Keynes who advocated boosting demand to avoid depression were influential in 1951.

Britain overseas

- Britain had granted independence to India, Pakistan and Palestine (Israel), but in 1951 still had a great deal of imperial territory and many Britons still went overseas to live and work in the colonies, but less so than in the pre-war period.
- Britain still relied on many imperial products in its basic diet.
- Britain still had conscription and its national servicepeople still defended the Empire. There were important bases in South East Asia and the Suez Canal was still seen as a British routeway.
- Imperial attitudes influenced attitudes to race within the UK and there was no legal bar to racial discrimination.
- Britain saw itself as a leading figure in the Cold War and saw Russia as its major enemy and the USA as the major ally. Its leaders did not see the future mainly in Europe but in being the link between the Commonwealth countries, Europe and the USA.

Society

- The war and the period of change from 1945 to 1951 saw considerable changes in British society. There had been more opportunities for the middle classes and grammar school educated officers, managers, politicians and civil servants were more common. Women had gained more opportunities during the war, though did not always maintain their progress once peace returned. There was still not equal pay for men and women, for example.
- The war and the post-war period had brought better medical care, education and welfare for the mass of the people. The post-war period saw a rise in the birth rate – the so called 'baby boomers'.
- Pre-war social customs and the numbers in domestic service or working in big country houses changed. There was less formality, fewer obvious class divisions and a more democratic outlook. By modern standards, though, society was quite restrictive. Homosexuality was punished more severely than in the war; married women were often not thought suitable for jobs in offices and banks and were expected to look after the home. Young people were expected to conform much more and there was very limited 'youth culture'. Much social change had to wait for the 1960s, but, for many, social life and culture had changed since the 1930s with greater social and physical mobility.

Chapter 4

Conservative domination, 1951–64

This chapter focuses on the reasons why the Conservatives were able to dominate British politics for thirteen years between 1951 and 1964 and considers the relative importance of Conservative strengths, Labour weaknesses and the role of the economy, social changes and individuals in explaining that dominance. The chapter also examines the reasons for the end of this dominance, considering the impact of scandals, leadership and Labour recovery. It addresses a number of key questions that relate to that dominance and its ending:

- Why did the Conservatives win the 1951 election?
- Why were the Conservatives able to dominate British politics for so long?
- How important a factor was Conservative leadership in maintaining power?
- How weak was the Labour party in the period 1951–64?
- Why did support for the Conservative party decline?

This chapter also explains how to understand the wording of an essay question through identifying the key words within it, and how to plan a response.

Timeline

1951	October	Conservative election victory, Winston Churchill returns as prime minister
1953		De-nationalisation of steel
1955	April	Churchill retires as prime minister, replaced by Anthony Eden
	May	Conservative election victory
1956	October	Suez Crisis
1957	January	Macmillan becomes prime minister
1957	July	Rent Act – removed controls on renting property in an attempt to create a free market in rented property
	July	Harold Macmillan's 'Never had it so good' speech
1958–89		Race riots in Notting Hill (west London), Nottingham, Bristol and other parts of London
1959	October	Conservative election victory
1960	February	Macmillan's 'Wind of Change' speech
1962	July	Macmillan's major cabinet reshuffle known as the 'Night of the Long Knives'
1963	March	Cabinet minister John Profumo lies to the Commons over an affair and is forced to resign in June
	October	Macmillan retires as prime minister
	October	Alec Douglas-Home replaces Macmillan

Overview

The Conservatives won a narrow victory over Labour in the 1951 general election but went on to remain in power for the next thirteen years. The party was led by Winston Churchill, who at 77 was not in good health and was largely a figurehead. The government continued the policy direction of the previous Labour government, but brought an end to rationing and dramatically increased the number of houses being built.

When Churchill retired in 1955 he was replaced by Anthony Eden. Eden called a general election soon after taking office, in which the Conservatives increased their majority to 60. This was partly due to the increasing prosperity that people were starting to feel after years of food rationing following the Second World War, but also because of the divisions within the Labour party over nuclear weapons. However, Eden's time in office was short-lived; the Suez Crisis in 1956 destroyed his credibility as leader both at home and abroad.

Eden was replaced by Harold Macmillan who was to remain as prime minister until his resignation in 1963. Macmillan became popular with the public through his television appearances and by the time of the next election, in 1959, voters had forgotten Suez, and 'Super-Mac', as Macmillan became known, increased the Conservative majority to 100. He was undoubtedly helped in this by the rising economic prosperity, which provoked Macmillan's famous phrase, 'Most of our people have never had it so good.'

However, by 1962 the party appeared to be running out of steam and, in an attempt to bring in some younger and fresher faces, Macmillan carried out a cabinet reshuffle, which has become known rather dramatically as the 'Night of the Long Knives'. Despite this, there were signs of increasing problems by 1963 as the economy began to stagnate, unemployment rose and Britain failed in its attempt to join the European Economic Community (EEC). In addition, the government became embroiled in a series of scandals, the most notorious of which involved the Secretary of State for War, John Profumo. Macmillan's Conservative government was losing its electoral appeal.

Nearing 70 and in declining health, Macmillan resigned in 1963 and, after a short process which involved, not a leadership election but 'taking soundings' among Conservatives, Lord Home emerged as his successor, although he had to resign his peerage to act as prime minister. His appointment was seen by many as an out-dated way of choosing a leader and some Conservatives announced they would not serve under him. In the October 1964 general election, faced by a younger and more energetic leader of the Labour party, Harold Wilson, the Conservatives were defeated and Labour came into office with a majority of four.

Why did the Conservatives win the 1951 election?

The debate on the 1951 election result has centred around the extent to which it was Labour weaknesses or Conservative strengths that determined the outcome. However, Table 1 below suggests that there might be a third element to the result: the electoral system.

Table 1 Election results, 1951

Political Party	Votes	Seats	Percentage of vote
Conservative	13,717,538	321	48.0
Labour	13,948,605	295	48.8
Liberal	730,556	6	2.5
Other	198,969	3	0.7

First-past-the-post system

A system by which a parliamentary candidate is elected if they win more votes than any other candidate in the constituency, with no account taken of the proportion of votes they won (i.e. whether they won a majority of the total votes).

Table 1 shows that Labour polled more votes than the Conservatives, yet won fewer seats because of the first-past-the-post system. What is also noticeable is the poor performance of the Liberal party. As a financially stretched party in decline, they decided to contest only 109 seats. This helped the Conservatives into power as many ex-Liberal voters turned to the Conservatives. Despite this, Labour had actually increased their popular vote by over 2 million since 1945, but the Conservatives had gained over 4 million.

How important were Labour weaknesses?

Although it is possible to argue that Labour failings in their two administrations of 1945–50 and 1950–51 were responsible for their defeat in 1951, this interpretation is not supported by their performance in the election. Their number of votes in 1951 was, at that point, the highest polled by a party in British politics, hardly a sign of a party in decline. Their governments had achieved a great deal and laid down some political principles that would be followed by all governments until 1979. However, despite its achievements, the Labour government was not as strong as it had been in its early years of office. There were a number of areas in both the party and its policies with which the public were dissatisfied.

The difficulties of dealing with the post-war economic and financial problems had exhausted many of the cabinet. In the popular mind they were associated with the policies of **austerity**, **rationing** and high taxation, which most of the public longed to see ended. The Labour government had taken Britain into the Korean War in 1950, which only added to the financial strains. Not only was the party exhausted, it was also divided. This division was seen most clearly in the imposition of charges for dental treatment, prescriptions and glasses, which appeared to undermine the principle that the NHS should be free at the point of treatment. Debates on this, and the reduction of Labour's majority to five in the 1950 election, encouraged some MPs to voice their concerns about economic and foreign policy, which further widened the divisions between the right and left of the party. The electorate was therefore faced with a party which was internally divided, while the Conservative party had recovered and reorganised itself after its defeat in 1945.

How important were Conservative strengths?

It would be wrong to see the result of the 1951 general election as mainly a vote against the Labour party as there were many positive aspects to the Conservative campaign. The party were undoubtedly shocked by their defeat in 1945, but by 1950 had put in place both policies and a reorganisation of the party that allowed them to recover and take advantage of Labour difficulties.

Accounts often overlook the vital work of Lord Woolton, who reformed party finances and local organisation, so that the party was in a stronger position to challenge Labour. He was aided by an influx of young talented politicians into the party, such as Reginald Maudling, who gave the party new ideas and dynamism. Labour's **nationalisation** of the iron and steel industry provided a contentious issue around which the party could challenge the government.

The party also offered an attractive programme. They promised to build 300,000 houses a year – a winning proposition given the serious housing shortage, despite Labour overseeing the building of an average of over 200,000 houses a year – and to give the people 'more red meat' at a time when meat was still strictly rationed. The party had also made it clear that they would not reverse Labour's achievements and were fully committed to the Welfare State. In practice, this meant that after a period of dramatic innovation, the Conservatives would consolidate. In 1945 the nation had wanted change and the abandonment of those associated with the failed policy of appeasement (see page 18); this time they abandoned the party associated with austerity. Finally, Winston Churchill was still a popular

Korean War, 1950–53

Communist North Korea, backed by Russia and China, invaded the non-communist South Korea in 1950. The resistance to the invasion was led by a US-dominated United Nations force, but with substantial British help. The war lasted until 1953 when the communist forces were driven back to the same position they occupied in 1950.

figure. Although he had lost the 1945 election, many still saw him as a hero for leading the country to victory in the war and wanted to thank him.

How important was the electoral system?

Table 1 on page 90 shows that Labour polled over 200,000 votes more than the Conservatives, but won 26 fewer seats. There were three interlinked key reasons for this:

1 **The nature of the British electoral system**
   In the 1945 election Labour had needed to poll only 30,522 votes for each seat it won, whereas in 1951 it needed 47,283 votes. In contrast the proportion of votes per seat for the Conservatives had declined from 46,892 in 1945 to 42,733 in 1951. This was the result of the first-past-the-post system (see page 90) whereby Labour piled up votes in safe seats, but the Conservatives won many of the marginal Labour seats.

2 **Boundary changes brought about by the 1948 Representation of the People Act**
   Boundary changes meant Labour had to win 2 per cent more of the popular vote to win the same number of seats because the redistribution of seats resulted in some of their seats becoming marginal or simply increased the number of votes they could win in already safe seats.

3 **The decline in the Liberal party**
   The problem for Labour was made worse by the decline in the Liberal party, whose vote fell from 2.6 million in 1945 to 730,556 in 1951. The Liberals did not contest every seat and many ex-Liberal voters turned to the Conservatives, helping them win Labour marginal seats.

The nature of the defeat should have given Labour encouragement that their period out of office would be short-lived, but they were to remain out of office for the next thirteen years, losing two further elections. The chapter will now examine the reasons why the Conservatives were able to remain in power for so long.

Marginal seats and boundary changes

Marginal seats are parliamentary constituencies where the number of votes cast for two parties are very close and where, when a few voters change their voting choice, the candidate elected will change.

The boundaries of constituencies are regularly reviewed to try to ensure that they contain approximately the same number of voters, but this may result in the boundary being moved to take account of population changes. The movement of the boundaries may result in one party gaining an electoral advantage as safe seats become more marginal or a party simply gains more votes in an already safe seat.

Activity

Using the information on pages 90–92 complete the table below to explain why the Conservatives won the 1951 election. You should:
- Explain how each factor helped the Conservatives win the general election.
- Award each a mark out of 6 for how important the factor was in helping the Conservatives: the higher the mark, the more important the factor.
- Explain why you have given the factor this mark.

Factor	How it helped the Conservatives win the 1951 election	Mark out of 6 for importance	Explanation of the mark
Labour weakness			
Conservative strengths			
Electoral system			

Why were the Conservatives able to dominate British politics for so long?

After the 1951 election there were thirteen years of Conservative government under four different prime ministers and a further two election victories. Most historians agree that one of the main reasons for this dominance was the rise in living standards, for which the Conservatives took the credit. However, it was also partially the result of both Labour weaknesses and Conservative strengths.

How important was the economy?

The Conservatives certainly had the advantage that much of the period was one of economic growth, which led to a rise in living standards. Given the low level of industrial output after the war some industrial growth was almost inevitable. Industrial growth was also stimulated by an increase in trade after the Korean War; countries had more money available to spend on goods rather than defence policy. However, the growth rate was not as impressive as other nations, as Table 2 illustrates, although both Italy and Germany started from a lower base.

Moreover, Britain's share of world trade shrank from 25 per cent to 15 per cent, while Germany's grew from 7 per cent to 20 per cent.

Some of this decline in world trade can be explained by Britain's defence expenditure, which amounted to 10 per cent of its GDP. The high cost of maintaining military bases and an independent nuclear arms programme meant that 34.5 per cent of funds for research and development was spent on defence rather than providing funds for industrial growth. It is therefore difficult to argue that the government aided industrial growth and their policies may have actually limited it, giving some justification to later Labour assertions that these were 'thirteen wasted years'.

In addition, the government was criticised for failing to modernise staple and traditional industries and instead prioritising investment overseas and maintaining a strong **sterling area**. The government defended its relatively poor performance by arguing that it was due to consumerism, with people spending money on goods rather than investing, or due to industrial disruption. But the number of hours lost to strikes was fewer than most countries.

This section will consider the rise in living standards and the reasons for the rise as well as how much, and how far, the government was responsible for this improvement. However, even if they were not responsible, they were able to persuade a sufficient number of the electorate that they were, with catchphrases such as 'Never had it so good' or 'Life is better under the Conservatives', which were used in the 1959 election campaign.

Wages and living standards

Although it was a period of relatively slow industrial growth, it is clear that most of the period was one of a continuous rise in living standards. This was largely the result of two main factors. First, wages rose faster than prices so that people were able to buy more with the money they earned. In 1951 the average weekly wage of an adult was £8.30, but by 1964 it had risen to £18.35. Second, Chancellors were able to cut income tax before both the 1955 and 1959 elections, reducing it by the equivalent of 2.5p in 1955 and by 3.75p in 1959, which helped to increase the amount of money people had available to spend and therefore improve the 'feel-good' factor. This increased purchasing power

Table 2 GDP growth rates, 1951–64.

Country	Percentage growth
Italy	5.6
Germany	5.1
France	4.3
Britain	2.3

GDP

GDP or Gross Domestic Product is the annual total value of goods produced and services provided. It is used as a measure of economic growth. Sometimes economists refer to GNP or Gross National Product, which also includes trade abroad.

available to the electorate was reflected in a 500 per cent rise in car ownership during the period and television ownership went up from 4 per cent of the population to 91 per cent. Similarly the purchase of labour-saving white goods, such as washing machines, also rose. These were all signs that austerity was over. As a result, there were fewer reasons for the electorate to vote for a change in government or policy as most were benefiting from these developments.

Credit

The improvement in living standards was also made possible by the greater availability of credit. People were able to borrow money and make small, monthly repayments spread over a number of years; they were thereby able to purchase items that would have been out of reach in the past. Coupled with the tax cuts, a consumer boom began and many were able to go on holidays abroad for the first time, adding further plausibility to Macmillan's claim (see below).

Housing

The improvement in living standards was most clearly seen in a housing boom. The government had promised to build 300,000 new houses per year and they were mostly able to meet their target, reaching 354,000 in 1954 and building some 1.7 million homes while in office. As a result of the building of new houses and the 1957 Rent Act, waiting lists for housing declined. The Rent Act abolished rent controls and resulted in more houses being available to rent, although it also led to rents rising, with some tenants finding it much harder to afford them.

The number of people who owned their own property rose from 25 per cent before the Second World War to 44 per cent by 1964. The government was able to claim credit for some of this as the housing boom had been made possible by the ease with which money could be borrowed and repaid over a long period of time. Macmillan certainly exploited this development when he said in 1957:

Let's be frank about it: most of our people have never had it so good. Go around the country, go to the industrial towns, go to the farms, and you will see a state of prosperity, such as we have never seen in my lifetime – nor indeed in the history of this country.

From a speech, 20 July 1957, in Bedford. Quoted in Michael Lynch, *Access to History: 1945–2007*, 2008, page 48.

Thus the middle classes, and even some of the upper working class, who had been major beneficiaries of these developments, had no reason to vote Labour as they had done in 1945.

Economic policy

Conservative economic policy remained consistent throughout the period and was very similar to that pursued by the preceding Labour governments. This was particularly noticeable under the chancellorship of R. A. Butler from 1951 to 1955. Increased borrowing allowed government expenditure, particularly on health, education and housing, to rise. The Welfare State saw increased spending throughout the period; the amount of GDP spent on it rose from 16.1 per cent in 1951 to 19.3 per cent in 1964. At the same time, the government attempted to achieve full employment while bringing about economic growth.

So similar were Butler's policies to those of Labour, that the term 'Butskellism' was coined; it brought together the names and policies of the Conservative Chancellor, who was on the left of the party, and Hugh Gaitskell from the right of the Labour party. This approach continued under Macmillan's leadership as successive chancellors attempted to avoid high

R.A. Butler, 1902–82

Butler was one of the most influential Conservative politicians of the period. He came close on three occasions to being chosen as leader of the party. He was very influential in developing Conservative policy after the 1945 election defeat. At various stages of his career he held the offices of chancellor (1951–55), home secretary (1957–62); deputy prime minister (1962–63) and foreign secretary (1963–64).

▲ Deputy Prime Minister R. A. Butler arriving at 10 Downing Street for a meeting in October 1963.

inflation or deflation, using interest rates and import controls to manage the economy. If spending or wages rose too rapidly, taxes and interest rates were increased and import controls prevented purchases from abroad; but if there was a fall in demand for goods, taxes and interest rates were lowered and import controls relaxed.

The result of such an approach has led many commentators to suggest that Britain did not have an overall economic policy, but instead followed a 'stop-go' approach as governments simply responded to economic developments, rather than developing a strategy that created consistent growth. As a result, the period was later described as one of stagflation, where industrial output declined, but inflation remained, with the result that the overall performance of the economy was not as strong as it could have been. Clamping down in a period when there was a balance of payment deficit slowed down recovery and growth, while cutting taxes increased spending and inflation, making a deficit more likely. This situation was made worse by a failure to direct enough investment into important industries, such as textiles and shipbuilding, with the result that they declined. Although industries such as aircraft, cars and chemicals were expanding, their production costs were high, making the goods expensive and uncompetitive in the export market. The government also did not invest sufficiently in industrial research and development, which further hindered growth.

Nevertheless, the government did introduce policies around credit and housing which improved people's standard of living. These, coupled with the natural recovery from both the Second World War and the Korean War and the move out of a period of austerity, contributed to an economic improvement. However, their policies towards industry and trade meant that the economy didn't grow as quickly as that of other powers.

Unemployment

Although Macmillan spoke of prosperity in his 1957 speech (see page 94), he was also aware of underlying problems in the economy: inflation and unemployment. The former was partially controlled by taxes and interest rates, but the latter was more difficult. The Conservatives had continued the Labour pledge of full employment, but although there were some years when unemployment did fall, the overall trend was upward and governments were never able to get the figure below 250,000, as Table 3 shows.

Table 3 Unemployment in Britain, 1951–64.

Year	Number of unemployed	Year	Number of unemployed
1951	367,000	1958	536,000
1952	468,000	1959	621,000
1953	452,000	1960	461,000
9154	387,000	1961	419,000
1955	298,000	1962	566,000
1956	297,000	1963	878,000
1957	383,000	1964	501,000

Not only did the high figures in many years cast doubt over the success of the government's policies, they also raised the question as to whether it was a period of prosperity and rising living standards for all.

The impact of the policies

Although there can be little doubt that living standards rose for most during this period, how much of that was due to government policies is debatable. Critics have argued that the success was built on heavy government borrowing and consumer credit, which was economically dangerous. It may even be argued that the government's economic policies hindered further growth and prevented the securing of a strong economic base – something that would haunt both Labour and Conservative governments in the 1960s and 1970s. Critics have argued that the government used tax adjustments in budgets just before elections to win votes, while the 'stop-go' economic policies also prevented the emergence of a coherent policy designed to bring about long-term economic growth. Therefore, although many saw their living conditions rise to levels that could not have been imagined before, the basis for that improvement was far from secure.

How important was social policy?

The Second World War had brought about massive social changes to which the Conservatives needed to adapt, particularly after their election defeat in 1945. The war had weakened and blurred class distinctions, and this was further reinforced by both the creation of the Welfare State and the growing affluence of the 1950s and 1960s. As R. A. Butler commented:

As in the days of Peel, the Conservatives must be seen to have accommodated themselves to a social revolution.

In many ways they were able to do this, increasing spending on welfare and building more houses (see pages 97–98), as well as introducing changes to the education system.

The three-tier secondary education system of grammar, technical and secondary modern schools had only served to reinforce class divisions. Although many Conservatives, particularly at a local level, disliked the comprehensive system, party policy accepted it. Edward Boyle, the Minister of Education, pushed for the abolition of the 11 plus and the first purpose-built comprehensive schools were constructed under the Conservatives. In fact, more comprehensive schools were opened in the second half of the twentieth century under the Conservatives than under Labour: a sign not only of official Conservative acceptance of change, but also of the consensus between the two main parties. This change was taken even further in 1963 with the Robbins Report which attempted to take the comprehensive principles into higher education by expanding universities and providing larger grants so that students were not deterred by a lack of funds.

Impact of policies

The greatest impact was in the field of education with over 6000 new schools and 11 universities built. There were some liberal reforms carried out by Butler as Home Secretary, most notably the 1957 Homicide Act, which greatly accelerated the process which ended the death penalty. However, in the social field the list of achievements, particularly when compared to the previous Labour governments, appears limited, despite the dramatic improvement in the supply of housing.

> **The comprehensive system**
>
> This was the education system that replaced the three-tier system and ended selection at the age of eleven. During the three-tier system, all children sat an 11 Plus examination to determine the type of school they would attend, be it a grammar school for the academically inclined, a secondary-technical for the more technically minded or a secondary-modern for those not suited to either of the others. The comprehensive system meant that all children attended the school in their local area whatever their abilities. The 11 Plus examination continued for those children whose parents wanted them to attend a different school to the comprehensive assigned to them.

How important a factor was Conservative leadership in maintaining power?

The Conservative party had four different leaders during the period from 1951 to 1964:

- Winston Churchill won the 1951 election, having lost in both 1945 and 1950.
- Anthony Eden won the 1955 election.
- Harold Macmillan won the election in 1959.
- Alec Douglas-Home lost the 1964 election.

However, the election results alone are not enough to judge the qualities of their leadership. Both Eden and Douglas-Home served as prime ministers for only a short time: Eden was forced out by public opinion, following the Suez Crisis, within a year of increasing the Conservative majority; and Douglas-Home lasted just under year before electoral defeat. This section will consider the leaders' importance in maintaining the Conservatives in power.

Was Churchill anything more than a figurehead?

In 1951 it was Butler, rather than Churchill, who was the driving force behind the party. Churchill was already 77 when he became prime minister for a second time and it appeared as if the election victory was a belated thank-you from the electorate for victory in the Second World War. There is little evidence to suggest he was more than a figurehead as he was frail and sustained in power by his reputation. This was made most evident in 1953 when he had a stroke and was absent for some time, but was scarcely missed! Instead it was Butler who provided the drive and ideas for this and subsequent administrations.

97

The Suez Crisis, 1956

This conflict between Britain, France and Israel against Egypt took place in October–November 1956. The Egyptian leader, Nasser, had nationalised the Suez Canal in order to raise money. Despite pressure Nasser would not reverse his policy and Russian support at the United Nations prevented action there. As a result, an Anglo–French attack was launched, but at the UN the USA condemned the action of the three powers and Russia warned that it was willing to use rockets against the invaders. Not only international pressure, but also opposition among the British people and attacks from the Labour party, particularly Gaitskell, forced a British withdrawal.

Butler had already played a significant role in helping the party recover after 1945, ensuring that it developed new and modern ideas. He was involved in the production of the 1947 party 'industrial charter', in which the Conservatives accepted the principle of a **mixed economy** of private and state, a further sign of their willingness to accept change. His association with the 1944 Education Act (see page 50) indicated that he was also concerned with social issues, an area that many perceived the Conservatives ignored. Once in office as chancellor, his policies were little different to those of Labour, but they did allow the Conservatives to appeal to the centre ground of politics. It was therefore Butler, rather than Churchill, who was responsible for modernising the party and helping Eden to secure victory in the 1955 election.

Why was Eden's premiership short-lived?

Anthony Eden replaced Churchill as prime minister in 1955 and soon after called an election that resulted in an increased Conservative majority, in part due to his personal appeal, particularly to many female voters, but also due to the work of Butler. Despite this, his administration was short-lived. This was due to one event: the Suez Crisis of 1956. Eden had been foreign secretary, on three separate occasions and with the press criticising his rather lacklustre domestic policy, he was determined to achieve success abroad. The events are covered in more detail on pages 171–172, but importantly for Eden, he had misjudged the mood of the people and was heavily criticised by the Labour party for his 'mad venture'.

Although Britain was not defeated militarily, Eden's decision to withdraw was seen as evidence of a lack of political will. With most of the rest of the world condemning British actions, it was a clear sign that the country was no longer a major power. Less than three months after the incident Eden stood down as prime minister. The official reason was ill-health and there was certainly some truth that he was unwell, but his own personal standing had been undermined by events and he was replaced by Harold Macmillan as leader. Given the damage the affair had done to the party, Macmillan was fortunate that he did not have to go to the electorate until 1959, as an election in the aftermath of Suez might have seen the Conservatives defeated.

Does Macmillan deserve his nickname 'Super Mac'?

Macmillan led the Conservative party from 1957 to 1963, during which time he won the 1959 election and increased the Conservative majority to 100, despite this being just three years after the disastrous Suez affair. Although he was fortunate to preside over a period of growing prosperity and affluence, at least until his latter years in office, his personal appeal to the electorate also played a crucial role. His appearances on television won him much support and despite satirists mocking him as 'Super Mac' he was able to turn this image to his advantage with the famous comment 'Never had it so good'. However, not all of the Conservative success should be attributed to Macmillan. The work of Butler as home secretary, with the Homicide Act (see page 96), gave the party the appearance of changing its traditional and often reactionary attitudes. The 1959 election was the high point for Macmillan:

■ By 1961 a balance of trade deficit was evidence of a downturn in the economy as the country was importing more than it was exporting.
■ By 1962 unemployment was rising and the number of days lost to strikes was increasing.

▲ Harold Macmillan pictured in his home in Surrey, 10 February 1969.

In order to try to breathe new life into a tired government, Macmillan reshuffled his cabinet in July 1962. The sacking of seven cabinet ministers and nine other ministers became known as the 'Night of the Long Knives', an over-dramatic comparison with Hitler's 1934 massacre of supporters (see pages 103–104). It did not have the desired impact and 'Super Mac' became 'Mac the Knife' as opinion polls saw Conservative popularity fall. Macmillan was also the victim of circumstances beyond his control.

Macmillan gained the reputation of a world-class statesman, in part through his realisation that the British Empire had to be dismantled, despite protests from within the party. He made this clear in 1960 with his call for the need to recognise 'the wind of change' blowing through Africa and grant independence to those who wanted it (see pages 189–191). However, it was also foreign affairs that further damaged his and the party's image. First, developments in the Cold War (see page 176) in the early 1960s revealed that Britain was no longer a major power. Second, the French vetoed Conservative attempts for Britain to join the EEC. The government was then hit by a series of scandals (see page 104), most notably the Profumo Affair in 1963. Although Macmillan cannot be blamed for the failings of one minister, critics suggested he was losing his grip and Lord Denning, a senior judge who produced a report on the affair, criticised him for not acting quickly enough:

It is the responsibility of the Prime Minister and his colleagues, and of them only, to deal with this situation: and they did not succeed in doing so.

Quoted in D. Childs, *Britain since 1945: A Political History*, page 142.

Not only had Macmillan been damaged by these events, but he was also ill and announced his intention to resign. Macmillan's final act as leader was to ask the party to follow 'customary processes' in choosing his successor, but this process damaged the party's image and contributed to its defeat in 1964.

Why did Douglas-Home become leader?

Macmillan's illness and tiredness following the scandals resulted in his announcement that he intended to resign. The leadership appeared to be a contest between Lord Hailsham (Quintin Hogg) and R. A. Butler. Many thought that this time Butler would finally become leader, but Macmillan did not wish to see him succeed and used his position to advise the Queen to invite Sir Alec Douglas-Home to be prime minister. Initially Macmillan had backed Hailsham, but eventually he believed Home was a safer choice.

The process of choosing a leader by sounding out the cabinet and MPs was seen as rather ridiculous in a democratic age, particularly as it brought to power a man of aristocratic background who was perceived by many to be out of touch with ordinary people. Douglas-Home was chosen by an 'old-boy' network, which included many old Etonians; a clear sign to many that the Conservative party had not changed its image. There was resentment among some party members, and Enoch Powell and Iain Macleod stated they would not serve under Douglas-Home. Although Douglas-Home was affable and popular with some in the party, he faced a revitalised Labour party, with a new programme, under the youthful and dynamic leadership of Harold Wilson. It was therefore perhaps unsurprising that Labour won the election that followed within a year of Douglas-Home taking office; what was more surprising perhaps was the narrowness of the Labour victory.

EEC

The European Economic Community, the forerunner of today's European Union, was established in 1957 and was made up of the France, West Germany, Italy, Belgium, the Netherlands and Luxembourg. It established a trading system between member states which had the minimum of controls, while members were also forced to impose tariffs on goods from non-member states so that they were uncompetitive.

Activity

1 Create a balance sheet for each of the Conservative leaders using the chart below:

Leader	Successes as leader	Failures as leader	Mark/10	Explanation of judgement
Churchill				
Eden				
Macmillan				
Douglas-Home				

2 Using the above chart and information from earlier in the chapter, consider how important leadership was in Conservative success in the 1955 and 1959 elections. Fill in the chart below to help you.

Leader	1955	1959
Leadership		
Economic policies		
Standard of living		
Social policies		
Other		

3 In which election was leadership more important?
4 Now look back to the 1951 election and make a list of factors that helped determine the result of that general election. Put them in order of importance and explain the reasons for the order you have chosen.

How weak was the Labour Party in the period 1951–60?

One reason for the Conservatives remaining in power for so long was the condition of the Labour Party. Although Labour's record in office between 1945 and 1951 was strong, the party was divided internally and less able to recover from defeat in 1951 than the Conservatives in 1945. The lack of unity continued for much of the period, the split being between the supporters of Gaitskell (known as the Revisionists, as they wanted to modernise the party) and the supporters of Aneurin Bevan (known as the Fundamentalists, because they wanted to maintain the traditional principles of the party), with the result that the party did not look like one of government.

Internal disputes

One explanation that has been offered for Conservative dominance in this period is the divisions within the Labour Party. Although Labour was fortunate that Attlee's successor, Hugh Gaitskell, was a talented politician and excellent public speaker, he was not able to unite the party. The party was divided over whether it wanted to move further to the left or right in British politics and Gaitskell was unable to resolve this.

Aneurin Bevan, 1897–1960

Aneurin Bevan was the son of a miner. He became minister of health in the Labour government of 1945 and was largely responsible for the establishment of the NHS and also housing policy, but then moved on to be Minister of Labour in 1951. However, he resigned from the cabinet over cuts to the NHS and the introduction of prescription charges. The left of the party saw him as their hero and although he was expelled in 1955 he became deputy leader in 1960.

Socialism

The key issue that divided the party was the future of socialism. Those on the left of the party (Bevanites) believed that the welfare measures introduced between 1945 and 1951 were just the first step along the road to a truly socialist Britain. They argued that there should be far more state control of the economy and society and disagreed with the moderate direction pursued by both Clement Attlee, the Labour leader from 1935 to 1955, and his successor, Gaitskell. In 1952 Bevan published *In Place of Fear*, which argued that:

It is essential that we should keep clear before us that one of the central principles of socialism is the substitution of public for private ownership. There is no way round this.

The left of the party also believed that the unions, which represented the working man, should have a real say in the development of party policy. This conflicted with those on the right of the party who wanted policy to be decided by the parliamentary party and not by the unions, many of which were led by powerful figures on the left of the party.

The party was also split over its attitude towards social reform and economic change. The most notable politician on the right of the party was Anthony Crosland who argued that the emphasis should be on social equality, rather than economic change, as capitalism had been 'reformed and modified almost out of existence'. This led to divisions with the left of the party over Clause IV of the Labour Party constitution about nationalisation. The left of the party wanted a greater commitment to Clause IV with its call to 'secure for the workers by hand or brain the full fruits of their industry and the most equitable distribution thereof that may be possible on the basis of common ownership of the means of production' and also to ensure the state had greater control over industry, the economy and society.

Nuclear policy

There were also divisions over Labour's nuclear policy. The left of the party wanted unilateral nuclear disarmament so that more money was available for social reforms, while others on the left argued that Britain should disarm so that the Soviet Union should not fall too far behind in the arms race with the West. The right of the party were opposed to unilateralism and wanted Britain to maintain its independent nuclear deterrent. However, on this issue Bevan was less radical and rejected unilateralism at the Party Conference of 1957. Nonetheless, he opposed the party's approval of the rearmament of Germany and its inclusion in NATO (see page 170), which he believed would alienate the Soviet Union. These divisions were so great that in 1955 Bevan was expelled from the parliamentary party for challenging official Labour policy.

These divisions came to a head at the 1960 party conference. Gaitskell had defeated Bevan for the leadership of the party in 1955 and believed that this gave him the go-ahead to take the party in a more centrist direction. Defeated for a third successive election in 1959, Gaitskell argued that the left had weakened the party with their unilateralist views, which he argued were unpopular with the country. However, the left of the party attacked the party's nuclear policy and at the party conference forced a unilateralist policy on the party using the block vote of the unions, which allowed the left-wing leaders of the unions to cast their votes on behalf of all the members of their

▲ Aneurin Bevan

Block votes

At Labour Party conferences each trade union and constituency party could cast a vote, the size of which depended on the size of its membership. The larger the union or constituency party, the larger its vote. Because the votes were cast as a single block, all the members of the union or constituency party were assumed to have the same opinion.

Activity

How important are internal divisions in weakening a political party? Look further ahead in the book to Chapter 6 (page 141) to see the impact that internal divisions had on Labour during the 1980s and the Conservatives during the 1990s. Why do you think an electorate is less willing to vote for a divided party?

union, despite the fact that the majority were moderates and did not agree with the policy. However, within a year the policy was abandoned. There were also divisions over nationalisation as the left accused Gaitskell of abandoning it as a priority.

Attitudes to Europe

A further handicap for the Labour party was its attitude towards Europe. Attlee had declared that Labour was opposed to Britain joining the EEC and in 1962 this stance was continued by Gaitskell, which hardly gave the party the appearance of modernisation and progression.

The 1959 general election

During the 1955 election campaign Attlee appeared both ill and tired in contrast to Eden, the new Conservative leader. Following Labour's defeat Attlee was succeeded by Hugh Gaitskell, a gifted politician. However, his death in 1963, at the age of only 57, meant that he never became prime minister.

Gaitskell was on the right of the party, but he believed that his victory in the 1955 leadership contest had given him the authority to lead the party away from policies such as unilateralism, which were not popular with the public. However, his period as leader coincided with divisions over the party's future and a poor election campaign in 1959. Labour stood a chance of winning in 1959 as the election was only three years after the Suez Crisis and the government's budgetary policies appeared unsound. However, the result was a disaster for the party as the Conservatives not only increased their majority to 100, but also came close to winning 50 per cent of the popular vote (see Table 4 on page 102).

Table 4 1959 general election results.

Party	Number of votes	Number of seats	Percentage of vote
Conservative	13,749,830	365	49.4
Labour	12,215,538	258	43.8
Liberal	1,638,571	6	5.9
Others	255,302	1	0.9

The Conservatives were fortunate that the election coincided with a period of economic recovery and allowed them to claim that 'Life is better with the Conservatives'. However, Labour also made mistakes. They promised an increase in state pensions without a rise in taxes, and when questioned about how it would be funded had few answers and were simply not believed. In contrast, the government had reduced income tax before the election and, with their record of improving living standards, appeared to offer security and prosperity. Added to the other problems faced by the Labour party it was not surprising that their performance was so poor, but it only added to the internal arguments that reached their climax at the 1960 party conference.

The death of Gaitskell in 1963 resulted in Harold Wilson being elected as leader of the Labour party. He presented a youthful and 'working-class' image, which was in direct contrast to Douglas-Home. He was able to dominate the direction of the 1964 election campaign and stress the need for modernisation of the economy with his emphasis on 'the white heat of technology'. Labour therefore entered the election expecting to win.

Activity

1 Make a list and put, in order of priority, the failings of the Labour party in the 1959 election. Explain your order.
2 How far can Labour's leadership be blamed for electoral failures?
3 Labour lost three successive elections in 1951, 1955 and 1959. You should now come to a conclusion about whether you think Conservative strengths or Labour weaknesses were more important in determining the outcome of the elections.
  a Complete the table below by entering any strengths or weaknesses of the two parties that you think influenced the outcome of the election
  b In the final column review your entries and decide whether you think the outcome was due to Conservative strengths or Labour weaknesses.
  c Having completed the chart, write a paragraph to explain whether you think Conservative strengths or Labour weaknesses were more important in determining the outcome of the elections.

Election	Labour strengths	Labour weaknesses	Conservative strengths	Conservative weaknesses	Reason for outcome
1951					
1955					
1959					

Why did support for the Conservative Party decline?

The last years of the Conservative government were damaged by a series of scandals which, although not the direct fault of the government, reflected badly on it and gave the appearance of a ministry that had lost control. However, it was not just the scandals that lost the government support and ultimately the 1964 election. There were a number of reasons for the loss of support: the economy was declining; the government had failed to secure membership of the EEC; and the leadership of the party no longer appeared to be strong after the 'Night of the Long Knives' and Macmillan's subsequent retirement.

The economy

If Conservative dominance had been based on the rising standard of living, then their defeat in 1964 was due, at least in part, to the worsening economic situation over which they presided. In 1959 they had been able to campaign on 'Don't let Labour ruin it', but now it appeared as if it was the present government who were failing. From 1961 onwards, the economy went downhill:

- There was a balance of trade deficit and government attempts to reduce it, such as a 'pay pause' and the establishment of the National Economic Development Council (NEDC) – an economic planning body made up of representatives from the government, trade unions and industrial managers – and the National Incomes Commission (NIC), which was to control incomes, had no noticeable impact.
- Unemployment began to rise and reached over 800,000 by the end of 1963, with the north and Scotland suffering particularly badly.
- There was a significant increase in the number of days lost to strikes, particularly in the docks.

Compared with much of the rest of Europe, which had faster rates of growth, Britain appeared to be lagging behind and this only added to the government's difficulties when its application for membership of the EEC was rejected in 1963.

EEC rejection

Both major political parties had been hostile to Britain joining the EEC when it had been established, but with the loss of Empire and the Suez Crisis, which both raised questions about Britain's status as a world power and damaged Anglo-American relations (see pages 97 and 171–172), politicians gradually began to change their views. For many in the Conservative Party, the most important reason for a change in attitude was the economic performance of the EEC, which was far better than that of Britain (see page 182). This became even more apparent with the worsening performance of the British economy after 1961. However, the French President, Charles de Gaulle, had serious reservations about Britain's sincerity and commitment to Europe and rejected its application. It was humiliating for Britain and revealed to many just how weak the country was.

Night of the Long Knives

The Night of the Long Knives is the name given to the reshuffle of the cabinet undertaken by Macmillan in 1962. The declining economy resulted in losses in by-elections throughout 1962, such as Orpington where the Liberals overturned a Conservative majority of 14,000 and won the seat by 7000 votes, similarly Labour captured the previously safe Conservative seat of West Middlesbrough. This growing unpopularity was also seen in falling opinion polls as Labour surged ahead and therefore Macmillan decided that a reshuffle was needed. This was particularly necessary as, compared with the young and dynamic men emerging in both the Labour party and around the US president, J. F. Kennedy, Macmillan's cabinet appeared old. The reshuffle saw a third of the cabinet replaced. Although there was some improvement in his ratings afterwards, it resulted in him being seen as 'Mac the Knife' and damaged the unity of the party, prompting a historian to comment:

Planning required either a government which commanded enough prestige to force its will upon people or a system in which people could be confident that they would be treated fairly. Macmillan did not possess either claim to authority after the ministerial changes.

T. O. Lloyd, *Empire to Welfare State: English History 1906–85*, 1986, page 381.

Perhaps the decline in his reputation was put even more clearly by the rising star of the Liberal party, Jeremy Thorpe, who made a play on words of the Bible, and said:

Greater love hath no man than this – that he lays down his friends for his life.

Macmillan never recovered his authority in either the party or country as shown in the opinion polls.

Scandals

The large number of scandals that befell the government in 1963 served only to make matters worse and have prompted the historian, Paul Adelman, to suggest that they delivered the 'coup de grace to the Conservative government'. Although the Profumo Affair is probably the most famous, there was also the Vassall Affair, the Philby Case and the Argyll divorce case. Each of the cases further weakened the government.

Scandals of 1963

- Vassall was a civil servant in the Admiralty who spied for the Soviet Union. There were rumours that senior figures in the Admiralty tried to protect him and although no evidence of a cover-up was found, it created distrust.
- Kim Philby was a senior official at the Foreign Office and had been passing information to the USSR and recruiting spies for them. He fled to Russia in 1963 to avoid arrest.
- In 1963 the Duke of Argyll sued his wife for divorce on the grounds of adultery. In court a list of 88 names was produced with whom it was alleged she had, at various times, had group sex. This was rumoured to include some government ministers and led to the famous radio comment from a comedian that she should have married Plymouth Argyll rather than the Duke of Argyll.
- The Profumo scandal caused the government the most problems. John Profumo's liaison with Christine Keeler was a security risk because of her links through sex work to the Russian embassy. Not only did Profumo deny the affair in the House of Commons, but it also became known that he had met her at the home of Stephen Ward, an osteopath who treated a number of Conservative MPs, and this damaged the Party by association.

- The inquiry into the Vassall Affair suggested that although there was no evidence of cover-ups, the government was not in control of its departments.
- With the Philby Case, the government took the blame for the security service's failure to identify a traitor in the Foreign Office for so long.
- With the Argyll divorce case, two government ministers were supposedly on the list of 88 with whom the Duchess had been involved sexually.
- The Profumo Affair raised issues of risks to national security through the Secretary of State for War, John Profumo, and his relationship with Christine Keeler, who was linked to a member of the Russian embassy. His initial denial of the affair and then admission that he had lied to parliament, raised doubts about Macmillan's control of the party and naivety in believing his minister. More importantly, it also reflected badly on both parliament and the party, raising questions as to the fitness of the government to lead. It appeared as if the government was out of touch with reality and this was only reinforced by satirists of the time.

Social problems

As class barriers were breaking down, Butler claimed that the Conservative party was aiding the process. A strong case can be made for his claim that:

We [Conservatives] have developed an affluent, open and democratic society, in which the class escalators are continually moving and in which people are divided not so much between 'haves' and 'have-nots' as between 'haves' and 'have-mores'.

Michael Lynch, *Access to History: Britain 1945-2007*, 2008, page 52.

The education system had given greater opportunity to all young people and the creation of a 'property-owning democracy', aided by credit, had done the same for adults. However, despite these developments, where working-class income often exceeded that of the lower-middle class, there were increasing tensions that the government struggled to manage

Social tensions and riots (1958–59)

The clearest evidence of social tensions were the race riots that broke out in 1958 as Britain struggled to start to adapt to being a multi-racial society. After the Second World War immigration from the Empire had been encouraged as workers were needed to fill the labour shortage. However, tensions developed as those people who had migrated to Britain were blamed for housing shortages in many of the poorer areas where rent was cheaper. Similarly, they were blamed for job shortages because of their willingness to work for lower rates of pay. In 1958–59 these tensions spilled over into riots in some of the main cities, including London, Bristol and Nottingham. The most notable outbreak of violence occurred at Notting Hill where white youths tried to attack properties owned and rented by black people. The police struggled to maintain order, but afterwards heavy prison sentences were imposed on those who provoked the violence.

The government set up the Salmon Inquiry, which concluded the trouble was due to increased immigration, and made no reference to the racism or discrimination suffered by the immigrants in matters such as housing or employment. The government responded to the inquiry report by passing the 1962 Commonwealth Immigration Act, which limited the number of immigrants, depending upon their ethnic origin. However, as the Act was moving through parliament there was a rush of immigrants to avoid the restrictions, which served only to further fuel the concerns of those who wanted greater controls on immigration.

Youth sub-culture

The other social problem facing the government was the development of a youth sub-culture. This included those young people who had interests and beliefs that did not conform to the majority of their age group. In some instances this escalated into violence, as seen in the clashes between 'mods and rockers' who often confronted each other in holiday resorts during bank holidays. Although there is no agreement as to the reasons for this development, it is likely to be a combination of a variety of factors. Many young people were benefiting from the greater affluence and had more money available to spend on the increasing variety of goods, such as transistor radios. This generation had also not lived through the war and did not feel constrained by the horrors and grim times of the past and as a result did not feel bound by traditional hierarchical structures and a respect for authority, which their elders still had. Moreover, new forms of entertainment, both musical, with 'rock and roll', and satirical television shows, challenged the established behaviour of deference.

However, not all young people gained from the increasing affluence and those who had missed out on the increasing wealth often felt alienated and developed a 'sub-culture' which resulted in the emergence of anti-social behaviour, seen in the fights that took place between the mods and rockers during the summer of 1964. Many were losing respect for those in authority because the increasing number of scandals usually involved those in government or senior roles within the civil service (see page 104) who therefore did not provide good role models.

All of this helped to undermine a Conservative party still closely associated with tradition and hierarchy and which was lampooned in the new satirical magazine, *Private Eye*, or on the television in programmes such as *That Was the Week That Was*. Despite attempts to modernise its image, the choice of Sir Alec Douglas-Home as Macmillan's successor in 1963 (see page 99) appeared to confirm to many that it was out of touch.

Mods and rockers

These were the terms used to describe the two groups whose fights characterised the summer of 1964. The 'mods' rode scooters and were usually more smartly dressed than their counterparts the 'rockers', who rode motorbikes.

Activity

1 Using the information on pages 103–106, complete the following chart to explain why the Conservatives had declined in popularity by 1963. You should:
- Explain how each factor caused the Conservative decline.
- Award each a mark out of 10 for how important its role was in the decline; the higher the mark, the more important the factor.

- Explain why you have given the factor this mark.

Factor	Explanation of role	Mark/10	Explanation of mark

2 Write a paragraph explaining which factor you consider to be the most important.

Historical debate

'Never had it so good' or 'Thirteen wasted years'?

This historical debate on the Conservative performance 1951–64 centres round the claims made by the two main political parties, which, given their partisan nature, suggests that the truth is likely to lie somewhere between. In 1957 Macmillan claimed in a speech to a Conservative rally in Bedford that 'most of our people have never had it so good', while Labour have described the period as 'thirteen wasted years'.

There is much to support Macmillan's claim as it was a period of continuously rising living standards and wages were certainly rising faster than prices, with wages going up 72 per cent and prices only 45 per cent. As the historians Alan Sked and Chris Cook have commented, 'Everyone from the middle-aged mum with her domestic appliances to teenagers with transistor radios' agreed that after years of austerity they had the right to take advantage of the improvement. The Conservatives had also, according to Churchill in 1954, 'improved all the social services and are spending more this year on them than any Government at any time'.

Certainly the years 1957–59 appear to be the high point of affluence and allowed the government to lower taxes and increase spending without causing serious economic and financial problems. However, even Macmillan in his speech warned that high public spending, rising living standards, full employment and low inflation were not all possible at the same time, so it would be unfair to argue that the government was not aware of problems in the economy.

Despite these warnings, there is still a different perspective to the economic and social policies that needs to be examined. Critics have argued that the governments did very little while in power, manipulating budgets for electoral gain and giving little impression of understanding how the economy worked. According to the alternative view, the governments were more concerned with maintaining Britain as a world power, whatever the cost to the economy, and paid little attention to the sluggish growth compared to Germany or other European states. These critics also argued that Conservative economic complacency ensured the necessary economic growth would not be generated: stop-go policies discouraged investment and too much money went into defence or abroad, as key industries, such as textiles or shipbuilding, were neglected. Even in the field of social reform critics argued that whatever growth there was did not reach the Welfare State. Pensions were updated, but erratically; and nothing was done to solve the problems of the NHS. In these accounts, Churchill's main concern was survival; Eden's priority was foreign policy; Macmillan, who was interested in social reform, presided over the period when an economic downturn impacted on expenditure; and Douglas-Home failed to change direction, perhaps justifying the title given to one book on this period, *The Stagnant Society*.

The two extracts below further develop the contrasting views outlined above. These passages focus on the 1950s, rather than the whole period, with the first passage supporting the view that it was a stagnant or wasted period, while the second supports Macmillan's claim that Britain 'never had it so good'.

Passage 1

The object of every economic system is to increase the supply and range of consumer goods and services available to its people, in other words to increase the standard of living as fast as possible. In the long run, this can only be done by expanding production. When Butler was Chancellor [April 1955] the cost of living was deliberately pushed up by raising purchase tax on a wide range of goods, and at the same time a number of measures were taken to discourage capital investment. Butler's policies were followed by his two successors; they were only reversed at the onset of the recession in 1958. What did this policy achieve? It did eventually succeed in slowing down the pace of wage increases which was one of the main factors behind the 1955 inflation. But it took nearly three years to do so, at the cost of a virtually complete industrial standstill and a number of financial crises and industrial disputes. It is too early to assess the long-term damage to the British economy from this period of enforced standstill, but it certainly left us with a lot of leeway to catch up.

M. Shanks, *The Stagnant Society*, 1961.

Activity

1 In light of the two passages and further reading, do you agree with the view that the 1950s were a period of great prosperity for people in Britain? Explain your answer.
2 Using the information in this chapter, find information to support the two views:
   (i) Never had it so good
   (ii) Thirteen wasted years
3 Which view do you find more convincing? Explain your choice.

Further research

In reading some of the material below you should consider the author's view of the period and the evidence they provide to support their claims.

R. Blake, *The Decline of Power*, 1985, Chapters 17–20.

P. Clarke, *Hope and Glory*, 2004, Chapters 7–8.

A. Marr, *A History of Modern Britain*, 2007.

K. Morgan, *Britain since 1945: The People's Peace*, 2001.

Passage 2

By 1959 the economy stood on the edge of a great leap forward. Macmillan said in July 1957 that people had 'never had it so good'. At the time he said it, it may not have been accurate; production figures in 1958 were no higher than in 1955. But between September 1958 and December 1959 there was a sudden explosive expansion, and Macmillan's slogan dominated politics and everyday life. Partly because the expansion was started by making credit easier to come by, and partly because of a change in people's wants, a great deal of the expansion was devoted to buying 'consumer durables'. A majority of families had a washing-machine, about one family in three had a refrigerator, and in the south the proportion was higher; about one family in three owned a car. In 1955 40% of homes owned a television set; by 1959 the figure had risen to 70%.

T. O. Lloyd, *Empire to Welfare State: English History 1906–85*, 1986.

Chapter takeaways

- Although the British public were disillusioned by the continuation of rationing and austerity after the Second World War, the 1951 election result produced only a small victory for the Conservative Party.
- The policies pursued by the Conservative Party were, in many respects, similar to those begun by the previous Labour governments; therefore as the Conservatives brought about an improvement in living standards there was no reason to remove them from office.
- Many people credited the Conservative government with the improvement in living standards and voted for them in the elections of 1955 and 1959.
- The Conservative Party was able to modernise and adapt to many of the significant social changes as class distinctions declined and social mobility increased.
- Social tensions, such as the development of a multi-racial society, culminated in a series of riots in cities in 1958–59 and the growth of a 'youth sub-culture', both of which damaged the Conservatives.

- Adapting to the major change in Britain's position in the world challenged the leadership of the Conservative Party. The Suez Crisis ended Eden's period in office.
- The loss of Empire was acknowledged by Macmillan in his 'Wind of Change' speech, and this culminated in Britain's failed attempt to join the EEC in 1963, which weakened the Macmillan administration.
- The failure of governments to increase growth in the economy as fast as other European countries further weakened the government's position by 1962.
- The final years of Conservative power were rocked by a series of scandals, most notably the Profumo Affair, but also the flight to Russia of Kim Philby, a senior official in the Foreign Office, which lessened trust in the government.
- By 1964 Labour had overcome many of the internal disputes over its direction and under the youthful leadership of Harold Wilson was in a strong position to challenge a tired Conservative Party.

Study skills: Understanding the wording of the question and planning an answer

Understanding the wording of a question

It is very important that you read the wording of the question you are answering very carefully. You must focus on the key words and phrases in the question; these may be dates, ministers' names or phrases such as 'how successful'. Unless you directly address the demands of the question you will not score highly.

The first thing to do is to identify the command words; these will give you the instructions about what you have to do. You may be asked:

- to **assess** the causes of an event
- **to what extent**, or **how far** a particular factor was the most important in bringing about an event
- **how successful** a government or prime minister was.
  Here are two examples:

> ### Examples
>
> 1 **Assess the reasons for Conservative dominance 1951–64.**
>
>   In this essay you would need to analyse a range of reasons why the Conservative Party dominated British politics in the period 1951 to 1964. However, in order to reach the highest levels you would need to weigh up – **assess** – the relative importance of the factors you have discussed and reach a balanced conclusion, not simply produce a list of reasons for their dominance.
>
> 2 **'The most important reason for Conservative dominance in the period 1951–64 was the improvement in the standard of living.' How far do you agree?**
>
>   Although this question, like the first, requires you to consider the reasons for Conservative dominance, you must consider the importance of the improvement in the standard of living and write a paragraph on the named factor, even if you argue it was not the most important. However, even if you think it was the most important, you must still explain why other factors were less important.

Planning an answer

Once you have understood the demands of the question, the next step is planning the answer. The plan should outline your line of argument – this means that you will need to think about your thesis before you start writing and the plan should help you maintain a consistent line of argument throughout the answer. Consequently, your plan should be a list of ideas and reasons relating to the issue in the question. Your plan should not be a date list of events, as this will encourage you to write a narrative or descriptive answer, rather than an analytical one.

Consider the first example above: 'Assess the reasons for Conservative dominance 1951-64'. A plan for this essay might take the following form:

1 **Increase in the standard of living**
Evidence of wages, consumer purchases and economic success at time of elections. Important as persuades voters Conservatives doing a good job, important as 1964 loss when economy weak, **therefore most important reason**.

2 **Timing of the elections**
Link to the above and 'feel good', avoid elections close to difficulties, such as Suez.

3 **Leadership of Macmillan**
His appeal, image and ability to convince electorate party responsible for rise in living standards and ensures elections at time of prosperity (link to 1 and 2). Important as under Douglas-Home lose, **but close result and therefore less important**.

4 **Reorganisation and modernisation of Conservative Party**
Recovery from 1945, new policies, social issues and attitudes, Butler, Woolton, therefore in a position to take advantage of points 1 and 5.

5 **Labour weakness**
Divisions within party, consensus and why change to Labour? Important as once united under young and charismatic leader win 1964, **but even under Gaitskell who was talented did not win, had to wait for economic downturn**.

6 **Conclusion**
Link between factors, but prosperity crucial and once achieved no need to vote Labour, but once in decline that changed.

The answer should not just list the reasons, but offer a comment about their importance and the conclusion should offer a clear line of argument which has been supported in the previous paragraphs.

Planning an answer should help you focus on the actual question and not simply write about the topic. In the first question it is wrong to write all you know about the Conservative governments of 1951–64, but not explain why they dominated. Under the pressure of time in the examination room it is easy to forget the importance of planning and just start writing, but that will usually result in essays that do not have a clear argument or that change their line of argument halfway through, making it far less convincing.

Question practice

The focus of this section has been on planning. Use the information in this chapter to plan answers to the following questions:
1 'The most important reason for Conservative dominance in the period 1951–64 was the improvement in the standard of living.' How far do you agree?
2 Assess the reasons why Labour lost three elections in the period from 1951 to 1964.
3 'The scandals of 1963 were the most important reason for the Conservative defeat in 1964.' How far do you agree?

Chapter 5

Labour and Conservative governments, 1964–79

This chapter deals with the efforts of Labour and Conservative governments to grapple with Britain's economic and social problems between 1964 and 1979. It considers how far the economic difficulties can be attributed to government policy and how far they were the result of long-term changes in British society. It also explores the efforts of successive governments to manage industrial relations and examines the extent to which trade union power contributed to the fall of both the Conservatives in 1974 and Labour in 1979. The main issues of this chapter are:

- Why did the Labour Party win the 1964 election?
- How effective was Harold Wilson as prime minister?
- How successful were the economic policies of the 1964–70 Labour government?
- How successfully did the Labour government deal with industrial relations?
- Did the result of the 1970 general election owe more to Labour weaknesses or Conservative strengths?
- How successful was Edward Heath as prime minister?
- How effectively did Wilson and Callaghan deal with the problems Britain faced between 1974 and 1979?

At the end of this chapter there is advice on how to write a good opening paragraph to an essay question. This is a vital skill. A good first paragraph demonstrates that:

- you understand the question
- the reader knows exactly how you intend to develop your argument.

Timeline

1964	October	Labour government under Harold Wilson takes office
1965	September	National Plan published
1966	March	General election gives Labour a 96-seat majority
1967	November	Government devalues the pound
		President de Gaulle again vetoes British membership of the EEC
1969	June	'In Place of Strife' abandoned in return for TUC pledge to monitor strikes
1970	May	Equal Pay Act enacted
	June	Conservatives win the general election
1971	August	The Industrial Relations Act becomes law
	October	House of Commons votes in favour of British entry to the EEC
1972	January	Miners' strike begins (ends February)
1973	January	Britain joins the EEC
1974	February	Miners' strike begins (ends March)
		Conservatives lose the general election; Labour takes office without a majority
	October	Labour wins a small majority in the general election
1975	June	Referendum on Britain's membership of the EEC
1976	March	Wilson resigns as prime minister and is replaced by Callaghan
	December	Britain accepts a loan from the IMF
1977	March	Lib–Lab Pact: the Liberals agree to support the Labour government in parliament
1979	January	The 'winter of discontent'
	May	Conservatives win the general election

Overview

The Labour government, elected with a tiny majority in 1964, began with high hopes of setting Britain on a new path of modernisation, technological development and planned economic growth. Although the government quickly ran into economic difficulties, many voters blamed these on the previous Conservative administration and, in March 1966, the Labour Party won a larger majority. However, the British economy continued to be less successful than the economies of its European rivals. The government believed that workers' pay increases were damaging British trade and tried to restrict them. But this upset the Labour Party's natural supporters – trade unionists, workers and left-wing activists – who argued that workers were being blamed unfairly and asked to make unreasonable sacrifices. So there were regular strikes against government pay policy. The trade unions were especially outraged in 1969 when the government tried to reform industrial relations. They were able to defeat the reform proposals. Despite signs of economic improvement from 1969, the Conservatives won an unexpected victory in the 1970 general election. Many of the Labour Party's supporters in the wider Labour movement were disillusioned with their government's failure to transform British society and by what they saw as its conservative economic policies. As a result, some local Labour Party organisations were taken over by extreme left-wing activists who hoped to be able to influence both the party's policies and its membership.

Heath's Conservative government took Britain into the European Economic Community (the EEC, now known as the European Union) in January 1973. The Tories also hoped to reduce the number of disruptive strikes with a comprehensive Industrial Relations Act, but the opposition of the trade union movement was so strong that the legislation became unworkable. The government's attempts to stimulate growth, combined with the impact of international crises, pushed up prices and led to demands for huge pay increases. Heath had two unsuccessful confrontations with the coal miners over pay and these contributed to his defeat in February 1974.

The return of Labour did not appear to improve matters. The economy seemed trapped in what became known as 'stagflation' – a mixture of stagnation and **inflation**; a period of low growth, rising unemployment and rising prices. The government continued to believe that high wage increases were to blame but this widened the arguments in the Labour movement over economic policy. Although the government reached an agreement with the unions over industrial relations, in 1978–79 several groups of workers went on strike demanding pay increases. This became known as the 'winter of discontent' and contributed to victory in the 1979 general election for the Conservative Party. Led by Margaret Thatcher, the Tories were determined to introduce a radical new economic strategy.

Why did the Labour Party win the 1964 election?

When Harold Macmillan resigned as prime minister in October 1963, the Labour Party had an opinion poll lead of 12 per cent over the Tories; and Harold Wilson, the new Labour leader, enjoyed a 60 per cent approval rating. But when the general election occurred a year later, the Labour Party achieved only a narrow victory (see Table 1). This means that historians have two questions to answer:

- Why did the Labour Party win in 1964?
- Why was the result so close?

Table 1 The 1959 and 1964 general elections.

	October 1959			October 1964		
Party	Votes	Seats	Candidates	Votes	Seats	Candidates
Conservative	13,749,830	365	625	12,001,396	304	630
Labour	12,215,538	258	621	12,205,814	317	628
Liberal	1,638,571	6	216	3,092,878	9	365

Explaining Labour's victory in 1964

The Labour Party enjoyed several advantages in 1964:

- Harold Wilson's leadership of the Labour Party.
- How the electorate regarded the Conservatives.
- The revival of the Liberal Party.
- Changes in British society during the 1950s.

Harold Wilson's leadership of the Labour Party

The Labour Party appeared to be much more united than it had been in either 1955 or 1959 (see pages 100–102). Their divisions over nuclear weapons, Europe and nationalisation had not disappeared. However, Harold Wilson, elected leader in February 1963, was able to gloss over them by presenting the Labour Party as modern, dynamic and progressive. The party's election manifesto promised a range of policies to promote faster economic growth and full employment, as well as improved welfare and health services, better housing and a programme of comprehensive education. These commitments echoed Wilson's pledge to 'harness science to our economic planning' and create a 'Britain that is going to be forged in the white heat of this [technological and scientific] revolution'. Wilson himself seemed to personify this new, progressive Britain in which talented people from humble backgrounds could succeed. He was a former teacher of economics at Oxford University, but he stressed how different he was from the Old Etonians who led the Tory Party by cultivating his image as a person of the people – a Yorkshire-born, grammar-school boy and football fan. He appeared to be just the kind of classless professional the country needed to tackle its economic difficulties.

How the electorate regarded the Conservatives

The Conservatives had been in power since 1951, and many voters blamed them for the growing economic problems which became apparent in the early 1960s (see page 103). The Tories did not seem to have the answers to the problems of rising unemployment, inflation, industrial unrest and the growing disparity in wealth between the regions of Britain. Labour claimed that the Tories had presided over 'thirteen wasted years'.

The Conservatives also seemed out of touch with a modern democratic society. Their new leader, Sir Alec Douglas-Home, was a Scottish aristocrat – the fourteenth Earl of Home – who had given up his peerage when he became prime minister in October 1963. Already 60 years old when he became prime minister, he appeared no match for the 47-year-old Wilson. Tories were implicated in 'sex scandals' too (see page 104). The electorate was given the impression that the Tories were an old-fashioned, self- indulgent elite.

The revival of the Liberal Party

The Conservative government's growing unpopularity in the early 1960s benefited the Liberal Party because many middle-class voters who wanted to register their protest were not prepared to vote for the Labour Party. This was shown by the by-election result in middle-class Orpington in 1962, when a Conservative majority of 14,700 was overturned by the victorious Liberal candidate who won with a majority of 7850.

The Liberal revival brought them more publicity, increased funding and some talented new recruits. As a result, they were able to contest many more seats in 1964 than they had done in 1959 (see Table 1 on page 112). They gained only three more seats but almost doubled their vote. This considerably affected the outcome of the election because, by taking votes from the Conservatives, they helped to hand victory to the Labour Party in many seats (for example, Dover, Wellingborough and Bolton East) even though the overall Labour vote fell a little.

Changes in British society in the 1950s

You have read in Chapter 4 how living standards in Britain improved during the 1950s. Having more money to spend made people, especially young people, more independent and less willing to accept traditional authority. These attitudes were encouraged by the cultural changes of the decade (see pages 105–106) in which plays, novels and television examined the class structure, satire poked fun at politicians, and pop music and cinema challenged attitudes to sex. Grammar schools gave bright pupils from underprivileged backgrounds unprecedented opportunities to enter universities and careers. All of this created a climate in which many people, especially the young, aspired to create a new, modern, classless Britain run with professional, scientific competence. The Labour Party benefited from this mood; opinion polls showed that it was significantly more popular with voters under the age of 44 although it lagged behind the Conservatives among older voters and women.

Why was the result so close?

If a mere 900 voters in eight crucial constituencies had voted Tory instead of Labour (or even not voted at all) the Conservatives would have won. Table 1 (on page 112) shows that the Labour Party actually secured fewer votes in 1964 than it had done in 1959, which suggests that the election was more a rejection of the Conservatives than an endorsement of Labour. The section above on the Liberal Party shows how the Labour Party could still win seats, despite losing votes. The opinion poll lead that Labour had enjoyed at the height of the Profumo scandal in June 1963 (see page 104), when they were 20 per cent ahead of the Tories, was gradually whittled away during the following year.

Douglas-Home's leadership

Sir Alec Douglas-Home turned out to be a more effective prime minister than many expected. For all his apparent bumbling, he appeared modest, decent and trustworthy, while Wilson had something of a reputation for political cunning.

Conservative tax cuts

The Chancellor of the Exchequer, Reginald Maudling, cut taxes in his 1963 budget. Although the cuts contributed to a trade deficit of £800 million, they also helped to narrow the gap between the parties as earnings rose and the number of unemployed people dropped from almost 900,000 in February 1963 to 300,000 by July 1964. Some opinion polls even showed a small Tory lead in the summer.

Attitudes to the Labour Party

Many voters still distrusted the Labour Party and its links to the trade unions and so strikes against the government's pay policies reduced its support. The party's internal divisions had not been fully resolved, and middle-class voters disliked its commitment to nationalisation. Very few of its leaders had held office before and some voters doubted their ability to handle crises, especially international problems, as the Conservatives continued to be regarded as more reliable on defence.

The Labour Party also fared less well than it hoped in some working-class areas in the Midlands where the Conservatives picked up votes because immigration was a sensitive issue. The most notorious result occurred in the Smethwick constituency near Birmingham, where the Conservative candidate ran an overtly racist campaign and succeeded in turning a 3500 Labour majority into a Tory victory by 1700 votes.

Activity

How is the outcome of the 1964 election best explained? Copy and complete the table below to help you answer this question.

You should:
- Award a mark out of 6 for how important each factor was in determining the outcome: the higher the mark, the more important the factor.
- Explain why you have given the factor the mark.

Factor	How it influenced the outcome of the election	Mark/6 for importance	Explanation of the mark
Attitudes to the Conservatives			
Home's leadership			
Attitudes to the Labour Party			
Wilson's leadership			
Liberal revival			
Social change			

How effective was Harold Wilson as prime minister?

Wilson faced a number of problems when he became prime minister:

- The Labour government had a majority of only four seats.
- The party's promises about modernising British society needed to be fulfilled.
- There were pressing foreign and colonial problems to deal with.
- Senior figures in the government were talented but several of them disliked one another.
- The economic situation was serious.

Wilson displayed a number of important characteristics as prime minister. He was:

- Highly intelligent, hard-working and had an excellent memory for detail.
- Perpetually optimistic, and resilient, patient and cool in a crisis.
- Personally kind, charming and generous.
- Distrustful of party ideology, preferring practical solutions.
- A leader who sought compromise rather than conflict.
- Acceptable to both wings of the party.

The Labour government's small majority

Wilson faced great difficulties with a majority of only four. However, in the March 1966 general election, the government was returned with a majority of 96. This was a major achievement and it showed that Wilson's leadership style had paid off. Wilson had avoided splits in the party. Labour won because they had managed to appear purposeful and resolute, and had avoided any damaging divisions. Many voters still blamed the Tories for the country's difficulties, and Wilson, by exuding self-confidence and authority, had made Edward Heath, Conservative leader since August 1965, seem dogged and ponderous.

▲ Harold Wilson at Chequers, the prime minister's country residence in Buckinghamshire, circa 1975.

Table 2 The March 1966 general election result.

Party	Votes	Seats	Candidates
Conservative	11,418,433	253	629
Labour	13,064,951	363	621
Liberal	2,327,533	12	311

The transformation of British society

Labour had promised the modernisation of society after 'thirteen years of Tory misrule'. To do this, the government enacted a series of reforms which had a major impact on British society. Wilson himself was not comfortable with some of them but allowed his more reform-minded colleagues to sponsor them. The reforms owed a lot to Roy Jenkins, the home secretary.

The Labour government's social reforms

Date	Act	Impact
Nov 1965	Murder	Temporary abolition of the death penalty, made permanent in 1969
Nov 1965	Race Relations	Discrimination in public facilities illegal
June 1967	Family Planning	Contraception available to all on the NHS, not just married couples
July 1967	Sexual Offences	Homosexual acts in private between consenting adults legalised
Oct 1967	Abortion	Abortion under certain conditions legalised
April 1968	Race Relations	Racial discrimination in housing and employment illegal
July 1968	Theatres	Censorship of plays by the Lord Chamberlain ended
May 1969	Voting	Voting age lowered from 21 to 18
Oct 1969	Divorce	Divorce process simplified and made less costly
May 1970	Equal Pay	Men and women to receive the same pay for the same work

There had been important social changes in the 1950s, which had resulted in changing attitudes:

- The increase in prosperity meant people travelled more and reduced the divisions between the social classes.
- There was more education, a higher standard of living and less respect for tradition.
- Youth culture, the civil rights movement in the US and more employment opportunities for women brought demands for equality.

The Labour government's radicalism lay not so much in its traditional policy of nationalising industry but in this major programme of social change, which introduced many of the ideas that modern Britain takes for granted, especially race relations.

However, traditionalists were outraged and thought that changes to the law on homosexuality, contraception and the legalisation of abortion encouraged promiscuous sex and created a 'permissive' society. Opinion polls showed that the death penalty for murder was popular, and the campaign led by Mary Whitehouse against what she regarded as excessive sex, violence and bad language in BBC programmes gained 400,000 supporters.

Race relations

Many new arrivals from the Commonwealth, finding only low-paid jobs, settled in less affluent areas. This was a problem for the Labour Party: immigration was often unpopular with Labour voters in inner-city areas. One reason was racial prejudice, but there was also fear that competition for jobs would mean lower wages. This was why the government tightened the rules on immigration in 1965 and 1968. Its Race Relations Acts did attempt to tackle discrimination but the enforcement methods were weak, making it difficult to secure convictions.

Education policy

Many Labour supporters opposed the existing system which divided children on the basis of an examination at the age of eleven, into academic achievers who went to grammar schools and the remainder, most of whom attended secondary modern schools. In 1965 Anthony Crosland, the education secretary, began the process of replacing the system with new comprehensive schools for children of all abilities. The comprehensive system led to bitter controversy in many areas where grammar schools had been seen as offering the sort of opportunity usually only open to those who attended independent schools.

In higher education there was a considerable period of expansion. Sir Alec Douglas-Home's government had begun to implement the recommendations of the 1963 Robbins Report which had called for a major expansion of university education to produce a sufficiently educated workforce to compete in the modern world. The Labour government, with its faith in scientific and technological advance, maintained this commitment. A major change was the introduction of the Open University, which Wilson thought one of his finest achievements and which offered adults the chance to work for a degree on a part-time basis.

Foreign and colonial issues

Wilson had managed to hold a balance between his left wing and the less radical Labour supporters in his social reforms, achieving a degree of change without seeming to be too extreme. Foreign and colonial policy issues were more of a strain.

The Vietnam War

Wilson believed that Britain's economic recovery and security depended on close alliance with America. The left regarded US policies as aggressive and imperialist and were especially bitter over Wilson's attitude to the Vietnam War. In April 1965, a few weeks after President Johnson committed US troops to fight in Vietnam, Wilson told the Commons that 'we have made absolutely plain our support of the American stand against the communist infiltration in South Vietnam'. But, to appease the left, he refused Johnson's requests to send British troops; in June 1966 he publicly criticised heavy US bombing of North Vietnam; and in 1967 he attempted to broker a peace deal. These actions irritated Johnson without going far enough to satisfy the Labour left.

Table 3 The numbers attending university courses in selected years.

Academic year	Men	Women
1951–52	79,422	22,590
1963–64	106,402	36,571
1969–70	176,169	66,842

The Vietnam War

After the defeat of the Japanese in 1945 the French tried to re-establish their colonial empire in Vietnam. They were defeated by Vietnamese communist nationalists in 1954 and an international conference at Geneva divided the country between a communist north and non-communist south. The communists in the north never accepted the validity of the Geneva decision and began a guerrilla war designed to reunite the country. South Vietnam relied on US help for survival and in 1965 US President Johnson sent American troops to defend it. America's use of heavy bombing and chemical weapons made the war highly controversial.

Southern Rhodesia

Wilson also attempted to balance different sections of opinion in his handling of the illegal declaration of independence in November 1965 by the white minority government of Ian Smith in the British colony of Southern Rhodesia (see page 191). The Labour left and the most independent Commonwealth states in sub-Saharan Africa wanted the government to send troops to crush the rebellion. Instead, the government used economic sanctions to try to end it, but it soon became clear that these were not working. Wilson, optimistically believing that he could find a workable compromise, twice tried personal diplomacy. He proposed a settlement that would have left Smith in power, provided that **majority rule** was introduced at some time in the future. Wilson's offer to Smith risked inflaming left-wing opinion in Britain, the unity of the Labour government and the future of Britain's multi-racial Commonwealth. Smith's refusal let Wilson off the hook, allowing him to maintain his stance as an opponent of the rebellion who had nevertheless striven to find a peaceful solution. Wilson's tactics were extremely risky but there were no easy solutions to the problem, which was not settled until 1980.

The Common Market

Wilson believed he could persuade the French President, Charles de Gaulle, who had vetoed Britain's application in 1963, to change his mind. He failed. In November 1967 de Gaulle repeated his veto. Wilson did, however, succeed in maintaining cabinet and party unity over Europe; the pro-Europeans were pleased by the application and the anti-Europeans by its failure.

Management of the Labour Cabinet

Wilson showed considerable political skill in avoiding splits on foreign issues and had used his cabinet effectively to pass major modernising social policy. As prime minister he faced considerable problems in managing difficult cabinet colleagues.

Wilson was anxious to avoid the internal squabbling that had weakened the party in the 1950s (see pages 100–102) and hoped to achieve this by giving ministerial jobs to senior party figures from all shades of opinion, not just to his associates and supporters. However, there were often bitter quarrels about policy and conflicts between personalities. As cabinet minister Barbara Castle observed in her diary in January 1968, 'We spend three-quarters of our time in these personal pro and anti intrigues instead of getting down to real jobs.'

Cabinet in-fighting reached a peak in 1969 when the government tried to reform industrial relations (see pages 124–136). But as Denis Healey, Wilson's minister of defence, admitted, such disputes were 'all too common in governments of all parties' and there were only four cabinet resignations during the life of the Labour government, a record similar to that of Macmillan.

Activity

1 Consider these statements about Harold Wilson as prime minister:
   (i) He was a superb politician, he kept his party together on difficult issues and managed his colleagues in the cabinet. He was a good communicator and knew what would gain votes. He modernised Labour's image and dealt well with party conflicts.
   (ii) He was a poor prime minister who allowed his cabinet to quarrel. His policies were often weakened by trying to compromise between left and right. He did not offer strong leadership.
   Copy and complete the table below to help you assess his leadership.

Issue	Evidence of success	Evidence of failure
Parliamentary majority		
Cabinet management		
Labour Party unity		
Social reform		
Foreign and colonial issues		

2 Which view do you find more convincing? Explain your answer.

Nationalised industries

In the 1940s, a number of major industries had been brought under government control. These included coal mining, civil aviation, telecommunications, transport, electricity, gas and water. This, it was hoped, would eliminate wasteful competition between firms offering the same service and allow the government to plan the efficient provision of resources on a national basis. However, it also meant that investment in the nationalised industries was subject to government expenditure cuts and it gave the trade unions increased power because strikes could cause national disruption.

How successful were the economic policies of the 1964–70 Labour government?

Britain's economic difficulties in the 1960s

Labour ministers were aware that, in the 1950s, Britain's economic performance had lagged behind that of its main competitors and argued that the Conservatives had failed to solve the problem (see page 103).

Their immediate problem, inherited from the Conservatives, was a balance of payments deficit of £800 million, a large sum in those days. They believed that this was a symptom of Britain's lack of competitiveness which could only be properly solved by producing goods that were better and/or cheaper than products from overseas. This required British firms to:

- Improve their efficiency by investing in new technology and machinery.
- Grant wage increases only if workers were more productive.

It also needed the government to:

- Use its revenue from taxation to develop and improve Britain's transport network.
- Maintain investment in the **nationalised industries**.
- Ensure that Britain had a well-trained workforce.

The balance of payments

When the country spends more on imports than it earns in exports, the balance of payments is in deficit. This was considered at the time to be a key indication of the effectiveness of economic policy and of how well the British economy was performing. It was important because international holders of sterling needed to have confidence in Britain's economic strength. If they sold sterling, the value of the pound would fall.

Lack of confidence in sterling could create a vicious circle. If British goods were not selling well abroad, fewer people abroad wanted pounds with which to buy them. Falling demand for the pound reduced its value, contributing to inflation. This also damaged the overseas earnings of the countries of **the sterling area** who used the pound to trade. If the pound fell too far in value, bankers around the world would quickly transfer their money from sterling into other currencies. This was called a run on the pound. Britain also depended on the so-called 'invisible' earnings of the City of London's banking and insurance services to boost its exports. These would be damaged if foreigners lost confidence in the stability of the British economy and its currency.

Government tax cuts risked a balance of payments deficit because, when people had more money, they often spent it on imports. It was difficult to reduce the import bill because Britain needed to import many of its industrial raw materials and much of its food. The solution to a balance of payments deficit was for British goods to be better and/or cheaper than those of their competitors.

Many economists also argued that Britain's trade unions contributed to the country's economic difficulties because:

- In times of inflation, union leaders used the threat of strike action to demand wage increases for their members.
- Unions strongly resisted attempts by the government to use its power to try to restrict pay increases or to make wage increases dependent on improved productivity.
- Any wage increase which was not linked to an improvement in productivity made industry's labour costs higher and increased inflation.
- High labour costs made goods more expensive and contributed to the balance of payments difficulties.
- High labour costs also reduced the amount of profit that employers could invest in research and development, new machinery and plant.

The Labour government had to take account of the demands of the trade unions because:

- The Labour Party was allied to the trade unions who provided most of its money.
- In the 1960s, almost half of the British workforce belonged to a trade union.

The economic policies of the Wilson government, 1964–70

The government had to take immediate steps to tackle the balance of payments deficit. If it failed to do so, it would gain a reputation abroad for economic incompetence which would discourage investment from overseas

Devaluation

Its advantages:

- People overseas would get more pounds in exchange for their currency so British exports would become cheaper and more competitive.
- Imports would be more expensive which, together with the boost to exports, could wipe out the balance of payments deficit.

Its disadvantages:

- Britain's international prestige would be damaged.
- The rise in import prices would contribute to inflation.

and damage the earnings of the City of London. The government was faced with an unpalatable choice between two contrasting solutions:

- **Deflation** – tax rises and/or cuts in government expenditure. These measures would take money out of consumers' pockets and reduce the spending power of industries and businesses, thereby decreasing the import bill. This would decrease the gap between imports and exports.
- **Devaluation** – reducing the exchange value of the pound. Since the Second World War the exchange value of the pound had been fixed and, since 1949, the rate was £1: $2.80. Reducing the value of the pound would make British products cheaper, boosting exports. This could solve the balance of payments crisis but, because Britain relied on many imports, the cost of living would rise.

Deflationary measures

As soon as he came into office, Wilson ruled out devaluation because:

- He believed it would reduce the savings of thrifty, working-class families – people he admired and whose interests he believed the Labour Party should be defending.
- He was aware that devaluation had destroyed one Labour government in 1931 and, in 1949, had severely damaged the Attlee government in which he had served.
- He didn't want the voters to associate Labour with what he called 'the easy way out' of economic difficulties.
- He knew that, with a tiny Commons majority, he would have to have another election before long. He told one of his Cabinet colleagues: 'Devaluation would sweep us away. We would have to go to the country defeated. We can't have it.'
- He did not want to upset the USA. They also had a balance of payments deficit and the US Treasury feared that if the British devalued, the currency traders would assume America was about to do the same and start a run on the dollar.

In autumn 1964, the chancellor of the exchequer, Jim Callaghan, negotiated international loans to prevent a run on the pound and, over the next nine months, introduced a series of deflationary measures which included higher taxes on tobacco and alcohol, and a temporary import surcharge. However, in return for US financial assistance he had to agree to maintain British Far Eastern bases. British forces were fighting in Borneo to defend the Commonwealth state of Malaysia against Indonesia. America, already embroiled in the war in Vietnam, wanted continued British support in the region.

The National Plan, September 1965

Wilson believed that better planning could, in the long term, make British industry more competitive. He created a new ministry – the Department of Economic Affairs (DEA) – to devise a plan to modernise and improve Britain's economy. The National Plan was published in September 1965 and set two ambitious targets for British industry.

- An annual growth rate of 3.8 per cent over six years.
- An increase in exports of 5.25 per cent each year to wipe out the balance of payments deficit.

The National Plan also required the government to:

- Create a new National Board for Prices and Incomes (NBPI) to ensure that wage increases would only be granted if accompanied by increases in productivity.
- Provide investment funds for the modernisation of British industry, the improvement of workers' skills and a programme of regional development.

Unfortunately, the National Plan never had much chance of success. There were three main reasons for this.

- The Treasury jealously guarded its role as the government's economics ministry and did not co-operate with the DEA.
- The recommendations of the National Plan for government spending were undermined by the Treasury's deflationary measures to solve the immediate economic difficulties.
- The NBPI had no power to enforce its decisions. It relied on the co-operation of the trade unions, who did not support a policy of wage restraint.

As a result of in-fighting, the Department of Economic Affairs was wound up in 1969. Nevertheless, the National Plan contributed to the Labour Party's victory in the March 1966 general election because it suggested that the government had a coherent vision for the future. They campaigned on the slogan, 'You *know* Labour government works'. The Chancellor's deflationary measures had reduced the balance of payments deficit and prevented a run on the pound, but critics were already pointing out that the government was struggling to impose wage restraints and that the DEA and the Treasury were pursuing contradictory policies.

Devaluation, 1967

The general election gave Labour a substantial majority (see page 116). But, in November 1967, the government had to accept the humiliation of devaluing the pound because there seemed no other way out of its economic difficulties:

- On 16 May 1966 the seamen began a strike, demanding a pay increase that exceeded the government's pay guidelines.
- The strike damaged British exports, and poor trade figures threatened another run on the pound.
- Although the strike ended early in July, the government once again chose **deflation** rather than devaluation to deal with the balance of payments deficit.
- There was more bad economic news in the autumn of 1967. Unemployment was unusually high. In 1964 there were 1.7 million people unemployed; by 1967 this had risen to 2.5 million. In addition, another balance of payments deficit put the pound under pressure again.

On 18 November the pound was devalued. Instead of being worth $2.80, it was now worth $2.40.

How successful was devaluation?

The trade figures were stubbornly slow to improve and the substantial balance of payments deficit remained. Nor did devaluation prevent cuts in spending. Roy Jenkins replaced Callaghan as chancellor but, despite devaluation, concluded that severe deflationary measures were still needed to cure the balance of payments crisis.

- In January 1968 the government announced that all British forces east of Suez (apart those in from Hong Kong and the Persian Gulf) were to be withdrawn by the end of 1971.
- Prescription charges, abolished in 1964, were reintroduced.
- The raising of the school-leaving age from fifteen to sixteen was deferred from 1971 to 1973, a change that undermined the educational reform the Labour government had believed essential to its plan to modernise Britain.

In the budget of March 1968 Jenkins, determined to overcome the balance of payments deficit, delivered another hefty dose of deflation, increasing taxation by £923 million. During 1969 there were signs of improvement. The balance of payments at last showed a surplus, the value of sterling rose and interest rates were reduced.

The economic record of the Labour government

It is possible to argue that, by its short-term focus on the balance of payments and the value of sterling, the Labour government was no more successful than the Tories had been in tackling the underlying weakness of the British economy.

- The rate of inflation had not been slowed, and unemployment was higher in 1970 than it had been in 1964.
- Britain's relative decline also continued, as Table 4 shows.

Arguably, the Labour government's failure to tackle Britain's long-term problems prevented it from achieving the ambitious aims it had set itself in 1964 of modernising the country and successfully planning a productive, competitive economy.

High defence expenditure and the investment in research and development

Britain devoted more of its national resources and more of its research and development budget to the military than other NATO countries (see page 170) apart from the USA. This reduced investment in other sectors of the economy.

Lack of investment

The Labour government did endeavour to improve Britain's transport network by building motorways in the north of England. It also encouraged the development of manufacturing sites in south Wales, Scotland, Merseyside and Tyneside. However, sustained improvement in industrial productivity was undermined by the government's deflationary policies which imposed cut-backs in government investment.

Table 4 Britain's percentage share of world exports of manufactured goods.

Year	Percentage
1950	25
1960	16
1970	11

Activity

Assess the economic policies of the Labour government 1964–70 by copying and completing the following table about the economic problems in Britain.

Policy	Why was it adopted?	How successful was it?
Deflation		
Devaluation		
National Plan		

How successfully did the Labour government deal with industrial relations?

Wilson had hoped to improve industrial relations and win trade union support for his efforts to modernise Britain but the economic difficulties of the 1960s opened a rift between the government and the unions. Wilson became convinced that:

■ Strikes for higher pay, many of them unofficial, were disrupting production, forcing up labour costs and contributing to inflation and Britain's poor export performance.
■ Industrial relations needed to be more strongly regulated if the government's efforts to control prices and wages were to succeed.

The trade unions argued that:

■ The country's lack of competitiveness should be blamed on employers and on government investment policies, not employees.
■ The government's attempts to limit wage increases unfairly penalised low-paid workers.
■ The right of unions to bargain freely with their employers should not be restricted by laws.

It was particularly difficult for the Labour government to reform industrial relations because the trade unions were their traditional allies and provided the Labour Party with most of its money. Their block votes at Labour Party conferences could often prove decisive in determining party policy (see page 101). The trade unions also exercised considerable economic power:

■ The **closed shop** requiring workers to join a particular union enhanced union bargaining power.
■ Strikes in nationalised industries could cause disruption throughout the country.

'In Place of Strife'

By 1968 Wilson was worried by press criticism of his failure to tame the unions and by the Conservatives' announcement of a plan to reform industrial relations. In April he asked Barbara Castle, a Cabinet colleague from the left of the party, to lead the newly established Ministry of Employment and Productivity and reform industrial relations. In January 1969 Castle's proposals, called 'In Place of Strife', were published.

The principal proposals were:

■ Employees would have a legal right to join a trade union.
■ The government could order a ballot to be held before a strike if it believed there was a serious threat to the national interest.
■ In an unofficial dispute the government could order a return to work for a 28-day 'cooling-off' period.
■ Disputes between unions could be referred to an industrial commission whose decision would be legally binding.
■ There would be financial penalties if the commission was not obeyed.
■ Workers who were unfairly dismissed would be entitled to compensation or to get their jobs back.

The TUC

The Trades Union Congress was founded in 1868 to provide a co-ordinated voice for the labour movement. It meets annually and elects a general council to run day-to-day business. It has close links with the Labour Party.

Activity

Find evidence for each of these statements about the Labour government and the trade unions in the chapter:
1 Wilson took a realistic view of the need to reform the unions.
2 Wilson's policy as regards the unions was a failure.

The TUC and left-wing Labour MPs were incensed by 'In Place of Strife'. As one trade union leader put it, legal sanctions would 'introduce the taint of criminality into industrial relations'. More than 50 Labour MPs rebelled when 'In Place of Strife' was debated in the House of Commons.

Resistance within the party, the TUC and even in the Cabinet led by Home Secretary, Jim Callaghan, caused Wilson to back down. A face-saving formula was devised by which the TUC gave a 'solemn and binding undertaking' that it would monitor strikes and disputes and offer 'considered opinion and advice'. The failure of 'In Place of Strife' contributed to the fall of the Labour government in 1970 and convinced many outside the Labour movement not only that trade unions had too much power, but that their resistance to change was a major obstacle to economic progress.

As traditional industries declined and **white collar employment** grew, some of the largest and most powerful unions lost members (see Table 5 on page 126). There was an increase in the membership of unions representing workers in the expanding **public sector** of government administration, health and teaching, but this was not matched by the **private sector** where many employers discouraged union membership. The changes to union membership can be seen in Table 6.

Table 5 Workers in selected British occupations.

Industry	1961	1971
Mining and quarrying	722,000	391,000
Manufacturing industries	8,383,000	8,136,000
Building and contracting	1,600,000	1,669,000
Transport and communications	1,673,000	1,564,000
Insurance, banking, finance	722,000	952,000
Professional, scientific	2,120,000	2,901,000

Table 6 Membership figures for selected unions.

Union	1960	1970
National Union of Railwaymen	334,000	198,000
Shop Workers	355,000	330,000
National Union of Mineworkers	586,000	279,000
Transport and General Workers	1,302,000	1,629,000
Science and Finance	25,000	221,000
Government Service	140,000	185,000
National Union of Teachers	225,000	311,000
Health Workers	54,000	90,000

Did the result of the 1970 general election owe more to Labour weaknesses or Conservative strengths?

Harold Wilson decided to hold a general election in June 1970 because the economy had begun to improve and the Labour Party was ahead in the opinion polls. The result was a surprise victory for the Conservatives.

Table 7 The general election of June 1970.

Party	% of vote won	Votes won	Seats won	Candidates
Conservative	46.4	13,145,123	330	628
Labour	43.0	12,179,341	287	624
Liberal	7.5	2,117,035	6	332
SNP	1.1	306,802	1	65
Plaid Cymru	0.6	175,016	0	36

Why the Labour Party lost in 1970

The Labour Party lost in 1970 for a number of reasons.

Wilson's complacency

An opinion poll taken just before the election suggested that Wilson had a 51 per cent approval rating, compared to 28 per cent for the Conservative leader, Edward Heath. Not surprisingly, Wilson exuded confidence during the election campaign, believing that his electioneering skills were superior to those of Heath. But Wilson was probably too relaxed. The publication of some poor trade figures just before election day dented Labour's claims that the economy was on the mend.

The disillusionment of Labour supporters

One senior cabinet minister Richard Crossman thought that the party was defeated in 1970 because too many Labour supporters did not bother to vote, and his colleague Barbara Castle 'sensed an undercurrent of detachment among our own activists and party audiences'. Membership of the party fell from 830,000 in 1964 to 680,000 in 1970, reducing the number of local activists willing to campaign for it. For many activists and MPs the government had been much too right wing, especially in its economic and foreign policies. They believed that:

- Britain's foreign policy had been too supportive of the USA, especially over Vietnam.
- Too much money had been spent on defence and not enough on welfare, education and economic regeneration.
- The policy of maintaining the value of sterling had benefited only the City of London and the USA.
- The working class had been made poorer by the government's policies.
- The government had abandoned its historic commitment to socialism and the interests of the working class, especially in its attempts to curb trade union power with 'In Place of Strife'.

The government had tried to win the support of working women by passing the 1970 Equal Pay Act but politically motivated young people – often those who had benefited from the expansion of university education – were more likely in 1970 to be found demonstrating against the Vietnam War than joining the Labour Party.

The failure of 'In Place of Strife'

Many voters who had supported the Labour Party in 1964 and 1966 had been impressed by Wilson's promise to modernise Britain. But the defeat of 'In Place of Strife' suggested to many that the trade unions were selfishly determined to preserve their power and influence and were more powerful than the government. For many voters, this was a sign of the government's wider failure even to improve, let alone transform, the nation's economic performance.

Why the Conservatives won

The Conservatives won for the following reasons.

Conservative policy proposals

The Conservatives had used their years in opposition to develop a distinctive set of principles to underpin their policies. The main ideas were:

- Industrial relations law would be reformed to reduce the number of disruptive strikes and inflationary pay settlements.
- There would be less state intervention in industry, especially if enterprises were loss-making.
- Attempts to control prices and incomes by law would end.
- Britain would apply to join the EEC.

These policies, by proposing that government should do less to manage the economy, challenged some of the assumptions that had been accepted by both parties since the Second World War. Wilson tried to mock them as prehistoric but by doing so probably only succeeded in drawing attention to their novelty.

Edward Heath's leadership

During the election campaign Heath relentlessly attacked the economic record of the Labour government, stressing that, since 1964, inflation, as measured by the **Retail Price Index**, had risen by 33 per cent and unemployment by over 200,000. The press almost unanimously agreed and attributed the Conservative victory to Heath himself. The *Daily Express* praised his 'guts and leadership'.

Heath had also dealt firmly a major challenge to his authority when, in 1968, he had sacked Enoch Powell from the **shadow cabinet**. Powell was a fierce opponent of both Commonwealth immigration and the Labour government's race relations legislation. In April 1968 he made a widely reported speech in which he predicted race riots. 'As I look ahead, I am filled with foreboding. Like the Roman, I seem to see "the River Tiber foaming with much blood".' Powell's speech was popular with many white working class people who felt threatened by immigration and Heath received thousands of letters of criticism for sacking him. However, the majority of Tory MPs rallied behind their leader.

Edward Heath
Heath became Conservative leader in August 1965. Like Wilson, he had attended a grammar school and won a scholarship to Oxford. He became an MP in 1950. A passionate European, he was widely praised for his handling of the negotiations for British entry to the Common Market (EEC) in 1961–62. He was a serious and reserved person who loved sailing and music.

Activity

'Labour lost, rather than the Tories won, the 1970 election.' Do you agree? Copy and complete the table below and then write two paragraphs explaining your conclusion.

Labour Party failings	
Labour Party strengths	
Conservative Party strengths	
Conservative Party weaknesses	

How successful was Edward Heath as prime minister?

Heath's aims

Heath's message during the 1970 election campaign was that the Labour government's economic management had been a failure. Once in power, he promised to:

- Strengthen the economy and curb inflation.
- Legislate to transform industrial relations.
- Create 'one nation', promising regional development, faster economic growth, better social services and the maintenance of full employment.
- Apply to join the EEC (Common Market), believing that membership would facilitate these objectives.

Heath told his party conference in October: 'We were returned to office to change the course of history of this nation – nothing less.' The Conservatives' 1970 policy proposals (see page 128) suggested that they would allow market forces to determine prices and wages, and would be less involved in managing the economy. But Heath did not regard high levels of unemployment as acceptable and believed that the government, by channelling investment appropriately, still had a significant role to play in regenerating run-down parts of the country. In practice, neither Heath's aims nor his economic policies were much different from Wilson's.

Heath's economic record

- The Conservatives inherited an inflation rate of approximately 5 per cent per annum but this had reached 10 per cent four years later.
- Although the level of unemployment was no higher in 1974 than it had been in 1970, the number of working days lost to strikes during the Conservatives' four years in power was double that of Wilson's six years.
- Heath inherited a balance of payments surplus but left a substantial deficit.

However, his years in power coincided with what one analyst has called a 'world economic blizzard'. Historians, in assessing Heath's record, must decide how much can be blamed on his decisions and how much on adverse circumstances.

▲ Edward Heath during his retirement in September 1992.

Joining Europe

Britain became a full member of the EEC on 1 January 1973. When parliament debated British entry in October 1971 both major parties had been divided over Europe. On the Conservative side 39 MPs voted against entry. The Labour Party opposed the terms of entry, but 69 of their MPs defied the party line and voted in favour of joining – this was enough to give Heath a comfortable majority.

Heath was a passionate advocate of European unity and believed that membership of the EEC would give British industry better access to Europe's markets and that European competition would stimulate modernisation and development. By 1970, Britain's application had a much better chance of success because President de Gaulle had left office in 1969 and the new French president, Georges Pompidou, was not opposed to British entry.

Nevertheless, Pompidou was determined that Britain should enter on French, not British, terms. His demands angered those in the Conservative

Party who were mistrustful of Europe, believing that it threatened Britain's independence. Britain had to:

- Sacrifice any remaining preferential trade deals with the Commonwealth.
- Accept the EEC's policy of heavily subsidising French farmers.

Membership had little immediate impact on Britain's economic performance and the country's relations with Europe have remained controversial ever since (for more on the controversy, see pages 158 and 160–161).

The Industrial Relations Act, August 1971

Heath believed the 1970 election victory had given him a popular mandate to legislate on industrial relations and there was considerable popular support for government action to curb strikes. The Industrial Relations Act aimed to balance the rights of individual workers with those of the unions, while reducing the likelihood of strikes. Its main provisions were as follows:

- Workers would have the legal right to join (or not to join) a trade union. This challenged the legality of the closed shop.
- The National Industrial Relations Court (NIRC) and the Industrial Relations Commission (IRC) were established.
- Trade unions were required to register with the NIRC and IRC. Those that did so would have improved rights of recognition by the employers.
- Members of registered unions would enjoy better protection against unfair dismissal.
- Unions which failed to register would be liable for claims for damages.
- The Act gave the government power to order a pre-strike ballot and impose a cooling-off period of up to 60 days.

The failure of the Act

Many of these regulations were similar to those of Labour's 'In Place of Strife' so it was no surprise that the Act was unpopular with most union members. The TUC set out to make the Act unworkable by telling its members to de-register and defy the NIRC. The Act increased the bitterness of confrontations between unions and employers. It also complicated Heath's efforts to negotiate with the TUC over strikes about prices and wages.

Many union leaders, especially at local or shop-floor level, were militant in the early 1970s and hoped not only to destroy the Industrial Relations Act but also to bring down the Heath government. When a legal judgement in 1972 ordered the release of some dock workers who had refused to appear before the NIRC, the credibility of the Act was seriously undermined.

Industrial relations under the Conservatives

Heath was less successful than Wilson had been in managing industrial relations (see Table 8). The frequency of strikes was partly a result of union hostility to the Industrial Relations Act but it was mainly a response to inflation. As prices rose, workers sought to increase their wages to prevent their living standards falling.

Table 8 Industrial relations under the Conservatives, 1970–74.

Year	Working days lost	No. of stoppages	Workers involved
1970	10,985,000	3,906	1,793,000
1971	13,551,000	2,228	1,776,000
1972	23,909,000	2,497	1,722,000
1973	7,197,000	2,873	1,513,000
1974	14,750,000	2,922	1,622,000

Inflation was particularly severe in the early 1970s for several reasons:

- In 1971 US President Nixon ended the system of fixed exchange rates which had existed since the end of the Second World War. This had the effect of devaluing the dollar and making British exports more expensive in the USA.
- In 1972 the pound was allowed to 'float' freely, its value determined by the money markets. Britain's poor industrial performance meant that, when the pound floated downwards in value, imports became more expensive.
- There was a worldwide increase in commodity prices: prices of raw materials, food and fuel.
- The Heath government aimed to stimulate growth. By cutting taxes and increasing public spending, especially in the 1972 budget, it stimulated a demand for goods and services but this also pushed up prices.

The miners' strike, January to February 1972

The miners enjoyed considerable public sympathy for doing a dangerous, dirty and poorly paid job, but their claim for a 47 per cent pay increase was well above both the government's wage policy and the 8 per cent offered by the National Coal Board. In January 1972, 280,000 coal miners came out on strike. The government was forced to declare a state of emergency and there were regular power cuts throughout the country. By February, the government was anxious for a settlement and appointed a commission of inquiry. This awarded the miners a large pay increase.

Why was the miners' strike successful?

- The miners were skilfully organised, especially by Yorkshire miners' leader, Arthur Scargill, who co-ordinated **flying pickets**: groups of miners who aimed to persuade others to join or support the strike and to travel to power stations and fuel depots to prevent the movement of coal by road.
- There were violent incidents, notably at the Saltley coke depot in Birmingham, where 15,000 massed **pickets** successfully prevented large supplies of fuel from leaving the depot. But the ugly confrontations did not seriously damage public sympathy for the miners.
- The government was poorly organised to cope with the strike and the severe winter weather meant that it had an immediate impact on the country's power supplies.

The success of the miners' strike was damaging for the government because:

- It encouraged other workers to strike for pay increases.
- Successful strikes added to inflationary pressure.
- The government looked weak in the face of determined union hostility.
- It emphasised the failure of the Industrial Relations Act.

Heath's U-turn, 1972

Heath's government began with the intention of reducing state intervention in industry and of refusing to rescue failing enterprises – those that one minister described as 'lame ducks'. But this policy did not last long. In January 1971 the aircraft division of Rolls-Royce, facing bankruptcy, was nationalised because it was regarded as vital to Britain's defence industry.

Heath was not prepared to allow unemployment to increase as the price of reducing government expenditure and this explains what has become known as his 'U-turn' in policy.

- In February 1972 the government granted £35 million to Upper Clyde Shipbuilders to safeguard its 3000 jobs.
- A new Ministry for Industrial Development was set up in April to provide aid to industry in deprived regions of the country as part of the government's plan to stimulate growth.
- Having failed to secure a voluntary agreement with the unions over wages and salaries, the government established statutory policies in November 1972 to regulate both prices and pay increases. These had some success but were destroyed by the oil price shock of October 1973.

The oil price shock of 1973 and the three-day week

In October 1973 two Arab states – Egypt and Syria – went to war against Israel to try to recover land lost in the war of 1967. The Middle Eastern oil-producing countries, angry at what they perceived to be Western support for Israel, cut back supplies and quadrupled their prices. Since Britain depended on oil for 50 per cent of its energy needs, this had a decisive impact on prices.

In November 1973 the miners began an overtime ban in pursuit of a pay claim that exceeded the government's limit. Heath tried negotiating directly with their leaders but the talks got nowhere. One militant miner told Heath that the aim of the strike was to bring down the Conservative government. On 13 December Heath went on television to declare a State of Emergency and announce the introduction of a three-day working week to take effect from 31 December:

- Electricity would be provided to industry and businesses only on three specified days per week.
- To save petrol a 50 mph speed limit was introduced on all roads.
- Television was required to close down at 10.30p.m. each evening.

Further talks to resolve the dispute failed and in February the miners voted 81 per cent in favour of strike action.

The February 1974 election

Heath responded by calling an election for 28 February on the issue of 'Who Governs Britain?' He hoped to get decisive support for his government's policies. But, as Table 9 shows, the result was unclear. Heath's efforts to form an anti-Labour coalition failed and, on 4 March 1974, Wilson became prime minister again.

Table 9 The February 1974 general election.

Party	% of votes won	Votes won	Seats won	Candidates
Conservative	37.9	11,868,906	297	623
Labour	37.1	11,639,243	301	623
Liberal	19.3	6,063,470	14	517
SNP	2.0	632,032	7	70
Plaid Cymru	0.6	171,364	2	36

Activity

How far do you agree that the Heath government was unsuccessful because of circumstances beyond its control?

1 List the factors that were outside the government's control.
2 List the government's policies and actions which were unpopular with the electorate.

How effectively did Wilson and Callaghan deal with the problems Britain faced between 1974 and 1979?

The Labour government faced a number of problems including dealing with a minority in the Commons, relations with the trade unions and changes and divisions within the Party and economic issues.

Minority government

After the indecisive February result it was inevitable that Wilson would soon hold another election to try to secure a majority.

Table 10 The October 1974 general election.

Party	% of vote won	Votes won	Seats won
Conservative	35.8	10,464,817	277
Labour	39.2	11,457,079	319
Liberal	18.3	5,346,754	13

But, as Table 10 shows, the result was hardly a ringing endorsement of the Labour Party. The government achieved a small overall majority of three seats in the October general election but won fewer votes than in February.

Relations with the trade unions

To demonstrate that the 1971 Industrial Relations Act had been unnecessary, the Labour Party and the TUC had reached an agreement in 1973 called the Social Contract:

- The unions agreed to co-operate in trying to control wage increases.
- The government promised to try to keep down prices and provide improved welfare benefits.
- There would be a return to free collective bargaining over wages and no statutory incomes policy.

But the Social Contract did not solve the nation's economic difficulties because wage increases continued to exceed the inflation rate and cynics suggested that 'the only give and take in the Social Contract was that the government gave and the unions took'. According to an opinion poll, Jack Jones, the leader of the transport workers' union, was regarded as the most powerful man in the country. However, the Social Contract did suggest that trade unions and government had some shared objectives. Their uneasy co-operation lasted until the winter of 1978–79 (see page 135).

The drift to the left in the Labour Party

The Labour Party had moved to the left during its four years in opposition. This was reflected in two Cabinet appointments, Michael Foot at the Department of Employment and Tony Benn as secretary of state for industry. The trend was also occurring at local level. The Party's shift to the left caused it considerable difficulties in the 1980s (see page 144).

Labour Party divisions over Europe

Wilson promised to renegotiate the terms of British membership of the EEC (or Common Market) and hold a referendum on the issue. The new terms, by which Britain's contribution to the EEC budget would be reduced, were announced in March 1975 and the date for the nation's first referendum was fixed for 5 June 1975.

Michael Foot and Tony Benn

Both children of politicians, Michael Foot and Tony Benn took the socialist ideas of the Labour Party very seriously.

Foot (1913–2010) was an intellectual who had edited the *Evening Standard* newspaper. He was deputy leader of the Labour Party in 1976–80 and leader in 1980–83. He believed strongly in social equality.

Benn (1924–2014) was the son of a Labour peer. He served as postmaster general under Wilson from 1964 to 1970 and minister for technology in 1974–79. He also opposed nuclear weapons and had strong socialist beliefs.

▲ Michael Foot (left) and Tony Benn (right) in their seats at the House of Commons during the State opening of Parliament, London, 20 November 1980.

Wilson sensibly allowed his Cabinet ministers freedom to campaign for either side. The result was a 2:1 vote in favour of continued membership because voters believed that the success of the EEC offered a way to overcome Britain's economic difficulties. This result, for a while at least, buried the issue of Europe and appeared to preserve Labour Party unity.

Wilson's resignation, March 1976

In March 1976 Wilson suddenly announced his resignation. Although he was only 60 years old, he was aware that his normally excellent memory was beginning to fail him. He later revealed that he had decided in March 1974 to serve no more than two more years. James Callaghan defeated five other senior Labour figures (all Oxford graduates) in the election to replace him.

Economic difficulties: stagflation

The Labour government had settled the miners' strike in 1974 by means of a 29 per cent pay increase and, with wages rising faster than growth, inflation reached nearly 30 per cent by the middle of 1975. The response of the trade unions was to demand ever bigger wage increases which created further inflation. A world recession hit British exports, economic growth slumped and unemployment steadily increased from 542,000 in 1974 to over 1.3 million two years later.

Denis Healey (chancellor of the exchequer, 1974–79) concluded that economic recovery depended on conquering inflation:

- His 1975 budget increased taxes and cut government spending programmes; he hoped that taking money out of the economy would reduce prices.
- In July 1975 the government introduced a formal incomes policy, setting a £6 per week ceiling on wage increases, with a freeze on higher incomes. The TUC reluctantly agreed to it, but the policy was opposed by some left-wing MPs.

■ A year later, the government imposed an even tighter squeeze, reducing the ceiling to £4 per week. The result was a gradual fall in the average level of wage increases from 26 per cent in 1975 to 15 per cent in 1976, and to 10 per cent in 1977.

Although the inflation level dropped economic recovery did not follow. Continuing poor productivity and high costs did little to boost exports and imports remained high, so that the balance of payments was in deficit.

During 1976 the government was faced by a severe crisis of confidence in the pound. Its falling exchange value threatened to push up the price of British imports and make inflation worse. The Bank of England bought pounds on the foreign exchanges in order to prop up its value, but this threatened to use up the nation's currency reserves. National bankruptcy threatened.

Callaghan realised that the onset of 'stagflation' had destroyed some of the economic assumptions that had prevailed since 1945. He told the Labour Party conference in September 1976:

We used to think that you could just spend your way out of recession and increase employment only by cutting taxes and boosting government expenditure. [However] it only worked by injecting bigger doses of inflation into the economy followed by a higher level of unemployment at the next step. The option [of spending yourself out of a recession] no longer exists.

The IMF loan, 1976

In September 1976 Healey decided he could only arrest the falling value of the pound by asking the International Monetary Fund (IMF) for a loan of $3900 million. But to secure it, the government would be required to cut government spending by approximately £2 billion. After exhaustive debate, Callaghan and Healey finally persuaded the Cabinet to accept the terms early in December.

Although the crisis deepened the rift between the Labour leadership and the left of the party, Callaghan had prevented a severe economic crisis becoming a political one. All too aware that a similar crisis in 1931 had destroyed the Labour government and kept it out of power for fourteen years, Callaghan succeeded in preserving the unity of his Cabinet and kept the government in office.

The Lib–Lab Pact, 1977–78

However, the severity of Britain's economic problems undermined public confidence in the government. In November 1976 a Gallup opinion poll gave the Tories a 25 per cent lead over Labour. By-election losses meant that the government's slim overall majority in the House of Commons disappeared. In March 1977 Callaghan negotiated a deal with the new Liberal leader, David Steel, by which the thirteen Liberals MPs agreed to support the government. The pact lasted until 1978.

The 'winter of discontent', 1978–79

The government's strategy for controlling inflation depended on the unions agreeing to pay rises of no more than 5 per cent. But the unions disliked Chancellor Healey's policies, believing that he had abandoned the Social Contract and that their members were suffering disproportionately from the

The International Monetary Fund (IMF)

At the end of the Second World War 30 countries (now 188) agreed to create a fund to help rebuild their national economies and to provide short-term loans to enable members to overcome balance of payments deficits. The IMF can impose strict conditions on its loans, requiring countries to implement programmes aimed at rapid debt-reduction.

David Steel

David Steel had been elected aged 26 as a Liberal MP for a Scottish seat in 1965. He was responsible for introducing the 1967 Abortion Act in parliament. He became Liberal leader in 1976 when a scandal forced Jeremy Thorpe to resign. Steel's decision to maintain the Callaghan government in office may have contributed to the Liberals' loss of two seats and a million votes in the 1979 general election.

government's counter-inflation strategy. In December, Ford workers won a 15 per cent pay increase after a three-month strike. They were followed by the lorry drivers, who went on strike in January 1979 demanding a 30 per cent rise. This affected deliveries and caused petrol shortages. More strikes and overtime bans followed when the National Union of Public Employees (NUPE), representing some of the lowest-paid local authority workers, demanded a 40 per cent increase. With workers such as refuse workers and gravediggers involved, and rubbish piling up in the streets, the impact of the strikes was dramatic and easy for the press, predominantly unsympathetic to both Labour and the unions, to sensationalise as symptomatic of the country's decline and the government's impotence in the face of over-mighty union power.

Callaghan appeared to be complacent and out of touch. He spent a week in early January at a summit in the West Indies, and photos of him basking in the sunshine contrasted badly with the wintry chaos in Britain. When he returned, he told reporters: 'I don't think that other people in the world would share the view that there is mounting chaos.' This was transformed into a damning tabloid headline: 'CRISIS? WHAT CRISIS?' The strikes were settled by pay increases adding to the public perception that the Labour government could neither control the unions nor manage the economy.

The end of the Labour government

The government had won the support of Plaid Cymru and SNP in parliament by promising to devolve some power to Wales and Scotland. But in March 1979 referenda in Wales and Scotland failed to win enough votes in favour for devolution to proceed. The nationalist MPs expected more support for devolution from the government and felt badly let down and, at the end of March, joined the Conservatives in voting against the government in a no-confidence motion which the government lost by a single vote.

▲ David Steel pictured next to his battlebus at the start of the election campaign in London, 9 April 1979.

Activity

Jim Callaghan wrote in his memoirs that 'the Labour government of 1974 to 1979 had no reason to feel ashamed, and much to be proud of'.

To what extent do you agree with him?

Copy and complete the following table to help you decide. You should:
- Award a mark out of 6 for how well you think the Labour government handled each of the problems it faced.
- Explain why you have awarded the mark.

Issue	Mark/6	Reason for the mark
The economy		
Europe		
Trade unions		
Party unity		
Devolution		

Historical debate

1964–79: Was Britain in decline?

The governments of 1964 to 1979 have been widely criticised because they disappointed people on both sides of the political spectrum. Those on the right claim that attempts to manage the economy were bound to fail because the market, not government, should determine prices and incomes. They also maintain that trade unions had acquired too much power, especially in the nationalised industries, and that making deals with them led to overmanning and inefficiency. Right-wing commentators reserve their greatest scorn for the Conservative government of Edward Heath, believing that, having begun with a policy of not interfering in the economy, he did not have the courage of his convictions.

Just as the right blames Heath for supposedly abandoning true Conservativism, the left castigates Wilson and Callaghan for not being true to socialism. In 1963 Wilson had promised 'to make far-reaching changes in economic and social attitudes which permeate our whole system of society' so his critics see the 1960s, in particular, as a missed opportunity. Wilson and Callaghan, the left argues, too eagerly embraced traditional economics and did not do enough to tackle the root causes of economic and social inequality. These critics criticise the Labour governments for being too close to the USA and for spending too much on defence, especially nuclear weapons, in the mistaken belief that Britain was still a major power. Nationalisation, they argue, should have been extended and the strongholds of privilege – the public schools, Oxbridge, the House of Lords, the monarchy – either abolished or radically reformed.

Wilson's defenders point out that the depth of the divisions in the Labour movement, culminating in the split in the 1980s, demonstrates his skill in maintaining party unity. He also preserved Commonwealth unity, despite the rancour caused by Rhodesia, and skilfully maintained Britain's relationship with the USA without committing British troops to the Vietnam War. Heath's achievement in taking Britain into the EEC was inspired by idealism about European unity. His economic difficulties can be attributed to the impact of worldwide recession, the oil price shock and the stubborn defence of vested interests by the trade unions just as much as to his policies. Callaghan can be credited with facing up to economic realities when he told the Labour Party conference in 1976 that it was no longer possible to 'spend your way out of recession' because doing so merely injected 'bigger doses of inflation into the economy followed by a higher level of unemployment'. He also skilfully navigated through a crisis in 1976 that had the potential to destroy his government and fatally divide the Labour Party.

The governments in the years 1964 to 1979 had the misfortune to be in power at the end of the post-war boom. As they were run by people who had experienced the Depression of the 1930s and privations of the Second World War, it is hardly surprising that these politicans continued to believe that governments had a duty to manage the economy and maintained the policies that appeared, at least until 1960, to have delivered unprecedented prosperity to Britain.

The two passages below offer contrasting views of post-war Britain.

Activity

1 In the light of these two passages and your further reading, how far do you agree with the view that the years 1964–79 were a period of decline?

2 Using information in this chapter, find evidence to support each of the following views:
   (i) The trade unions exercised too much power.
   (ii) Governments failed to do enough to tackle the root causes of Britain's economic problems.

3 Which view do you find the more convincing? Explain your choice, using both passages.

Further research

David Childs, *Britain Since 1945*, 7th edition, 2012.

Andrew Marr, *A History of Modern Britain*, 2007.

Alan Sked and Chris Cook, *Post-War Britain, A Political History, 1945–92*, 1993.

Dominic Sandbrook, *White Heat, A History of Britain in the Swinging Sixties*, 2006.

Dominic Sandbrook, *State of Emergency, 1970–74*, 2010.

Dominic Sandbrook, *Seasons in the Sun, 1974–79*, 2012.

Passage 1

All the findings of opinion polls and other surveys suggested that the overwhelming majority of ordinary citizens were convinced that the period since the end of the war in 1945 was a time of comfort and content. While there were periods of internal stress, notably concern over the alleged 'ungovernability' of the unions at the time of the 'winter of discontent' in the late seventies, Britain was a relatively stable society internally. It was also, for most ordinary citizens, a time of prosperity. National income doubled between 1948 and 1976. The average citizen's standard of living rose accordingly, as income and social expectations mounted steadily. Take-home pay rose persistently during the inflation of the 1960s and early 1970s. By 1961 there were 7 million homes owned by their occupiers; by 1987 the total was 14.5 million. Surveys of opinion invariably revealed that very few people ever wished to live anywhere but in Britain.

Adapted from Kenneth O. Morgan, *The People's Peace*, 1990.

Passage 2

Some will argue that, although Britain has declined in economic terms, it has not done so in other respects; in particular, its institutions have adapted and survived better than those of most European states. To a degree, they are right. Yet the decline in the economy means that Britain is less able to support the things its citizens want and need – better education and training, better health care, better transport systems, better law enforcement, and defence forces adequate to our commitments. In one or all of these areas, many European, and some non-European, states have caught up with, or overtaken, Britain. It is baffling that a nation with so much talent at its disposal has decayed so much.

Adapted from David Childs, *Britain Since 1939, Progress and Decline*, 1995.

Chapter takeaways

- Labour only just won power in 1964 but, by March 1966, the British public was sufficiently convinced about their competence as a government to give them a large majority.
- The leadership of the Labour government followed traditional policies for tackling Britain's economic problems and faced repeated balance of payments crises.
- The trade unions disliked the government's attempts to control pay rises at a time of rising prices.
- The Labour government suffered a humiliating defeat in 1969 in its attempt to regulate industrial relations.
- Wilson's government enacted a series of liberal social reforms.
- Heath's government tried to adopt a new strategy for managing Britain's economy but carried out what its opponents called a 'U-turn' in 1972.

- The Industrial Relations Act of 1971 was an ambitious attempt to regulate industrial relations but was defeated by opposition from the Labour movement.
- Britain joined the EEC (Common Market) in 1973.
- The coal miners played a large part in the defeat of Heath's government in 1974.
- The Labour Party, although its leadership continued to follow traditional economic policies, moved decisively to the left in the 1960s and 1970s.
- The decision of the Callaghan government to apply for a loan from the IMF, and the 'winter of discontent', contributed to the victory of the Conservatives, led by Margaret Thatcher, in 1979.

Study Skills: Writing an introduction and avoiding irrelevance

The types of question set for AS and A Level essays will be the same and therefore all the advice in this section applies to both examinations.

Writing an introduction

Having planned your answer to the question, as described in the previous chapter, you are in a position to write your crucial opening paragraph. This should set out your main line of argument and briefly refer to the issues you are going to cover in the main body of the essay. The essays will require you to reach a judgement about the issue in the question and it is a good idea to state in this vital opening paragraph what overall line of judgement you are going to make.

It might also be helpful, depending on the wording of the question, to define in this paragraph any key terms mentioned in the question.

Consider the following question:

Example

Assess the reasons for the fall of Edward Heath's government in 1974.

In the opening paragraph of an answer to this question you should:

- Identify the issues or themes that you will consider – these might be political, social, economic, individuals.
- State your view as to which of the factors was the most important.

This type of approach will help you to keep focused on the demands of the question rather than writing a general essay about Heath. It might also be helpful to occasionally refer back to the opening paragraph.

This approach will also ensure you avoid writing about the background to the topic, for example explaining Heath's early life and career, which has no relevance to the question set. Another mistake is to fail to write a crucial first paragraph and rush straight into the question. Readers appreciate knowing the direction the essay is going to take, rather than embarking on a mystery tour where the line of argument becomes apparent only in the conclusion.

The following is a sample of a good introductory paragraph:

> Heath's campaign slogan in the February 1974 general election was 'Who Governs Britain?' This made the election a choice between himself and the coal miners whose pay dispute had caused the government to order a three-day working week. The result was a defeat for Heath, but it was not a victory for the Labour opposition. In 1970 the two main parties had won 89.4 per cent of the vote; by 1974 this had dropped to 75.0 per cent. This shows that the main reason for Heath's fall was the increasing public distrust of politicians from either main party to manage the economy, a feeling which had been growing since the early 1960s. Heath, like Wilson before him, had continued to believe that the government could, and should, regulate prices and incomes. But by 1974, it was becoming increasingly clear that this no longer worked. Heath's own policies contributed to his fall, in particular the bitterness caused by the 1971 Industrial Relations Act and the inflationary impact of the 1972 budget. However, he was also the victim of bad luck. Nixon's 1971 devaluation of the dollar and the 1973 oil price shock worsened Britain's inflation and undermined the government's economic policies.

The paragraph offers a view as to the most important reason for Heath's fall, but also outlines some of the other factors that the essay will consider. It remains focused on the question throughout the paragraph and shows some understanding of the key developments and events that occurred during his premiership. The answer shows a sound knowledge of the 1974 campaign and is able to use that knowledge to put forward a clear argument.

Avoiding irrelevance

You should take care not to write irrelevant material as not only will it not gain marks, but it also wastes your time. In order to avoid this:

- Look carefully at the wording of the question.
- Avoid simply writing all you know about the topic; remember you need to select information relevant to the actual question, use the information to support an argument and reach an overall judgement about the issue in the question.
- Revise *all* of a topic so that you are not tempted to pad out a response where you do not have enough material directly relevant to the actual question.

Consider the following question:

> **Example**
>
> **How successful were the economic policies of the Labour governments of 1964–70 and 1974–79?**
>
> You should:
>
> - Consider the economic aims of the government so that you establish some criteria against which to judge the policies.
> - Explain the policies and how far they dealt with the economic problems.
> - Differentiate between policies that were a success and those that were a failure.
> - Consider the economic policies in their wider context; were they also designed to tackle social issues?
> - Assess how successful the policies were in each area.

The following is a sample of an irrelevant answer to the question above:

> The Labour governments of 1964–70 and 1970 were largely successful in their economic policies. Their greatest achievement was in the field of education where they were able to move towards comprehensive secondary education and introduce the Open University so that people could receive a university education at home. Social conditions also continued to improve as the standard of living continued to rise so that more homes owned white goods than ever before.

The answer confuses economic policy with domestic policy and therefore the focus is on issues such as education and improvements in living standards. At best these have only a limited relevance to the actual question set and if the answer continues to focus on these issues, rather than the governments' handling of the balance of payments deficit, the growing industrial unrest and industrial inefficiency, it will score low marks. The response shows little understanding of the question and is largely irrelevant. It is important to have a clear grasp of the basic concepts and the requirements of the question, otherwise an answer can become irrelevant.

Chapter 6

Thatcher and the end of consensus, 1979–97

This chapter explains why Thatcher won the 1979 election and remained in office for so long. It considers the problems faced by Britain's first female prime minister and how she managed her Cabinet. It assesses the economic and social policies and how far they ended the consensus or broad agreement between the parties about how Britain should be governed. It explains why her style and policies brought such different reactions and why she was so controversial as a national leader. The reasons for her resignation are considered and the end of Conservative rule under her successor, John Major, in 1997 is explained. The main issues of the period to be considered are the following:

- Why did Thatcher win three general elections in a row?
- How successful were Thatcher's economic and social policies?
- How successfully did Thatcher deal with industrial relations?
- How successful was Thatcher's management of her Cabinet?
- Why did Thatcher inspire such passionate support and hatred?
- Why did Thatcher resign as prime minister in November 1990?
- Why were the Conservatives under Major so badly defeated in 1997?

This chapter explains how to avoid writing descriptive answers and how to write analytically; it provides advice about the crucial opening sentence of each paragraph.

Timeline

1979	May	Conservatives win 43-seat majority in the general election
1981		Inner-city riots: Brixton, London (April) and Toxteth, Liverpool (July)
1982	April–June	Falklands War
1983	June	Conservatives win 144-seat majority in the general election
1984	March	Miners' strike begins
1985	March	Miners' strike ends
1986	January	Resignation of Michael Heseltine in Westland affair
	October	The 'Big Bang' in the City of London
1987	June	Conservatives win 102-seat majority in the general election
1990	March	Violence at anti Poll Tax demonstration in Trafalgar Square
	October	Britain joins the Exchange Rate Mechanism
	November	Thatcher resigns; replaced by John Major
1991	April	Poll Tax replaced by Council Tax
1992	February	Maastricht Treaty signed
	April	Conservatives win 21-seat majority in the general election
	September	'Black Wednesday': Britain leaves the ERM
1993	July	Parliament ratifies the Maastricht Treaty
1994	July	Tony Blair elected Labour leader
1995	July	Conservative Party leadership election won by John Major
1997	May	Labour Party wins 179-seat majority in the general election

Overview

Thatcher's first government (1979–83) was dominated by the economic issues. Thatcher brought a new attitude to government based on very firm beliefs in reducing state intervention and promoting private enterprise. She was determined to reduce inflation and believed that she could do this by severely restricting the amount of money spent by the government. The cuts, combined with tax increases and high interest rates, were blamed for a rise in unemployment, which rose to unprecedented post-1945 levels. The government's popularity plummeted, there were criticisms of the policy in the Cabinet and, worst of all, there were damaging inner-city riots. Thatcher's personal popularity was restored in 1982. This was partly because the economy began to recover from the worst of the slump, but mainly because of victory in the Falklands War.

After a landslide electoral victory in 1983, Thatcher's government carried out its most extensive phase of reform, privatising major nationalised industries and challenging some Labour-controlled inner-city municipal councils. A series of laws between 1980 and 1984 reformed industrial relations, limiting the use of the strike weapon. The defeat of the coal miners after a prolonged and bitter strike completed her attempt to reduce what she saw as over-mighty trade union power. The economy was booming in mid-1980s, in part because of the deregulation of the City of London in 1986 and the tax-cutting policies of the Chancellor of the Exchequer, Nigel Lawson. Unemployment, however, remained higher than it had been in the preceding decades.

Following Thatcher's third victory in 1987, the government reformed schools and universities and brought in some changes to the National Health Service. The policy, begun in 1980, of allowing tenants to buy their council houses continued. By the end of the decade, difficulties mounted. Inflation returned, there were disagreements among ministers about Britain's relationship with the EEC. In 1988 the government took the unpopular decision to replace the local property tax with a payment by all adults, known as the 'Poll Tax'. By November 1990 Thatcher had lost the support of a sufficiently large section of her party, triggering a series of events which led to her resignation.

Her successor, John Major, lacked her force of personality and had a less aggressive style. He initiated some important domestic changes, but his period in office was dominated by his party's divisions over Europe. Major successfully negotiated some concessions for Britain in the 1991 Maastricht Treaty (see Chapter 7, page 183), which committed the member states to closer European union. He went on to win an unexpected election victory in April 1992, but with a much reduced majority.

The humiliation of having to withdraw from the Exchange Rate Mechanism (see page 183) reduced confidence in the ability of the Conservatives to manage the economy, and the prolonged parliamentary discussions to ratify the Maastricht Treaty revealed deep Conservative divisions over Europe. By 1997 the Conservatives faced a revitalised and modernised Labour Party which won an overwhelming victory in the general election.

Why did Thatcher win three general elections in a row?

Margaret Thatcher was the only prime minister in the twentieth century to win three successive general elections. Her popularity with a large number of voters, including many who traditionally had supported Labour, undoubtedly contributed to her successes, as did the continued support of much of the media, but her victories were also assisted by a range of other factors.

The 1979 election

Table 1 The 1979 general election (total electorate 41,093,264).

Party	% of vote won	Votes won	Seats won
Conservative	43.9	13,697,690	339
Labour	36.9	11,532,148	269
Liberal	13.8	4,313,811	11

▲ Margaret Thatcher during her first stint as prime minister, circa 1980.

The 1979 election was decided largely in London, the south of England and the Midlands where approximately 40 seats changed hands from Labour to the Conservatives. These voters were punishing Labour for its perceived failure to deal with inflation, unemployment and the 'over-mighty' trade unions, culminating in the depressing scenes of the so-called 'winter of discontent' (see page 135).

The previous decades had created an enlarged middle class who felt increasingly resentful about strikes and trade union power. The piling up of rubbish during strikes in 1979 seemed symbolic of a decline in standards.

- As in previous elections, the Liberal vote was also significant in determining the outcome. Although the Liberals held on to most of their seats in their strongholds, their total vote dropped by over a million because some voters blamed them for keeping Callaghan's government in office since 1977.
- In many constituencies in the Midlands and south, the collapse of the Liberal vote was enough to hand the seat to the Conservatives even though the Labour vote did not significantly decline (and, in some cases, even increased).
- The Labour Party succeeded in retaining its traditional support in the industrial areas of the north, Scotland and Wales where it won twice as many seats as the Conservatives. This explains why it received more votes than it had done in October 1974.

As the *Financial Times* observed on the day after the election, 'this is a very divided country'.

The 1983 election

Table 2 The 1983 general election (total electorate 42,197,344).

Party	% of vote won	Votes won	Seats won
Conservative	42.4	13,012,315	397
Labour	27.6	8,456,934	209
Liberal	13.7	4,201,115	17
SDP	11.6	3,570,834	6
(Liberal/SDP Alliance)	(25.4)	(7,780,949)	(23)

The rise in unemployment and economic problems had reduced the popularity of the government by 1981, but the election of 1983 saw another Conservative victory, even with a reduced popular vote. The victory in the Falklands War was seen as a sign of Britain's greater confidence and unity. It increased the personal popularity of Thatcher in her own strongholds. However, the disastrous split in Labour and the selection of Michael Foot as leader in November 1980 played an important part in the outcome. Foot lacked an assured manner on television and his belief in unilateral nuclear disarmament, further nationalisation of industry and government regulation seemed old fashioned. He and his policies made little appeal outside traditional Labour voters. The more moderate elements in the Party split away to form the SDP in March 1981, massively damaging the Labour Party. The Labour manifesto was described as 'the longest suicide note in history' because it was so out of touch with the country as a whole. The Alliance between the Liberals and the SDP – the beginning of the modern Liberal Democrats – succeeded in splitting the anti-Thatcher vote. This allowed Conservative gains in some traditional Labour seats in the north.

The 1987 election

Table 3 The 1987 general election (total electorate 43,181,321).

Party	% of vote won	Votes won	Seats won
Conservative	43.4	13,763,066	376
Labour	31.7	10,029,778	229
Liberal	12.9	4,173,450	17
SDP	9.7	3,168,183	5
(Alliance	22.6	7,341,633	22)

The Conservative Party won more votes than in 1979 or 1983 but lost 21 seats. The particular elements that allowed for victory in 1983, such as the weakness of the Labour leadership and the split in the party, were no longer as important and there was no 'Falklands factor' or 'winter of discontent'. However, there had been policies that were popular among key sections of the electorate and there was the sense that the economy was doing well.

The Conservative Party

When Thatcher called an election in June 1987 the Conservatives were well ahead in the opinion polls.

- The government's policies of selling council houses and shares in privatised industries (see pages 148 and 151) appealed to many middle-class and skilled working-class voters.

The Falklands War, 1982

In April 1982 the Argentinian dictator, General Galtieri, sent forces to capture the British colony of the Falkland Islands, 400 miles from the coast of South America and 8000 miles from Britain. Argentinia had always claimed the islands, but the population was almost entirely British. Thatcher immediately sent British forces to recapture the islands. A short war followed in which some 655 Argentinians and 255 British servicepeople died and the Argentinian forces surrendered in June (see also pages 173–174).

The Alliance

In 1981 four former Labour Cabinet ministers – David Owen, Shirley Williams, Roy Jenkins and Bill Rodgers – disillusioned by the Labour Party's move to the left, had defected and founded the Social Democratic Party (SDP). This new party formed an electoral pact with the Liberals – known as the Alliance – for the 1983 and 1987 general elections. In 1988 the two parties merged to form the Liberal Democrats (Lib-Dems).

- These people were either better off, or believed that the government supported their desire to increase their wealth and status.
- Unemployment was falling and the pound was strong.
- In both 1983 and 1987 the Conservatives benefited from a split in the left-wing vote.

The Labour Party

The Labour Party had not fully recovered from its defeat in 1983 but its new leader, Neil Kinnock, had very publicly criticised prominent left-wingers and brought the party back towards the centre.

Labour polled over 1.5 million votes more than in 1983 and won 20 more seats. However, Kinnock's style had limited appeal to many voters. He was often long-winded in speeches and Thatcher seemed to be the stronger leader with a very firm hold over her colleagues and a growing international reputation. Labour was more affected by the Alliance who contested every seat in 1987, splitting the anti-Conservative vote.

Activity

1 From the information on pages 142–144 make a list of possible explanations for the results of the three elections.
2 Give each factor a mark out of 6 for its importance (1= not very important, 6 = very important).
3 Now draft the first paragraph of an answer to the following essay question: 'The personality of Mrs Thatcher was the main reason for the Conservative election successes 1979–87.' How far do you agree?

How successful were Thatcher's economic and social policies?

Since 1945 all parties had agreed that, whatever the cost, unemployment, which had been high in the 1930s, should be kept low by government spending. This had been the central idea of the influential economist J. M. Keynes ('Keynesianism') and had been the basis of government thinking in the post-1945 era. There was also a broad agreement that the nationalised industries that had been created by Labour from 1945 to 1951 were necessary to maintain the essential services Britain and its economy needed – coal, gas, electricity, railways. There had also emerged a consensus that government should try to control prices and wages and enter into direct negotiations with trade unions in periods of 'emergency'. Right-wing economists were challenging 'consensus politics' by the late 1960s and were influencing several politicians on the right wing of the Conservative Party by the early 1970s. Particularly prominent among these was Sir Keith Joseph, a major influence on Thatcher.

Inflation

Retail prices had doubled between 1973 and 1979. Thatcher and her key adviser, Keith Joseph, were convinced that economic recovery depended on conquering inflation. Inflation in her view:

- Hit social stability by eroding middle-class savings and causing strikes for higher wages.
- Made British industry over-priced, due to the 'spiral' of rising prices and rising wages.

- Reduced incentives and enterprise because higher prices led to higher taxation; business should be as free from tax and restriction as possible in order to thrive.
- Was fuelled by government spending and lack of effective control of the money in circulation.
- Was a direct and very harmful result of 'Keynesianism', which had to be abandoned as a principle.
- Could only be tackled by reducing the money in circulation – a belief that came to be known as 'monetarism' – not by further attempts to control wages and prices by government, which had been unpopular and had largely failed.

Also, it was a moral and not just an economic issue as it prevented people from being thrifty and providing for the future in an independent way.

Sir Keith Joseph and monetarianism

Joseph was a Conservative intellectual and theorist much influenced by free market economists such as Milton Friedman in the US. He rejected the post-war trend to increase government interference and wanted the market to be allowed to determine wages and prices, believing that governments should help this by reducing money supply. This would mean deflation and a reduction in jobs in the short term, but would establish the basis for economic growth in the long term. Joseph was influential but not a good communicator and was opposed by many in the Conservative Party who feared the social consequences of this policy.

Taxation policies

In June 1979 the Chancellor of the Exchequer, Sir Geoffrey Howe, significantly shifted the tax burden from direct to indirect taxation. But the government's initial measures worsened inflation:

- They honoured the pay awards made by Callaghan's government to some lower-paid workers.
- The VAT increase pushed up the price of goods.

As a result, Howe resorted to the deflationary methods used by previous governments to tackle inflation. The 1980 and 1981 budgets:

- cut government expenditure
- reduced government borrowing
- increased taxes.

Howe described his 1981 budget as 'the most unpopular in history'.

Howe's policies and economic problems

Howe's policies had a positive impact on inflation but also contributed to an economic downturn:

- The rate at which prices rose was reduced from 18 per cent in 1980 to 4.5 per cent in 1983.
- Manufacturing output fell by 14 per cent and many firms went out of business.

Direct and indirect tax

Direct taxes are levied on an individual's income. Usually taxes are levied on the wealthy at a higher rate. Indirect taxes are levied on goods bought. They include VAT (Value Added Tax) – a duty on all goods and services – and also the duties paid on petrol, alcohol, cigarettes, for example, so the amount people pay depends on what they buy, not on their income. In many cases, indirect taxes hit hardest those on lowest incomes.

■ Unemployment more than doubled between 1979 and 1983 to over 3 million (see Figure 1).

■ The government did not act to support industries which were facing problems.

■ High interest rates which boosted overseas confidence made conditions difficult for anyone with loans to pay.

■ The value of the pound increased which made exports dearer, though it boosted the financial sector.

The social cost of the tough economic conditions became evident when, in April 1981, riots broke out in Brixton, south London, and, in July, in the Toxteth area of Liverpool – places of high unemployment, poverty and racial tension. Over the next three weeks further rioting occurred in six other major cities. Thatcher was deeply shocked but did not accept that her economic policies were to blame.

Although unemployment continued to rise, Britain's growth rate and productivity began to show signs of recovery by 1982. Thatcher and her supporters claimed that this was because the government's tough policies were working. Weaker businesses were failing, but stronger ones thrived. Wage demands and inflation were falling (see Figure 2), Britain was becoming more competitive. Critics argued that the increase in North Sea oil production, turning Britain into a net exporter of oil by 1980, was a significant cause of the improvement.

It was not possible for Thatcher to reduce government expenditure as a whole. It rose by almost 13 per cent between 1979 and 1990 in real terms. Nevertheless, government spending was reduced as a percentage of the economy as a whole, as Figure 3 shows. Although there were many economic factors affecting unemployment, many people saw the reduction of government spending as the cause of the high unemployment of the mid-1980s.

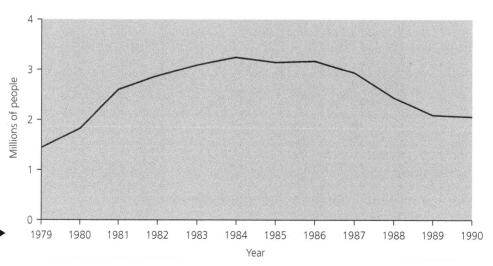

Figure 1 Unemployment, 1979–90. ▶

Source: ONS

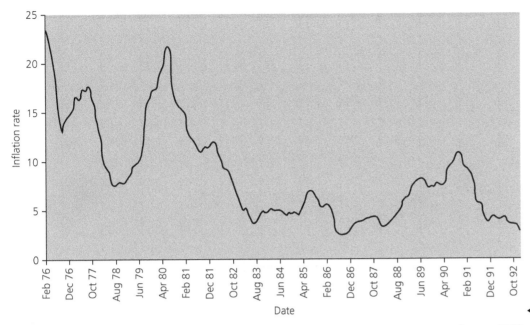

Figure 2 Inflation rate (%), 1976–92.

Source: ONS

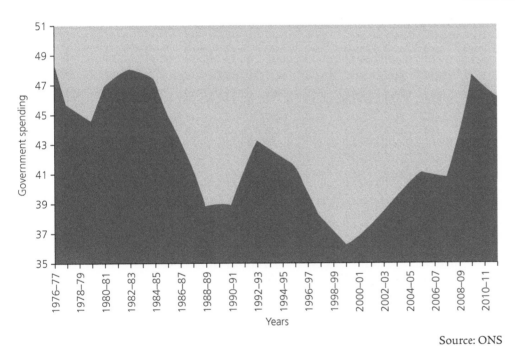

Figure 3 Government spending as a percentage of GDP, 1976–2010.

Source: ONS

Privatisation

Following the emphatic 1983 election victory, the government accelerated the sale of Britain's state-owned enterprises and utilities into private hands. Thatcher believed that privatisation 'was fundamental to improving Britain's economic performance'. She maintained that nationalised industries:

- Were inefficient and over-manned.
- Would be better able to raise investment capital once released from government control.

She also argued that the sell-off would raise revenue with which to fund tax cuts and boost investment and enterprise.

Privatisation was immensely popular with those who bought the shares in the new companies. When Thatcher came to power Britain had 3 million private shareholders and by 1990 there were almost 11 million. She hoped that her policy would reward the people she admired – hard-working, thrifty families whose small shareholdings would give them a modest stake in the future of capitalism. But because the government tended to undervalue the assets of each industry being privatised, the value of the shares usually climbed steeply immediately after issue. This encouraged many shareholders to sell their allocation quickly at a profit, usually to the big financial operations rather than to other small shareholders.

Thatcher's privatisations

Date	Company
October 1979	British Petroleum
February 1981	British Aerospace
October 1981	Cable and Wireless
February 1982	National Freight Corporation
November 1982	Britoil
February 1983	Associated British Ports
July 1984	Enterprise Oil
August 1984	Jaguar Cars
December 1984	British Telecommunications
1985 onwards	British Shipbuilders
December 1986	British Gas
February 1987	British Airways
May 1987	Rolls-Royce
July 1987	British Airports Authority
December 1988	British Steel
December 1989	Water utilities

Tax cuts and deregulation

Nigel Lawson, chancellor of the exchequer from 1983 to 1989, continued Howe's policy of shifting revenue from direct to indirect taxes, reducing further both the top and basic rates of income tax. Capital gains and inheritance taxes were also reduced so that British incomes were more lightly taxed than incomes anywhere else in Europe. However, indirect taxes such as VAT, petrol tax and other duties were increased. The Financial Services Act of 1986 deregulated the London stock market in the so-called 'Big Bang' of October 1986. This revitalised the City of London's money market by ending the Stock Exchange's monopoly on share dealing. The Chancellor's policies produced what was called 'Lawson's Boom'. It seemed that the gap between the very thriving and high-earning financial sector, based in London, and the economically struggling areas of traditional industry and mining in south Wales, central Scotland and much of the north of England, had got even greater.

The economic record of the Thatcher governments

The government's economic policies were highly controversial at the time and have remained so ever since. Thatcher's supporters argue that:

■ She succeeded in bring down the rate of inflation.

Deregulation of the City of London and the 'Big Bang'

Before October 1986, the City of London's financial markets were subject to a number of regulations which had made it difficult for them to compete with overseas banking centres, especially New York. The abolition of the regulations came into effect on 27 October 1986, a day which was nicknamed the 'Big Bang' (comparing it to the creation of the universe) because of the increased amount of trading expected.

- Privatisation improved performance, lowered prices and offered consumers more choice.
- Deregulation of the City ensured that London remained at the centre of a global financial market.
- The extension of shareholding gave many more people a stake in the success of the economy.

Critics of her policies maintain that:

- Such economic success as there was in the 1980s came from the bonanza of North Sea oil, not from Thatcher's policies.
- Too many privatised services and utilities were run for the profit of a few big shareholders rather than in the interests of the customers.
- Deregulation of the City encouraged a selfish, 'get-rich-quick' attitude among bankers and currency dealers that contrasted badly with the bleak prospects for the unemployed and disadvantaged in society.
- The social cost of the policies – pushing up unemployment and destroying communities hit by the fall in manufacturing – outweighed the benefits.

'Look champ, I know what I'm doing. In a few years he'll slow down and take a nap'

▲ This cartoon from the *Guardian* in 1981 shows a version of the famous hare and the tortoise race, in which Thatcher is delaying the British tortoise, already overburdened with attempts to reduce inflation (including Chancellor Howe as a jockey), as she explains her policies – while all the time the hare (inflation) is running away.

The social policies of the Thatcher governments

The Thatcher governments were prepared to take a critical look at major aspects of British life and institutions and to challenge assumptions and vested interests. The policies caused great controversy.

The NHS

The government's reforms were aimed at making the National Health Service, which had grown to be one of the major employers in the state and to take a considerable proportion of government spending, more efficient by applying business principles to its administration:

- Hospitals were allowed to become self-governing NHS trusts in control of their own budgets.
- NHS services were expected to compete with one another to provide the most efficient and cost-effective service to general practitioners (GPs).
- GPs also became fund-holders with their own budgets to manage.

The government's supporters argued that these changes injected some much-needed financial discipline into the NHS.

Its critics argued that it was the first stage in the privatisation of the NHS, in which the profit motive would take priority over patient care, and that business methods were inappropriate for a public service.

Schools

The quality of Britain's secondary school education had been a matter of concern for some time, in particular the two-tier qualification system of O Levels and CSEs. There was a feeling that Britain was lagging behind other countries and that teachers were not being subject to the quality control common in other jobs. At the age of sixteen, more academic pupils took O Levels, which had status, while the remainder took CSEs, which did not lead easily to further training or education. These were both replaced in 1986 with the GCSE – a qualification open to all levels of ability. In 1988 there was a bigger change when the government introduced a national curriculum with regular national testing of pupils at different stages of their school careers. State schools were given the right, if most of the parents agreed, to opt out of control by their local education authority and become grant-maintained schools with complete control over their budgets and operation. There were concerns:

- Thatcher was very doubtful but was persuaded by Sir Keith Joseph that GCSEs would not lead to lowering of standards.
- Some argued that GCSEs were not academically rigorous enough.
- The content of the national curriculum, especially in subjects such as English and History, caused disagreement and some thought setting down what should be taught was too restrictive and testing was too frequent.
- Some maintained that Thatcher was not being consistent. Allowing schools to control their own budgets suggested an extension of freedom from government control, but the imposition of the national curriculum meant that the Department of Education in London decided what schools could teach.

Universities

Thatcher maintained that universities needed to be more economically self-sufficient and do more to serve the economic needs of the country:

- Her government cut university budgets in 1981, forcing universities to seek alternative sources of revenue and accept more students.
- In 1988 a University Funding Council was created to ensure that university education reflected the needs of the economy rather than concentrating on pure research.
- Some university staff lost their security of tenure.
- The government also removed the polytechnics – higher education institutions which specialised in vocational courses – from local authority control and brought them under the control of the Universities Funding Council.
- The government did not abolish grants for young people to attend places of higher education.

The changes were controversial, and in 1985 Oxford University refused to grant Thatcher an honorary degree, something given to the six previous Oxford-educated prime ministers since the war.

Council house sales

Thatcher wanted to create what she called 'a property-owning democracy'. She wanted to reward those who shared the values she admired – hard work, self-reliance and initiative – by enabling them to own their own homes. She believed that owning property gave people a stake in their communities and made them less likely to support 'socialism'. This explains why one of her government's first actions was to allow long-term council tenants the right to buy their houses. To encourage home ownership she also insisted that home owners should continue to get tax relief on their mortgages. During her premiership the amount of government money spent on subsidising mortgages doubled and property ownership increased by 12 per cent.

Activity

1 Copy and complete the table below:
   (i) Assess how successful you think each of Thatcher's social policies were in meeting her aims.
   (ii) Award a mark out of 6 (with 6 being the most successful) for each policy.
   (iii) Then explain why you have awarded each mark.

Policy	Aims	Evidence of success	Evidence of failure	Mark/6	Reason for mark
NHS					
Education					
Housing					

2 Based on your completed table, write a paragraph to explain how successful you think her social policies were.

How successfully did Thatcher deal with industrial relations?

Thatcher's aims

Thatcher knew she would have to tackle the power of the trade unions. She believed that:

- The existing laws on industrial relations had been 'abused to protect **restrictive practices** and over-manning, to underpin strikes, and to coerce workers into joining unions and participating in industrial action against their better judgement'.
- Union power made British firms uncompetitive because high labour costs and restrictive practices meant that business was lost to more efficient overseas companies.
- Jobs would become available once British industry adjusted to market conditions and unions lost their power to control labour conditions.

Thatcher's legislation

Thatcher benefited from the lessons of the 1971 Industrial Relations Act, which incorporated all the measures to restrict union power in a single Act, making it easy for the unions to mobilise their opposition. In contrast, Thatcher adopted a piecemeal strategy, introducing restrictive measures stage by stage:

- The Employment Act of 1980 outlawed secondary picketing and increased the rights of employees who refused to join unions. Government money was made available to encourage unions to hold secret ballots.
- The 1982 Employment Act restricted sympathy strikes and allowed closed shops only if a ballot showed 85 per cent support. Anyone sacked for not joining a union became entitled to high rates of compensation.
- The Trade Union Act of 1984 required unions to hold secret ballots of their members before launching industrial action.

> ### Secondary picketing, the closed shop, sympathy strikes
>
> **Pickets** are groups of striking workers who congregate outside their place of work to demonstrate and to dissuade or prevent other workers and supplies from entering. Secondary pickets adopt the same tactics outside workplaces linked to, but not directly involved in, the dispute.
>
> The **closed shop** made membership of a certain trade union compulsory for all workers in a particular trade or profession.
>
> A sympathy strike is one in which workers not involved in a dispute take strike action to support workers who are on strike.

Table 5 Statistics for unemployment, strikes and trade unions in selected years.

Year	Maximum unemployed in year	Working days lost in strikes	Union membership
1979	1,464,000	29,474,000	12,128,000
1980	2,244,000	11,964,000	12,173,000
1981	2,772,000	4,266,000	11,601,000
1984	3,284,000	27,135,000	10,082,000
1985	3,346,000	6,402,000	9,855,000
1989	2,074,000	4,128,000	8,652,000
1990	1,850,000	1,903,000	8,405,000

The statistics in Table 5 show that, with the exception of the year of the miners' strike (1984–85), the number of working days lost to strikes dropped considerably. The government's legislation undoubtedly played a part in this. But other factors also influenced the trend:

- The high levels of unemployment deterred strike action. Workers were less ready to strike knowing that they could easily be replaced from the large pool of unemployed.

■ Thatcher's economic policies accelerated the social and economic changes
that had been affecting trade union membership since the 1960s (see
pages 124–125). Table 5 shows that union membership continued to fall,
making it more difficult for the unions to mobilise effective strike action.

The miners' strike, 1984–85

The National Coal Board was facing a loss of £250 million for 1983–84 alone.
To demonstrate that the government was serious about refusing to support
loss-making nationalised industries, a pit closure programme was essential.
This was bound to provoke opposition from the powerful mining unions who
had successfully challenged the Heath government. The coal strike began in
March 1984 in response to an announcement that twenty uneconomic pits
were to close, with the loss of 20,000 jobs. The dispute became exceptionally
bitter and violent because neither side was prepared to compromise.

Preparations for the strike

The government prepared carefully before taking on the coal miners:

■ In 1981 a secret Whitehall committee was set up to organise the
stockpiling of enough coal to keep the power stations running through a
long dispute.
■ The Central Electricity Generating Board built up large stocks of coal and
oil in the power stations.
■ Home Secretary, Leon Brittan, set up a National Reporting Centre in New
Scotland Yard as soon as the strike began. This was to ensure central
control of policing, co-ordinating intelligence and the movement of police
officers to trouble spots.

Why the miners' strike was defeated

■ The miners were not united. Those who wanted to continue working
formed a break-away union – the Union of Democratic Mineworkers – in
December 1984.
■ The strike, which began in March, was held in spring and summer when
there was less demand for coal. This deprived the miners of a key weapon,
as coal stocks remained adequate.
■ The Labour Party was reluctant to support the NUM leader Arthur
Scargill who received little public sympathy and was widely seen as an
extremist.
■ Although there was widespread sympathy for the miners, violent incidents
on the picket lines undermined public support.
■ Other workers had suffered from economic change. Mining suffered from
cheaper power sources and falling demand, but many saw it as impossible
to continue to subsidise the industry regardless of its importance in
British industrial history and the communities that depended on it.
■ The government was prepared to use considerable force to protect the right
of miners who wanted to work and it was not swayed by the scale of unrest
and violence.
■ In April 1984, Arthur Scargill refused to hold a national ballot of miners
on whether to continue strike action. This deprived the strike of legal
legitimacy and alienated many mine workers.

Arthur Scargill and the miners' strike

Arthur Scargill was leader of the
National Union of Mineworkers
(NUM). He had pioneered the
use of 'flying pickets' which had
been successful in the 1972 strike
against the Heath government
(see page 131). Scargill saw the
strike as an opportunity to inflict
another defeat on a Conservative
government. He wanted a national
strike, but some mining areas
voted against strike action. Scargill
sent flying pickets to deter them
from working and prevent the
movement of coal. As a result,
miners fought with each other and
with the police.

The impact of the strike

NUM membership dropped from 250,000 in 1979 to under 100,000 by 1987, and the union ended the strike virtually bankrupt. The miners' strike divided opinion about Thatcher more than any other issue. To her supporters, she was successful in terms of:

- Forcing the miners to come to terms with the fact that much of their industry was unsustainable.
- Demonstrating that trade union power could not be used to defeat the government.

However, Thatcher's enemies believed that she had wantonly destroyed livelihoods and historic communities, some of which have never recovered.

How successful was Thatcher's management of her Cabinet?

Thatcher's first years in power were extremely difficult because, although she had some clear, simple convictions, she did not have the backing of many senior members of the party.

- She had few allies in her **Shadow cabinet**. Many were older and more experienced, and had been loyal members of Heath's government. They saw themselves as 'one-nation' Conservatives. This meant that they wanted to maintain unity by ensuring that government spent money to maintain welfare and employment. They shared the Labour Party's view that the government should actively manage the economy. Thatcher wanted to roll back the state and put more emphasis on private initiative and enterprise and later contemptuously called these 'one-nation' Conservatives 'wets'.
- She had limited experience of government. Her only cabinet post had been as Minister of Education under Heath.
- Her gender divided opinion among Conservative MPs.

However:

- She did succeed in establishing a small band of loyalists. The most prominent were her deputy, William Whitelaw, and Keith Joseph, her main economic adviser.
- She was also backed in the Commons by an energetic group of supportive MPs.
- She was very popular with the grassroots members of the party where her emphasis on economic prudence, defeating socialism and restoring Britain's greatness went down well.

How Thatcher achieved mastery of her cabinet

When she chose her first cabinet, Thatcher felt obliged to appoint a number of 'wets' to senior positions in her government, including Jim Prior, Francis Pym and Michael Heseltine.

But she made sure that allies (soon nicknamed the 'dries') who shared her views about economic policy occupied key ministries. Geoffrey Howe became chancellor of the exchequer and Keith Joseph was given the Department of Trade and Industry. She then made sure to promote other supporters. In 1981 Thatcher strengthened her control over economic policy by moving Jim Prior from the Department of Employment and replacing him with the loyal Norman Tebbit and by sacking two other 'wets'. This enabled her to promote more of her supporters, including Nigel Lawson and Cecil Parkinson. At first

---

Activity

Why was Thatcher able to reduce trade union power? Find reasons in the chapter and list them in order of importance, explaining each one.

Brighton bombing

On 12 October 1984, the Irish terrorist organisation the IRA (Irish Republican Army) tried to kill Thatcher and her cabinet by bombing the Grand Hotel in Brighton where they were staying for the Conservative annual conference. There were five deaths and 31 were injuried but the Prime Minister and her senior colleagues survived. Thatcher showed personal bravery and care for those hurt.

she was careful to keep the support of key figures like the deputy prime minister William Whitelaw, but after 1983 the prestige of winning a second election and her strength in the Falklands War allowed her to be more commanding. The leading 'wet' Francis Pym was immediately sacked as foreign secretary and replaced by Geoffrey Howe. The new chancellor, Nigel Lawson, was to play a key role in implementing Thatcher's radical economic policies. Thatcher's immense hard work and thorough preparation won admiration and she did not suffer woolly thinking or weakness of argument in cabinet discussion. She could also use her considerable charm. Her courage in the Brighton bombing incident won respect. However, the downside was resentment about her inflexibility of style and unwillingness to accept alternative arguments without confrontation.

The growth of opposition to her style of leadership

By the mid-1980s, Thatcher had achieved such domination that critics thought her Cabinet had been completely cowed. Her loyal supporters admired her firmness and conviction, but her mastery of the Cabinet made her increasingly intolerant of disagreement from even her most loyal supporters.

- Michael Heseltine, one of the last surviving Cabinet 'wets' who was not afraid to express his independent views, resigned in January 1986 over the Westland Affair. Thatcher survived the difficulties this caused her, but he became a potential alternative leader for those within the party who disliked her.
- In December 1987 she lost the calming and unifying figure of William Whitelaw who retired after suffering a stroke.
- In 1989 she fell out with both Nigel Lawson and Geoffrey Howe over economic policy and Britain's role in Europe.
- Howe's resignation speech in November 1990 (see page 159) played a significant part in her downfall.

> ### Michael Heseltine and the Westland Affair
>
> In January 1986 there was a very public row over the future of Britain's last helicopter manufacturer, Westland, which was in financial trouble. Defence Secretary Heseltine wanted it to join a European consortium. Thatcher and trade and industry secretary Leon Brittan wanted it to be taken over by a US firm. Both Heseltine and Brittan resigned.

Activity

Assess the effectiveness of Thatcher's style of leadership.

Copy and complete the following table to help you decide. Look at the problems and consider how well she dealt with them.

Problem	Solution: successful or not?
Lack of supporters in 1979	
Concerns about a woman leader	
Lack of experience in government	
'Wets' in the Cabinet who opposed changes	

Why did Thatcher inspire such passionate support and hatred?

Support

To her supporters, Thatcher was a resolute, clear-sighted leader who brought about extensive, much-needed change and arrested the national decline symbolised by the industrial unrest and rampant inflation of the 1970s. They believed that she was implementing a coherent set of principles and policies called 'Thatcherism', defined by Nigel Lawson in 1981 as 'a mixture of free markets, financial discipline, firm control over public expenditure, tax cuts, nationalism, "Victorian values" (of the self-help variety), privatisation and a dash of populism'. Such a programme was, her admirers believed, not only necessary but was radically different from the approach of all governments since the Second World War. They also credited her with influencing similar changes around the world, especially in the USA under President Ronald Reagan (see pages 176–177). There were many in Britain who had strong economic reasons to support her, particularly those who benefited from council house sales, privatisation and the deregulation of the City.

She was also admired for her personal toughness in the face of adversity. In 1980, she responded to claims that she might copy Heath's U-turn by telling the Conservative Party conference: 'You turn if you want to; the lady's not for turning.' This defiance cemented her 'iron lady' image, as did her single-minded focus on victory in the 1982 Falklands campaign (see pages 173–174 and box on page 143) and her unwavering hostility to the USSR (see page 179). Her determination and self-confidence made her different from the run-of-the-mill politicians and even some critics acknowledge the clarity and resolution she displayed in tackling crises.

Criticism

Thatcher's policies were controversial from the start. Shifting the emphasis of the tax system from direct to indirect taxation was criticised for disproportionately hitting the poor. Those who lost their jobs in the industries which were hit hardest by her policies, especially the coal mines, became implacable opponents. And there were also some in the prosperous middle classes who felt that she had created a culture of vulgar greed which rewarded acquisitive selfishness, but ignored the plight of dispossessed people. They were disturbed by the growth of 'cardboard cities' made up of desperate and homeless people sleeping rough with only cardboard boxes for shelter. Some Church of England bishops publicly drew attention to the problems of the inner-city poor. In October 1987, intending to show her disapproval of the culture of dependency that had grown up with the **Welfare State**, Thatcher remarked in an interview that 'there is no such thing as society'. To her opponents, this remark simply confirmed her heartlessness.

Why did Thatcher resign as prime minister in November 1990?

Thatcher fell from power for four interconnected reasons:

- The impact of the poll tax.
- Economic difficulties.
- Divisions within the cabinet over policy towards Europe.
- Her growing personal isolation and unpopularity.

The poll tax

Since 1925 the principal source of local government revenue had been 'the rates' – a tax on the owners of property and businesses. Thatcher calculated that more than half of the local electorate did not pay rates and believed that the system was 'manifestly unfair'. She thought there would be more interest in local politics and in controlling local council spending if more people paid

---

Activity

Using the material you have read so far in this chapter, explain which of the following judgements on Thatcher's policies you agree with more:
- 'Thatcher's policies were successful in restoring the country's economy.'
- 'The damage to society caused by Thatcher's policies outweighed any economic benefits.'

local taxes. Because of the rise in house prices, many people lived in homes which were worth a lot but they themselves had little money. The Local Government Finance Act of 1988 introduced the Community Charge, which quickly became known as the 'poll tax'. It replaced the rates with a flat-rate tax on every individual, although there were to be concessions for the least well off.

However, some members of the cabinet and a number of Tory MPs opposed the poll tax because they believed it would be hugely unpopular. It was first introduced in Scotland in 1989 and millions of Scots, encouraged by the Scottish National Party, refused to pay it.

On 31 March 1990, the day before it was due to take effect in England and Wales, there was a massive demonstration against it in Trafalgar Square in London which turned into a violent riot in which 300 people were arrested and 400 police officers were hurt.

Thatcher's decision to press ahead with the policy despite warnings from within her Cabinet and party suggested to her critics that her style of government was increasingly dictatorial and alienating voters.

Economic difficulties

In October 1987 a stock market crash wiped 24 per cent off share prices. Chancellor Nigel Lawson thought this might trigger a recession so, in his 1988 budget, he reduced income tax rates. However, this stimulated a consumer spending boom which pushed up prices. By June 1989 inflation was running at 8.3 per cent. Lawson tried to control inflation, not by the monetarist policy of cutting government expenditure, but by raising interest rates and in October 1989 these had reached 15 per cent. Britain's home-owning mortgage payers, the very people Thatcher most admired and who had hitherto benefited from her policies, found themselves paying heavily for the houses they had been encouraged to buy. Thatcher had so often preached that inflation was responsible for Britain's post-war economic decline that her claim to have wrought an economic miracle now began to look unconvincing.

Divisions over Europe

Since the late 1960s the countries of the European Union had wanted to move towards closer economic union with the aim of merging their currencies into a single European monetary system. Thatcher accepted the Single European Act of 1986, believing that it was an essential step towards the kind of free market in Europe she believed in. But she later regretted doing so because it committed the member states to work towards closer monetary and political union. This she did not want, as she made clear in her speech at Bruges in September 1988: 'We have not successfully rolled back the frontiers of the State in Britain, only to see them re-imposed at a European level with a European superstate exercising a new dominance from Brussels.'

The following year, with the economy in difficulties, Lawson and Foreign Secretary Geoffrey Howe were keen for Britain to join the Exchange Rate Mechanism (ERM) which aimed to create European monetary stability by minimising the exchange rate fluctuations between members. Thatcher, however, disagreed and was fortified in her opposition by her unelected economic adviser, Alan Walters:

- In June 1989, she demoted Howe by moving him from the Foreign Office and giving him what some regarded as the meaningless title of deputy prime minister.
- In October 1989 Lawson, exasperated by Thatcher's resistance and resentful of her reliance on the advice of Walters, resigned as chancellor.

This rift weakened her authority and made her more isolated because she had alienated two important political allies. However, early in October 1990, Britain joined the ERM because she had been reluctantly persuaded by John Major, the new chancellor of the exchequer, that membership would help combat domestic inflation and reduce the high interest rates. Yet speaking in parliament at the end of the month, she denounced plans for the further integration of Europe with the words 'No, No, No'. This delighted the European sceptics in the Tory Party but frustrated some of her own ministers.

Thatcher's growing personal isolation and unpopularity

The government's difficulties were reflected in the opinion polls and some election results:

- In April 1989, in a by-election in the Vale of Glamorgan, Labour overturned a 6200 Tory majority and won by 6000 votes.
- The elections to the European parliament, held in June 1989, told a similar story. The Conservatives won 33.5 per cent of the vote to Labour's 38.7 per cent.
- In the Mid-Staffordshire by-election of March 1990, a Conservative majority of 14,600 became a Labour majority of 9400.
- By June 1990, the Labour Party was sixteen points ahead of the Tories in the opinion polls.

Many Tory MPs feared that the Conservative Party would lose the next election if Thatcher remained in charge. In the autumn of 1989 Anthony Meyer, a little-known Conservative MP, challenged her for the leadership of the party. In a ballot of Conservative MPs, he won 33 votes, and a further 30-odd abstained. The result was unimportant; the fact that there had been a challenge at all and that there was a core of MPs willing to vote against Thatcher indicated that she would be in difficulties when challenged by a credible candidate.

Her fall was triggered by Geoffrey Howe. This was unexpected because he had been one of her staunchest allies and was the only minister with an unbroken record of cabinet service since 1979. But he had also endured years of bullying and hectoring from her and had come to dislike the strident tone of her anti-European speeches and her policy towards Europe. His resignation speech on 13 November 1990 to the House of Commons caused a sensation. Television cameras had only recently been admitted to the Commons chamber, which added to the sense of drama, but his words made it clear that Thatcher's government was badly divided. He called obliquely for a challenge to her leadership: 'The time has come for others to consider their own response to the tragic conflict of loyalties with which I have myself wrestled for perhaps too long.'

The Conservative leadership election

Michael Heseltine took Howe's speech as his cue to challenge Thatcher and, the following day, announced his candidacy for the leadership of the Conservative Party. Thatcher won the contest, but not by a large enough margin to avoid a second round of voting. She tried to drum up support but was advised by a succession of cabinet ministers that she could not win. She announced her intention of resigning on 22 November and on 28 November she resigned as prime minister and was replaced by John Major.

Activity

Copy and complete the table below to assess the reasons for Thatcher's fall. Give a mark out of 6 for each factor, using 6 as the top of your scale and then explain your mark.

Factor	Explanation of how it contributed to Thatcher's fall	Mark/6	Reason for mark
Poll tax			
Relations with her ministers			
Attitude of her MPs			
State of the economy			
Divisions over Europe			

Why were the Conservatives under Major so badly defeated in 1997?

Major faced three main problems when he became prime minister:

- He lacked authority.
- Conservatives were divided about Britain's role in Europe.
- The Labour Party was revitalised under New Labour.

Major's lack of authority

He lacked authority with the Conservative Party as:

- Major was elected by Conservative MPs because the majority of Conservatives did not want Heseltine, whom they blamed for engineering the fall of Thatcher.
- Thatcher's supporters voted for him because she had recently appeared to mark him out as her successor.
- He was affable, reliable and conscientious and may well have appealed to those MPs who had become tired of Thatcher's bossiness.

He lacked authority as prime minister because he had limited experience. An MP since 1979, he had been in the cabinet only since June 1987. He was briefly foreign secretary from June to October 1989 and then chancellor of the exchequer. His uncharismatic personality was soon ridiculed in the media.

Major gained some credit for the unexpected victory of the Conservatives in the April 1992 general election. His vigorous campaigning, often speaking to crowds standing on a plastic container, won him some admiration, but the Conservative majority was slashed to 21 seats. This gave him two problems:

- Conservative MPs who disagreed with his policies could threaten him with defeat in parliament.
- Any by-election defeats would increase the danger of a parliamentary defeat.

Conservative divisions about Britain's role in Europe

The Conservative 'Eurosceptics' loathed the European Community's moves towards closer monetary and political union. But there was also a sizable section of the party who believed that Britain should play its full part in

Maastricht Treaty, 1991

The treaty by which the members of the European Community committed themselves to full integration of their currencies, foreign policy and defence.

The Social Chapter

This was an addition to the Maastricht Treaty by which the European Union could issue directives on working and employment conditions.

Europe. In December 1991 the European member states signed the Maastricht Treaty, committing themselves to full integration. Europe would have a common currency, foreign policy and defence and the community would be known as the European Union. Major succeeded in negotiating British opt-outs from two key aspects, the Social Chapter and the single European currency. But he had a fierce battle to secure ratification of the Treaty by the British parliament. He faced an unlikely alliance between the sceptics in his own party, supported by Thatcher, and the Labour Party. During prolonged parliamentary wrangling, the Conservative rebels twice succeeded in inflicting defeats on the government. Major had to force the ratification bill through parliament by telling his MPs that, unless they voted in favour, the government would resign.

Black Wednesday

By September 1992, the measures to curb inflation had tipped the British economy into depression. As unemployment rose, businesses went under and GDP diminished, it was clear that the exchange rate was too high:

- The pound fell sharply in value as international bankers sold it at its artificially high rate before it was devalued.
- Major and his chancellor, Norman Lamont, tried unsuccessfully to sustain the pound's value by pushing up interest rates and getting the Bank of England to buy pounds.
- But these desperate efforts failed and, on 16 September, which became known as 'Black Wednesday', Britain withdrew from the Exchange Rate Mechanism (ERM) (see page 183).

This episode not only ruined the Conservatives' reputation for sound economic management but it emboldened the Eurosceptics. The subsequent signs of economic recovery only reinforced their view that Europe had little to offer Britain.

Major's leadership election, 1995

Major was severely weakened by the public displays of dissent from the Eurosceptics, in both the parliamentary party and the cabinet. Once, during the Maastricht ratification process, he was caught off guard complaining about 'the bastards' in his cabinet. Although he did not name them, he did not sack them either. It seemed that he was not in control of either his party or his government. In 1995 he tried to face down his critics by holding an election for the party leadership. He was challenged by John Redwood, a leading Eurosceptic and widely assumed to be one the 'bastards'. Major won easily but the fact that a third of the party had not voted for him emphasised how divided the Tories were.

'New Labour'

Neil Kinnock, who was the Labour leader from 1983 to 1992, had done a great deal to make the party electable after its disastrous defeat in 1983. In particular, he had expelled the members of the extreme left who had infiltrated the party in the 1970s. However, he was blamed for over-confidence in the Party's performance in the 1992 election and resigned shortly afterwards.

Following the brief leadership of John Smith who had been popular and moderate, the 41-year-old Tony Blair, who had been an MP only since 1983, became leader in 1994. He set about reconciling the Labour Party to Thatcher's reforms and in April 1995 succeeded in abolishing Clause IV of the Party's 1918 constitution by which it was pledged to nationalise British industry. As part of the modernisation of its image, the party was rebranded as 'New Labour'. Blair appealed to hitherto Conservative-supporting businessmen and City bankers by reassuring them about Labour policies, and won the support of leading figures in the media, especially Rupert Murdoch, owner of the *Sun* newspaper.

The 1997 general election

The election resulted in the worst defeat for the Conservatives since 1906. The Labour Party won a parliamentary majority of over 180 seats – not only larger than any won by Thatcher, but also bigger than its historic win in 1945.

Table 6 The 1997 general election.

Party	% of vote	Votes	Seats
Labour	43.2	13,518,184	418
Conservative	30.7	9,590,916	165
Liberal-Democrat	16.8	5,242,517	46

Why the Conservatives lost

- Major's struggle with the Eurosceptics had reinforced the perception that he was weak.
- The Conservatives' reputation for economic competence had been badly tarnished by the fiasco of withdrawal from the ERM.
- The Conservative Party looked sleazy. A series of revelations about the sexual indiscretions of some MPs and the accusation levelled at MP Neil Hamilton that he had accepted cash from Mohamed Al-Fayed, the owner of Harrods, to ask questions in parliament on his behalf, undermined public confidence.
- After such a long period of Conservative rule many felt it was time for a change of style and policy.

Why Labour won

- Blair's youth and optimism appealed to voters.
- Its media presentation was slick and effective.
- Blair's reform of Clause IV and his wooing of businessmen and media tycoons made nonsense of the Tory campaign message that he and the Labour Party were socialists in disguise.

Activity

Construct a table like the one below to assess how and why the Conservatives lost the 1997 election. Give a mark out of 6 for each factor, using 6 as the top of your scale, and then explain your mark.

Factor	Explanation of role	Mark/6	Explanation of mark
Image of Major			
Divisions over Europe			
Conservative economic policy			
Sleaze and scandals			
New Labour			
Image of Blair			

Historical debate

Thatcher's impact on Britain

The two passages below show how much historians disagree about Thatcher and her policies.

Further research

John Campbell, *Margaret Thatcher, Volume 2, The Iron Lady*, 2008.

David Childs, *Britain Since 1945*, 2012.

Andrew Marr, *A History of Modern Britain*, 2007.

Charles Moore, *Margaret Thatcher, The Authorised Biography, Volume One: Not For Turning*, 2013 (NB This book only covers her life up to 1982).

Alan Sked and Chris Cook, *Post-War Britain, A Political History, 1945–92*, 1993.

Margaret Thatcher, *The Downing Street Years*, 1993.

Richard Vinen, *Thatcher's Britain, The Politics and Social Upheaval of the 1980s*, 2009.

Passage 1

Margaret Thatcher's 'conviction politics' led her more readily to destroy than to create, and her abiding narrowness of vision prevented her from seeing the likely medium- and long-term consequences of her policies. In using the power of the state negatively – to resurrect as much unbridled capitalism as a decade of power in an elective dictatorship could encompass – Thatcherism morally impoverished and desensitized a nation. Despite, or perhaps because of, the extraordinary political triumphs of Margaret Thatcher, Britain by the late 1980s had become a more grasping, greedy and mean-spirited society. Hers is a legacy to live down.

Eric J. Evans, *Thatcher and Thatcherism*, 1997, page 124.

Passage 2

When Margaret Thatcher was asked what she had changed about British politics, she answered, 'Everything'. It was uncharacteristically immodest of her, but it was true. After she became prime minister in May 1979, she changed the atmosphere of the cringe that successive ministries of both parties and industrial management had exhibited towards the trade unions ever since the Second World War. She changed the sense of embarrassment that Britons felt towards the concepts of productivity and profit. She changed British reliance on manufacturing industry just in time, inaugurating the services and information technology industry revolutions. She changed the ownership structure of vast industries, exchanging the nebulous concept of 'national' ownership for the more efficient, purer (and ultimately fairer) one of shareholder ownership. She changed the way we financed the European budget ... Margaret Thatcher stuck to the practice of saying what she meant and meaning what she said. When she said the lady wasn't for turning, she wasn't. When she said the Falklands must be liberated come what may, they were. When she said that people would be allowed to buy their own council houses, they were too. When she told European politicians that she wanted a rebate on the billions Britain overpaid the EEC, she held out till she got one. British politics throws up very few giants, but in her record-breaking 11-and-a-half years in the premiership – the longest continuous period of anyone since 1827 – Margaret Thatcher showed herself to be one such.

Adapted from an article by historian Andrew Roberts in *The Week*, 25 February 2009.

Chapter takeaways

- Thatcher won three consecutive election victories. She was aided by a range of factors, including a divided Labour opposition, victory in the Falklands War and improvements in the economy.
- Thatcher's period in office is usually seen as ending the period of political consensus in which governments controlled prices and wages and entered into negotiations with trade unions. Instead the Conservatives would follow a policy of monetarism and lower direct taxation. These policies were controversial and caused social disquiet.
- The privatisation policy gave ordinary people the opportunity to buy shares as former nationalised industries were sold off and this, along with public sector reforms, has been seen by some historians as a social revolution. However, whatever their consequences, they were controversial policies.
- The government introduced legislation to reduce the power of trade unions. This led to clashes with unions, the most notorious of which was the miners' strike, for which the government had prepared so that it was able to defeat the miners' union.

- When Thatcher first became prime minister her cabinet contained a balance of those on the left and the right of the party, but over time she removed those who disagreed with her views. However, she became more isolated and this contributed to her downfall.
- Thatcher's fall from power was the result of a number of long- and short-term factors, including her growing unpopularity among the party and fears that she had become an electoral liability. There were also unpopular policies, particularly the poll tax and Europe.
- Major unexpectedly won the 1992 election, but with a much reduced majority. This gave many Conservative backbenchers more influence and the growing divisions over Europe seriously weakened him.
- The 1997 general election witnessed a landslide Labour victory. The image of Blair contrasted with that of Major and after eighteen years of Conservative rule many were ready for a change.

Study Skills: Avoiding descriptive answers, writing analytically and the crucial importance of the opening sentence of each paragraph

The types of question set for AS and A Level essays will be the same and therefore all the advice in this section applies to both examinations.

Avoiding descriptive answers and writing analytically

What is meant by a descriptive answer? This is when an answer has relevant supporting knowledge, but it is not directly linked to the actual question. Sometimes the argument is implicit, but even here the reader has to work out how the material is linked to the actual question. Instead of actually answering the question, it simply describes what happened.

In order to do well you must write an analytical answer and not simply tell the story. This means you must focus on the key words and phrases in the question and link your material back to them, which is why the plan is crucial as it allows you to check you are doing it. You can avoid a narrative answer by referring back to the question as this should prevent you from just providing information about the topic. If you find analytical writing difficult it might be helpful to ensure that the last sentence of each paragraph links back directly to the question.

Consider the following question:

> **Example**
>
> **To what extent did Conservative divisions over Europe cause Thatcher to fall from power in 1990?**
>
> In order to answer this question you would need to consider the following issues about the Conservative divisions over Europe:
>
> - What European issues divided the Conservatives?
> - Why did they disagree about them?
> - In what ways did Thatcher make the divisions worse?
>
> Then you would need to consider other factors such as:
>
> - The impact of the 'poll tax'.
> - The state of the British economy in 1990.
> - The mood among the Tories about her leadership.
> - Michael Heseltine's ambition.
>
> A very strong answer will weigh up the relative importance of each factor as it is discussed, a weaker answer will not reach a judgement until the conclusion, and the weakest answers will either just list the reasons or, worst of all, just describe them.

The following is a sample descriptive answer for the question above:

> The Treaty of Rome in 1957 created the original Common Market and, even back then, the countries who joined it wanted to create a European Union eventually which would have a common currency and even, perhaps, a federal European government rather like the United States of America. Britain joined the European Economic Community (as it was called then) in 1973 and voted to stay in when a referendum was held in 1975. The Single European Act was signed in 1986 and this committed the member states to closer monetary and political union. The Exchange Rate Mechanism (ERM) was created as a first step towards a common European currency and Britain joined the ERM in October 1990 because John Major, the new Chancellor of the Exchequer, thought it would help to bring down inflation but he joined at too high a rate and Britain had to leave on Black Wednesday in 1992.

This paragraph outlines some of the facts about the European Union and the moves towards greater unity among the members, but it does not answer the question. The answer has described some of the developments of the European Union but has not explained attitudes to them in the Conservative Party. It needed to explain how these divisions weakened Thatcher. It also needed to weigh up the importance of divisions over Europe against the other factors that contributed to Thatcher's fall.

The opening sentence of each paragraph

One way that you can avoid a narrative approach is to focus on the opening sentence of each paragraph. A good opening sentence will offer a view or idea about an issue relevant to the question, not describe an event or person. With a very good answer you should be able to read the opening sentence of each paragraph and see the line of argument that has been taken in the essay. It is therefore worth spending time practising this skill.

Activity

How far were the government's preparations the most important reason for the defeat of the miners' strike in 1985?

Look at the following ten opening sentences. Which of these offer an idea which directly answers the question above and which simply impart facts?

1 Thatcher's government learned from the experience of the strikes of the early 1970s and made a series of careful preparations which undermined the effectiveness of the strike.
2 The strike gave the Labour Party's leader, Neil Kinnock, a dilemma.
3 Scargill's controversial leadership of the NUM contributed considerably to the miners' defeat.
4 The lack of unity among the miners was crucial because it undermined strikers' morale and allowed the government to portray the strikers as extremists.
5 Scargill got financial help from Colonel Gaddafi of Libya.
6 There was regular violence on the picket lines.
7 Thatcher gave pay rises to the railwaymen and the pit overseers.
8 The co-ordination of the police action by the government played a major role in deciding the outcome of the strike.
9 Some miners continued working.
10 The way the strike was reported in the media had a decisive impact on public opinion.

Question practice

In order to practise the skill of directly answering the question, write six opening sentences for the following essays:
- 'The most important reason for Thatcher's election victories was that her opponents were divided.' How far do you agree with this view?
- To what extent was Britain economically stronger in 1990 than it had been in 1979?

Chapter 7

Britain's position in the world, 1951–97

This chapter deals with Britain's role in a series of international crises as well as its Cold War relations with the USA and the USSR, and its later attitude to Russia. It also considers the impact of the United Nations on British policy, the nature of the independent British nuclear deterrent and Britain's relationship with Europe. The chapter also analyses the loss of Britain's colonial empire and the changing nature of the Commonwealth. The main issues dealt with include the following:

- How successfully did Britain respond to international crises?
- How close was the relationship between Britain and the USA?
- How important were Anglo-Russian relations?
- How has Britain's overseas policy been influenced by its role in the UN?
- Why has Britain's relationship with Europe proved controversial?
- Why has the British nuclear deterrent been controversial?
- How successfully did Britain deal with the problems of decolonisation and the changing nature of the Commonwealth?

This chapter will consider the importance of essays having a good conclusion. It will explain the need to reach a supported judgement, which is based on the argument and view offered in the rest of the essay. It will consider how to weigh up factors and reach a balanced judgement about the relative importance of factors and the approach to be taken when the question puts forward a named factor as the most important reason.

Timeline

1953	July	Armistice in the Korean War (begun 1950) signed
1956	July–Nov	Suez Crisis
1957	May	British hydrogen bomb tested
1958	January	EEC established
1961	August	Britain applies for membership of EEC; vetoed by France in 1963
1962	December	USA agrees to supply Britain with Polaris missiles
1965	November	Southern Rhodesia makes unilateral declaration of independence
1967	May	Britain's second application to join the EEC; vetoed by France in November
1973	January	Britain joins the EEC
1975	June	British vote 2:1 in favour of remaining in EEC
1980	March	Mugabe's ZANU party wins power in Zimbabwe
1982	April–June	Falklands War
1983	October	US invasion of Grenada
	November	US cruise missiles deployed in Britain
1990	August	Iraqi invasion of Kuwait
1991	Jan–Feb	Gulf War to expel Iraq from Kuwait
1992	February	Maastricht Treaty signed
	November	Anglo-Russian trade and defence agreements
1995	Aug–Sept	NATO bombing of Bosnian Serbs

Overview

Two themes dominated British overseas policy in the years from 1951. The first was the Cold War and the shared hostility of the western world to Soviet communism. The 1949 North Atlantic Treaty, by which the USA undertook to defend western Europe, became the cornerstone of Britain's foreign policy. The second theme was Britain's declining world significance as it adjusted, sometimes painfully, to post-war economic difficulties, the loss of its empire and its new relationship with Europe and the Commonwealth.

Throughout the period British politicians liked to claim that they enjoyed 'a special relationship' with the USA. The two nations had strong ties of language, culture, trade and history, and these were reinforced by the Cold War. But their interests did not always coincide, and Britain's views were usually ignored if they clashed with those of the USA. As the United States increasingly assumed the role of 'world policeman' in the post-war world, Britain, and Europe generally, became less important to the USA. Nevertheless, Britain remained an important NATO ally and provided valuable political, and sometimes military, support to America.

During the Cold War, the USSR was regarded as the West's principal potential enemy, so Britain's relations with Russia were mostly hostile, although both nations were anxious to avoid war. There were occasional periods when relations with the USSR improved, but because Britain remained firmly aligned with the USA any co-operation was never more than cautious, lukewarm and limited. The collapse of the USSR in 1991 brought a brief, unprecedented period of better Anglo-Russian relations, but this lasted only until the end of the century.

How successfully did Britain respond to international crises?

Britain faced some important challenges and this section deals with four of them: the Korean War; the Suez Crisis; the Falklands War and the First Gulf War.

The Korean War

After the defeat of Japan in 1945 the Korean peninsula had been divided at the 38th parallel between a communist north and a pro-American regime in the south. In June 1950, North Korea launched a full-scale invasion of South Korea, which almost succeeded in conquering it. The USSR was boycotting the UN over its refusal to recognise communist China, which enabled the US to organise a coalition of sixteen countries, including Britain, fighting under the UN flag to repel the invasion. In September a daring US landing behind North Korean lines forced the communists to retreat and America then launched an invasion of the North. As a result, China sent huge forces into Korea and pushed the US-led forces back to the 38th parallel. The war then became a stalemate with neither side able to defeat the other and an armistice was signed in July 1953.

Britain joined the US-led United Nations' force in Korea because the Labour government and its foreign secretary Ernest Bevin believed that communist aggression needed to be challenged to prevent another world war:

- Participation would, as one official put it, 'demonstrate to the Americans that we were one of the two world powers outside Russia'.
- The war was the first major challenge to the credibility of the UN of which Britain was a founder member.
- If Britain failed to join the war this might imperil the US commitment to the defence of Europe and the newly formed NATO alliance.

The USSR, 1922–91

In 1917 the Communist Party seized power in Russia. The new regime, which lasted until 1991, comprised fifteen different territories of the old Russian empire, and from 1922 was called the Union of Soviet Socialist Republics (USSR). Stalin's dictatorship between 1929 and 1953 built up the power of the Soviet state and made the USSR into a world power.

North Atlantic Treaty Organisation (NATO)

In April 1949, the countries of the West, fearful that the USSR wanted to conquer western Europe, signed the North Atlantic Treaty creating a permanent military alliance. The original members were: the USA, Canada, Britain, France, Belgium, Denmark, Iceland, Italy, Luxemburg, Holland, Norway and Portugal. Greece and Turkey joined in 1952, West Germany in 1955 and Spain in 1982.

How successful was British involvement?

Britain had shown it would take part in defending independent states, supporting the UN and working alongside the USA. The North Korean invasion was defeated and South Korea protected. However, political and strategic control of the war remained firmly in American hands and underlined that the British were junior partners.

- British and Commonwealth forces made an important contribution but they were dwarfed by the American commitment. By the time the war ended, Britain had suffered almost 700 killed in action but America had lost nearly 34,000.
- Britain influenced the fateful decision in September 1950 to invade the North but the majority of the troops involved were American.
- In December 1950, British Prime Minister Clement Attlee flew to Washington because he was mistakenly fearful that Truman might use nuclear weapons in Korea. Although he was given a private undertaking that the British government would be consulted before America considered using the bomb, it was a promise that would lapse when Truman left office.

There were advantages and drawbacks to British participation:

- Britain had demonstrated its loyalty to the USA.
- Britain had helped to check communist aggression and to establish the UN as an effective agency.
- As a result of the war, NATO established a permanent military bureaucracy that even more firmly tied the USA to the defence of Europe.
- The increased defence expenditure added to the difficulties of Britain's economy, which was still struggling to recover from the impact of the Second World War.

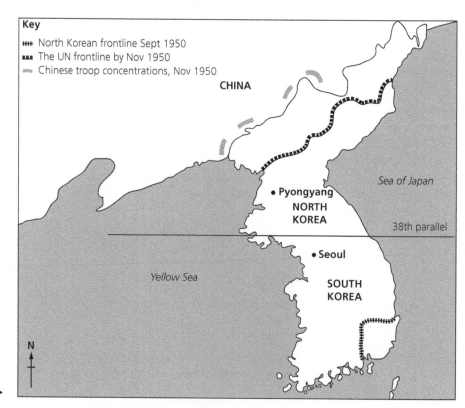

Front lines in the Korean War, 1950. ▶

How successfully did Britain deal with the Suez Crisis?

The Suez Canal was a vital sea route by which Middle Eastern oil was transported to Europe and British forces reached their Far Eastern bases. Since 1875 the British government had been the majority shareholder in the company running it.

In 1952 the pro-British King of Egypt was overthrown by a group of military officers who blamed him for the feeble performance of the Egyptian army in the war against the new state of Israel in 1948–49. One of the officers, Gamal Abdel Nasser, proclaimed himself president of Egypt in 1954. Determined to remove British influence, Nasser immediately negotiated the withdrawal of British troops from their remaining base in the zone around the Suez Canal. Nasser was an Egyptian nationalist, not a communist, but was prepared to buy arms and accept aid from the USSR.

In December 1955, the American and British governments agreed to lend Egypt the money to build a large dam designed to help modernise its economy. But they soon had second thoughts because Nasser was reluctant to follow pro-western policies. In mid-July 1956 the offer of the loan was withdrawn. Nasser responded by taking control of the Anglo-French company that ran the Suez Canal. America sponsored a series of diplomatic manoeuvres to try to solve the crisis peacefully, but without success.

British Prime Minister Anthony Eden, who had taken office in 1955, regarded Nasser's seizure of the canal as an outrage. He believed that:

- It was the first step in a plan to establish Egyptian domination of the Middle East.
- Nasser would allow the USSR to extend its influence in the region.
- The US accepted that continued British influence in the Middle East was essential to preventing the area falling under Soviet control.

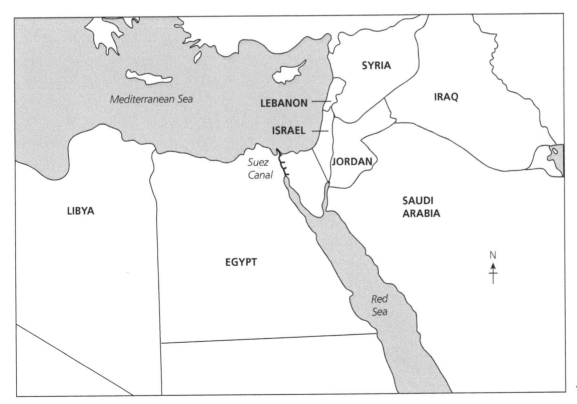

◀ Location of the Suez Canal.

■ Because nearly a third of the ships using the canal were British, and more than two-thirds of the oil supplied to western Europe passed through it, Nasser's action amounted to having 'his thumb on our windpipe'.

Eden concluded that Nasser had to be challenged, by force if necessary, and hoped to use the crisis to overthrow his regime. France also disliked Nasser because he was assisting the rebels fighting to end French colonial rule in Algeria.

In late October and early November French and British troops, in collusion with Israel, attacked Egypt. The Anglo-French invasion failed: Nasser responded to the invasion by sinking ships in the canal, preventing its use. President Eisenhower, who had not been consulted about the attack, insisted on the withdrawal of the invading forces. Humiliated by both Nasser and Eisenhower, Anthony Eden, the British prime minister, resigned in January 1957.

Britain found itself opposed by much of world opinion:

■ Nasser's action was not illegal. Even the British Cabinet recognised that 'his action amounted to no more than a decision to buy out the shareholders', whom he promised to compensate.
■ The USSR condemned the invasion as imperialist.
■ The US wanted to see the crisis resolved peacefully; President Eisenhower was furious about the invasion because he had repeatedly made it clear to Eden that he opposed the use of force. He felt deceived by the collusion between Britain, France and Israel. The invasion coincided with the USSR's invasion of Hungary to crush the efforts at reform there and the Suez invasion made it difficult for him to condemn the USSR.

Activity

Use a table like the one below to help you analyse the impact of these two crises on Britain and its relationship with the USA.

	Korean War	Suez Crisis
Advantages to Britain of involvement		
Disadvantages to Britain of involvement		
How the crisis affected British relations with the USA		

How successfully did Britain deal with the Falklands crisis?

On 2 April 1982 Argentine forces invaded and captured the Falkland Islands, a British colony in the South Atlantic approximately 400 miles from the Argentine coast and 8000 miles from Britain. Argentina's brutal military dictatorship believed that Britain would not have the will or means to retake the islands. The British government had to decide whether to risk military defeat by attempting to recapture the islands or suffer a loss of prestige by abandoning the islands' British population to Argentinian rule.

On 5 April Thatcher's government dispatched a task force of ships and troops to retake the islands. On 2 May a British submarine sank the *General Belgrano*, an Argentine cruiser, with the loss of 360 lives, and a few days later, an Argentine missile destroyed HMS *Sheffield*, a British warship, killing 20 crew members. On 21 May British troops landed on East Falkland, approximately 50 miles from the capital, Port Stanley. As the troops advanced, the Argentine air force continued to attack British ships, sinking several, but losing planes in the process. On 14 June, British forces entered the capital and the Argentine forces surrendered.

Why was Britain successful?

- Thatcher reacted swiftly to the invasion. A task force was assembled quickly and set sail three days after the invasion.
- The UN Security Council, at Britain's request, demanded the withdrawal of Argentine forces, ensuring that Britain's actions were justified in law.
- The European Community was persuaded to impose sanctions on Argentina.
- The opposing sides in the war were not well matched: the Argentine air force pilots were brave and skilful and succeeded in hitting a number of British targets, but also suffered heavy losses; the Argentine navy played little part in the conflict, possibly cowed by the loss of the warship *General Belgrano,* and the conscript Argentinian troops on the islands were less capable than the trained professionals in the British forces.
- The attitude of the Reagan administration was of the utmost importance. President Reagan, despite his personal regard for Margaret Thatcher, did not think the islands were worth a war; and his secretary of state, Alexander Haig, made intensive efforts to mediate. These were unsuccessful, but they did give the British forces time to reach the South Atlantic. The US Defence Secretary, Caspar Weinberger, was strongly pro-British and provided the task force with weapons, vital military intelligence (such as details of signals traffic from Argentina) and the use of the US air base on Ascension Island, an essential staging post for the build-up of British forces.

◀ Location of the Falkland Islands.

Was the war a success?

■ Thatcher's personal political fortunes were transformed by the war and the Falklands victory contributed to her landslide election victory in 1983 (see pages 143–144).

■ Thatcher liked to boast that her policies had restored Britain's 'greatness'; defeat would have ended any lingering pretensions that Britain was still a 'great' power.

■ Many admired the resolution and skill that both Thatcher and the British armed forces had displayed.

■ The war reinforced the lesson of Suez – that Britain could not go to war without the active support of the USA.

■ Defending the islands against any future attack required Britain to garrison troops and rebuild the airport – at a combined cost estimated in the mid-1980s to be approximately £1.5 million per islander.

■ The issue of the sovereignty of the islands remains unresolved despite the replacement of the Argentine dictatorship by a democratic government in 1983.

■ Critics of the war regarded it as a costly enterprise of little real significance, which also left Britain with the substantial costs of maintaining a military presence and continuing to defend the islands.

How successfully did Britain deal with the 1991 Gulf War?

On 2 August 1990 Saddam Hussein, leader of Iraq, invaded and conquered Kuwait. He claimed that Kuwait had always been part of Iraq's territory. The United States were worried that Iraq would go on to seize Saudi Arabia's oil fields, giving it control of most of the world's supply. US President George H. W. Bush (president from 1989–93) responded by building a strong coalition against Iraq. This involved troops from Arab nations, including Saudi Arabia and the United Arab Emirates. The war had United Nations support. The bombing of Iraqi defences and troop concentrations began on 17 January 1991 and the ground assault on 24 February. Hostilities were over within 100 hours. Britain was involved to support both the US and a UN resolution and also because Kuwait was a long-standing British ally.

Britain deployed more than 53,000 servicemen to the allied coalition, the third largest military contribution after the USA and Saudi Arabia.

■ The war successfully liberated Kuwait.
■ It strengthened US–British relations.

Although Thatcher was forced to resign before the US-led invasion began, her reputation for decisive defence of international law and stability was strengthened by her actions in the run-up to the war. Thatcher believed the invasion was a clear case of aggression in violation of the UN Charter. She told the media, 'You cannot have a situation where one country marches in and takes over another country which is a member of the United Nations.'

A legend has developed that Thatcher stiffened the resolve of President Bush by telling him: 'This is no time to go wobbly.' But the reality is that Bush and Thatcher differed only in emphasis. He wanted to take time to build the widest possible coalition against Iraq and give time for UN and diplomatic pressure to end the invasion, if possible, without war. Thatcher, with the Falklands in mind, wanted to act immediately.

RAF planes played a significant part in the bombing campaign and British troops were also involved in the ground assault. The war cost 47 British deaths. The Gulf War demonstrated that British armed forces could still play a significant role in supporting US initiatives.

The operation seemed successful, but there were problems:

- Saddam Hussein was allowed to maintain control of Iraq. He took revenge by persecuting his domestic enemies, especially the Kurdish population in Iraq, a minority group who had risen in revolt against him.
- The war was seen by many in the Middle East as British and American imperialism, despite the coalition with Arab states.
- Prime Minister John Major demonstrated that Britain still had diplomatic influence by enlisting US and European support for his plan to create 'safe havens' for the Kurdish population, to be guarded by allied troops and protected by allied aircraft enforcing a 'no fly' zone.
- Iraq continued to be an issue for Britain and the USA and in 2003 much more controversial joint action was taken which resulted in the removal of Saddam Hussein.

Activity

To what extent do you agree that the British responded skilfully to the crises of the period 1951 to 1997? Copy and complete the following table to help you plan your answer. Award a mark out of 6 for how skilfully you think each crisis was handed, with 6 for the most skilful. Then assess each crisis.

Crisis	Mark/6	Evidence of skilful handling	Evidence of poor handling
Korea			
Suez			
Falklands			
Kuwait			

How close was the relationship between Britain and the USA?

The British regarded themselves as the most important ally of the USA and the relationship did seem to be close:

- Britain and the USA had strong ties of language, culture, trade and history.
- Winston Churchill, speaking in the USA in March 1946, had claimed 'a **special relationship** between the British Commonwealth and Empire and the United States'.
- They had fought alongside each other in the Second World War when hundreds of thousands of US troops had been stationed in Britain.
- The two countries had co-operated to defeat the USSR's attempt to dominate Berlin by cutting off road and rail links in 1948–49.
- The relationship was reinforced by membership of NATO after 1949 and by co-operation over nuclear weapons and secret intelligence during the Cold War.

The Cold War

After 1945, the USA and the USSR were the world's major powers and they quickly became rivals. They had different ideologies and political systems, and each feared that the other wanted to dominate the globe. The period between 1945 and 1990 is known as the time of the Cold War because, despite regular crises, both the USA and the USSR were anxious to avoid a war with each other.

The Berlin crisis, 1961

During the Cold War Germany was divided into an eastern communist state and a democratic western state. The capital city, situated in East Germany, was similarly divided. In 1961 the East German authorities built a wall around West Berlin to prevent it being used as an escape route to the West. There followed a tense but brief stand-off between the US forces stationed in West Berlin and the Russian troops in East Berlin. The Berlin Wall remained until 1989.

The Cuban missile crisis, October 1962

During 1962 the USSR shipped nuclear missiles to Cuba to support the communist regime that had taken power there in 1959. US President Kennedy was determined to have the missiles removed and, resisting the advice of his military to invade Cuba, imposed a naval blockade around the island. After a tense thirteen-day stand-off, which brought the world close to nuclear war, a deal was struck by which the Soviet missiles were withdrawn and America agreed, at a future date, to withdraw some NATO missiles from Turkey.

Although to America, Britain was an important ally, there were some factors which reduced the closeness of the alliance:

- The decline in Britain's economic power meant that it could offer only limited military assistance to the USA.
- The USA had security concerns outside Europe, in the Pacific and Latin America. These were areas where Britain could offer only limited assistance, especially once it gave up its Far Eastern bases in the early 1970s.

Anglo-American relations in the 1950s

In 1951–53 British forces were fighting alongside America in the Korean War. Relations during the war were close, but Britain was clearly subordinated to US decision making.

The Suez Crisis in 1956 demonstrated that Britain could no longer act independently of, and certainly not in opposition to, the United States. Despite Eisenhower's fury, the crisis did little permanent damage to Anglo-American relations because Macmillan exploited his wartime friendship with Eisenhower and made it clear that the US alliance was central to Britain's foreign policy. After Suez, America found itself increasingly taking over Britain's role as guardian of Western interests in the Middle East.

Anglo-American relations in the 1960s and 1970s

During this period Britain's standing as a world power was reduced by its economic difficulties and by the rapid **decolonisation** of its empire (see pages 187–191). This meant that the importance and value of Britain to America diminished but the relations between the two nations remained mostly harmonious.

President Kennedy (president 1961–63) regarded Macmillan as a political father figure and consulted him for advice during the 1961 Berlin crisis and the 1962 Cuban missile crisis, but Britain did not play an active role in either case.

Harold Wilson (prime minister 1964–70) tried to broker peace in the Vietnam War (see page 118) in 1967, but the failure of his attempt illustrated how little influence Britain had over US policy. Wilson succeeded only in irritating Johnson (president 1963–69) who was already disappointed that no British troops were fighting alongside America in Vietnam.

During the premiership of Edward Heath (1970–74) relations with the USA were distinctly cool. Heath believed that Britain's future lay with Europe and wanted Britain, instead of claiming special status in Washington, to be part of a Europe-wide partnership with the USA. However, warmer relations were restored by the personal chemistry between James Callaghan (prime minister 1976–79) and Jimmy Carter (president 1977–81).

Reagan and Thatcher

Ronald Reagan and Margaret Thatcher not only shared a warm friendship, but they agreed about most policy issues:

- In the 1982 Falklands War US logistical and intelligence assistance was vital to Britain's victory (see pages 173–174).
- Thatcher reciprocated in April 1986 by allowing the USA to use British-based F111s to bomb Libya in retaliation for terrorist actions against American targets.

■ Both Thatcher and Reagan opposed United Nations sanctions against the **apartheid** regime in South Africa (see page 181).

There were three principal areas of disagreement between them. It was an indication of Britain's reduced status in Washington that Thatcher's objections on all three issues were ignored:

■ Thatcher was dismayed by Reagan's willingness to bargain away the West's nuclear deterrent in his talks with the reformist Soviet leader, Mikhail Gorbachev.
■ Thatcher disliked Reagan's Strategic Defence Initiative idea.
■ In October 1983 America invaded Grenada, a member of the Commonwealth, to remove its communist government. Thatcher was outraged because she had advised Reagan against invasion.

Anglo-American relations in the 1990s

Britain and the USA co-operated strongly in the First Gulf War (see pages 174–175) and also in the conflict in the Balkans in 1995.

After some initial disagreement, the European NATO powers, including Britain, co-operated with the USA in a bombing campaign against the Serbian population in Bosnia in retaliation for the 1995 massacre of Muslim people in the Srebrenica refugee camp, and also co-operated in bringing about the Dayton Peace Accords, which ended the conflict.

Reagan's Strategic Defence Initiative (SDI)

In 1983 Reagan, who disliked nuclear weapons, suggested that the USA should develop lasers capable of shooting down incoming missiles. His plan quickly became known as 'Star Wars'. The Soviet leaders, fearful of Western technology, believed the plan could make their nuclear arsenal redundant. Thatcher disliked it because she believed that nuclear weapons had kept the peace since 1945.

Conflict in the Balkans

The collapse of communism in eastern Europe in 1989 triggered the break-up of the ethnically mixed state of Yugoslavia. In 1991 Slovenia and Croatia declared themselves independent but the Serbian population, the largest ethnic group, were determined to resist the independence of Bosnia, an area where both Serbian and Muslim people lived. A vicious three-year war followed in which the Serbian group tried to destroy the Muslim population in a genocidal policy called 'ethnic cleansing'. UN and Western efforts to end the fighting failed, making them look weak and indecisive. The 1995 Srebrenica massacre prompted stronger US intervention. This resulted in the Peace Accords, signed in Dayton, Ohio, and the division of Bosnia into two separate republics loosely united under a central administration.

The state of Anglo-American relations in 1997

At the end of the century Britain was one among many US allies. Washington valued British diplomatic and military support in times of crisis, but British politicians exercised little influence over American decision making. Britain still relied on the USA to supply its nuclear deterrent (see pages 185–186), and usually exercised its influence in the UN Security Council in co-operation with America. Britain was an important but junior ally of the United States.

There were periods when Anglo-US relations were close, notably under Thatcher, but even under her there is little evidence to suggest that she sacrificed British interests to support the USA.

Activity

To what extent do you agree that Anglo-American relations were more friendly in the 1980s and 1990s than they were in the period from 1950 to 1980?

Prepare your answer by copying and completing the table below.

	Evidence of co-operation	Evidence of disagreement
Korean War		
Suez Crisis		
1960s: Berlin, Cuba, Vietnam		
1970s		
1980s		
1990s		

How important were Anglo-Russian relations?

During the early years of the Cold War the Western powers, including Britain, had been fearful that the USSR wanted to invade, or at least destabilise, Western Europe and that a third world war was imminent. However, Stalin's death in March 1953 raised hopes that relations with the USSR might improve.

Peaceful co-existence

The new Soviet leader, Nikita Khrushchev, initiated a policy of **'peaceful co-existence'** with the West. This meant he wanted, if possible, to avoid war but to continue competition with the West for influence around the world:

■ In October 1955, the British and Russian navies exchanged goodwill visits.
■ Khrushchev visited Britain in April 1956.
■ Harold Macmillan (prime minister 1957–63) went to Moscow in February 1959.

But these signs of a thaw in relations did not fundamentally change the mutual hostility between Britain and the USSR. Throughout the Cold War, Britain and Russia accused each other of imperialism:

■ From the mid-1950s the USSR started bidding for the support of the nations of the Asia and Africa as they emerged from European colonial rule.
■ The West regarded the communist states of eastern Europe as part of a Soviet empire.

The 1960s and 1970s

As Britain withdrew from its colonial empire, Russia regarded it as less important and concentrated their attention on the USA. However, Britain continued to regard the USSR as its principal potential enemy:

■ Each side was involved in espionage – in September 1971 Britain expelled 105 Soviet diplomats accused of spying.
■ Britain and the rest of NATO were concerned about the build-up of Soviet forces after the Cuban missile crisis.

Thatcher and USSR

Margaret Thatcher, dubbed the 'iron lady' by the Soviet media, made no secret of her anti-communism and was determined to retain Europe's nuclear defences, but this did not prevent her from saying in December 1984 that she liked the reformist Soviet leader, Mikhail Gorbachev, and that 'we can do business together'. She had several meetings with Gorbachev, visiting Moscow in 1984 and hosting a return visit, which did much to calm Russian concerns about America and the Star Wars (SDI) initiative (see page 171).

The collapse of the USSR

The collapse of the USSR in December 1991 brought about an entirely new Anglo-Russian relationship. The new Russian president, Boris Yeltsin, was grateful for the immediate diplomatic support he had received from Britain when Soviet hardliners had tried to seize power in August 1991. And British efforts during the 1990s helped pave the way for Russia to join the exclusive club of the world's leading industrialised nations, which, with Russia's accession, became known as the 'G8'. In November 1992 Yeltsin visited Britain to sign a set of wide-ranging agreements on trade and military co-operation. He thanked John Major (prime minister 1990–97) for his 'profound understanding of Russia and its reforms'. The importance of London as a financial centre soon made it an attractive place for some Russian businessmen – who had become very rich by taking advantage of Yeltsin's liberalisation of the economy – to live and invest in.

> ### The 'G8'
>
> The 'G8', or Group of Eight, began life in 1975 as the 'G6' when the heads of government and finance ministers from France, West Germany, Italy, Japan, the UK and the USA met to discuss economic problems. It became the 'G7' when Canada joined in 1976, and the 'G8' when Russia joined in 1998. There is no formal structure to the group, but members are expected to share democratic values. Russia was expelled in 2014 following its invasion of the Crimea.

Anglo-Russian relations during the period

Britain's relations with the USSR during the Cold War varied from outright hostility short of war to cautious, lukewarm and limited co-operation. During the Soviet period·there were trade links, British tourists could visit the USSR and Russia occasionally allowed cultural or sporting groups to visit the West. But with Britain firmly aligned with the USA, the USSR was regarded as Britain's principal potential enemy – an attitude reinforced by ideological hostility, propaganda and regular crises, although both sides were anxious to avoid a direct confrontation.

Activity

How far do you agree that relations between Britain and Russia were characterised more by hostility than friendship?

Copy and complete the table below to help you decide your view.

Evidence of hostility	Evidence of friendship

How has Britain's overseas policy been influenced by its role in the UN?

Britain's role in the UN

Britain, as one of the 'Big Three' victorious powers at the end of the Second World War, played a key role in establishing the United Nations in 1945.

The United Nations organisation

The UN's executive body is the Security Council. It has five permanent members, the USA, the USSR (now Russia), China, France, and the UK. It also has ten (originally six) non-permanent members each elected for a two-year term. All members of the UN have a seat, and equal voting rights, in the General Assembly, but its resolutions are largely advisory.

Britain has played an important, though largely non-political, role in key UN agencies. Since the inception of the International Court of Justice at The Hague (which arbitrates between nations on matters of international law) one of the fifteen judges has always been British. Britain has also always been a member of the Economic and Social Council, which oversees a huge range of activities and co-ordinates the work of specialist agencies such as the World Health Organisation.

United Nations membership

Year	Number of member states
1945	51
1950	60
1960	99
1970	127
1980	154
1990	159
2000	189

Along with China, the USSR and the USA, British diplomats were involved in drawing up the UN Charter. The key principles of the Charter were strongly influenced by the democratic values of the Western powers, and provided for:

- Maintenance of international peace and security.
- Prevention of aggression.
- Peaceful settlement of international disputes.
- Addressing economic, social and cultural problems.
- Promotion of human rights and fundamental freedoms for all, without distinction as to ethnicity, gender, language, or religion.

As a founder member, Britain also became one of the five permanent members of the Security Council, giving it considerable power and influence because each permanent member has a **veto** over Security Council decisions that are otherwise binding on all members.

The influence of UN membership on British policy

Membership of the United Nations has had a significant influence on British overseas policy because it has been important to British governments to present their actions as conforming to the principles of the UN. As global media coverage of international events has increased in speed and intensity, it has become ever more important for British governments to obtain UN backing to ensure the support of other nations and domestic public opinion for their policies. This was easier to do in the 1950s when Western nations dominated the membership but, once the European colonial empires broke up, the majority of nations were from outside Europe.

While Britain retained its colonial empire, its governments found themselves criticised, often by nations in Africa and Asia, as imperialist and in violation of the UN's commitment to human rights and freedom for people of all races. Britain has used its Security Council veto sparingly but almost always when their policy appeared to lay them open to the charge of imperialism:

- The British veto was first used, in conjunction with France, during the Suez Crisis (see pages 171–172) when the USA and the USSR accused them of trying to re-establish colonial power over Egypt.
- Between 1963 and 1973, Britain vetoed six Security Council resolutions on Rhodesia (see pages 118–119) because the Afro-Asian nations accused Britain of supporting white supremacy.
- In April 1986 Thatcher's government supported the USA in vetoing a resolution criticising the US bombing of Libya. Many in Africa regarded the bombing as an example of Western imperialism.

Britain found the taint of white imperialism hard to escape even during the 1970s and 1980s, despite granting independence to most of its colonial Empire. Together with the USA, Britain regularly incurred the wrath of the most independent Commonwealth states in sub-Saharan Africa and Asia by vetoing resolutions against white **minority rule** in southern Africa. In the 1990s, many Muslim people in the Middle East perceived the UN resolutions, which legalised military action in Iraq in which Britain participated, as similarly imperialist.

Activity

Use the material you have studied so far in this chapter to answer the following question:

To what extent has British foreign policy been conducted in accordance with the principles of the UN Charter?

Copy and complete a table like the one below to help you plan your answer.

	Evidence that the policy conformed to Charter	Evidence that the policy did not conform to Charter
Korean War		
Suez Crisis		
Falklands War		
Gulf War		
Bosnia		
South Africa		

Why has Britain's relationship with Europe proved controversial?

The nature of Britain's relationship with Europe has divided opinion in the United Kingdom ever since the 1950s. However, in the immediate aftermath of the Second World War Britain's relations with Europe caused little domestic controversy. Britain:

- Played a central role in creating the Organisation for European Economic Co-operation (OEEC) set up in 1948 to administer Marshall Aid, the huge American aid package to help rebuild war-torn Europe.
- Was one of the original signatories of the North Atlantic Treaty in April 1949.
- Was a founder member of the Council of Europe, established in May 1949 to promote unity and human rights.
- Committed itself to the defence of Europe by a series of treaties with France, Belgium, Holland, Luxembourg, West Germany and Italy.

It was with the development of the European Economic Community in the 1950s that more controversy emerged as moves towards European unity appeared to threaten **national sovereignty**. British interest was limited. Britain played no part in:

- The European Coal and Steel Community (ECSC), established in 1952 by France, West Germany, Italy, Belgium, Holland and Luxembourg.
- The 1955 meeting at Messina that led to the 1957 Treaty of Rome by which the ECSC countries established the European Economic Community (EEC) in 1958.

The Conservative governments of the 1950s did not join the EEC because they:

- Hoped to make the colonial Empire and the Commonwealth into a trading bloc that would be stronger than the EEC.
- Disliked the commitment to closer union contained in the Treaty of Rome.
- Did not believe that France and Germany could overcome centuries of hostility quickly enough to make the EEC a success.

The UN and the apartheid regime in South Africa

The most independent Commonwealth states in sub-Saharan Africa and Asia (and many liberals in the West) regarded the racial discrimination of the South African regime as morally offensive. They believed that it could be undermined by a programme of economic sanctions. The American and British governments, especially those of Reagan and Thatcher, valued South Africa for its mineral wealth and its strategic importance as an important Cold War ally. They believed that the black nationalist movement in the country was communist, and sanctions would hit the country's black population hardest.

Domestic divisions over Britain's role in Europe

Britain's relations with the EEC became a difficult issue in British domestic politics in the early 1960s. Harold Macmillan (prime minister 1957–63) realised that Britain's colonial empire had no future and tried to establish a new relationship with Europe:

- Initially, he took the initiative in establishing the European Free Trade Association (EFTA) in 1960 as a rival to the EEC that would not infringe national sovereignty.
- By 1961 the scale of Britain's economic difficulties (see page 103) convinced him and the pro-Europeans in both major parties that Britain needed to join the Common Market in order to compete with the countries of Europe.

Both major political parties had influential groups opposed to Britain joining the Common Market because they believed, for different reasons, that membership of the EEC would limit Britain's freedom to make its own decisions:

- The left of the Labour Party wanted to extend nationalised control of the British economy and did not want to join an organisation committed to free enterprise.
- The Conservative Party had a faction that looked back nostalgically to the days of Empire and opposed entry because it would jeopardise and perhaps even entirely sever Britain's remaining ties with the Commonwealth.

These divisions were starkly apparent when parliament debated the terms of British entry in 1973. Edward Heath's Conservative government could only secure a majority with the support of pro-European Labour MPs (see page 129). When Labour returned to power in 1974, Harold Wilson (prime minister 1974–76) chose to tackle the divisions within the Labour Party by holding a national referendum over membership in June 1975. The 2:1 vote in favour demonstrated that the majority of British people accepted the pro-European argument that membership was vital to overcoming Britain's economic difficulties. For the rest of the decade, the British role in Europe was not a major issue in domestic politics.

Why did British attitudes towards Europe change between 1950 and 1975?

With Britain joining the EEC in 1973 and a referendum in 1975 supporting continued British membership, it is worthwhile reflecting why attitudes towards closer European co-operation had changed:

- The loss of Empire encouraged Britain to look towards Europe.
- The economic success of the EEC compared with EFTA was important given Britain's lacklustre economic performance (see Chapters 4 and 5).
- The premiership of Heath, who was a pro-European.
- Encouragement from the USA for Britain to join.
- The retirement of de Gaulle in 1969 made British entry possible, as he had previously opposed Britain joining.

Thatcher, the Conservative Party and Europe in the 1980s

One of the politicians playing a key role in campaigning for a 'yes' vote in the 1975 referendum was the newly elected Conservative leader, Margaret

The EEC and EFTA

The EEC was a single trade area with a common external **tariff** and became known as the Common Market. In 1960 seven European countries outside the EEC – Britain, Denmark, Norway, Sweden, Austria, Switzerland and Portugal – created the European Free Trade Association (EFTA). This had a looser structure than the EEC. It abolished tariffs between its members but allowed them to set individual tariffs on trade with non-members, enabling Britain to maintain its Commonwealth trading links. EFTA was never as strong as the EEC.

Thatcher. But once she became prime minister in 1979 she began to have doubts about Britain's role in Europe:

- In 1980, convinced that Britain was making a disproportionately large contribution to the EEC budget, she demanded a rebate, exclaiming, 'I want my money back!' It took four years of negotiation before she succeeded and the process damaged relations with other member countries.
- Thatcher and her supporters thought that Conservative economic policy, rather than membership of the EEC, had brought about economic recovery from the difficulties of the 1970s.
- In September 1988 in a speech in Bruges she spoke for many on the right of the Conservative Party who regarded closer European integration as a threat to British sovereignty when she denounced what she called 'a European super-state exercising a new dominance from Brussels'.

But there were also members of the Conservative Party who believed that Britain should continue to play a major role in Europe:

- They believed that the benefits to Britain of closer integration with the economies of Europe outweighed the disadvantages.
- By 1989 some of Thatcher's senior ministers believed that inflation could best be tackled by Britain joining the Exchange Rate Mechanism (ERM). This issue contributed to her downfall (see page 147).

Major, Maastricht and Conservative divisions in the 1990s

The Eurosceptic wing of the Conservative Party, which grew during Major's premiership, was emboldened by two issues in the early 1990s:

- Britain's humiliating withdrawal from the Exchange Rate Mechanism in 1992 (see page 161) and subsequent economic recovery confirmed them in their view that Britain did not benefit from European membership.
- The Maastricht Treaty brought together the Conservatives who wanted to leave the EEC with those who believed that the EEC should be no more than a trade partnership because of its implications for British sovereignty. They feared that the Treaty was another step towards making Europe into a federal state governed from Brussels.

The pro-Europeans maintained that Eurosceptic fears were exaggerated and that:

- Britain benefited from being part of the world's largest single market.
- The free movement of goods, capital and labour removed obstacles to business within Europe.
- Common regulations on goods, working conditions, the environment and crime benefited all member countries.
- The European Union attracted more investment into Britain from outside Europe than Britain could achieve alone.

Throughout the post-war period, and into the twenty-first century, the British people have been divided about how far the country should co-operate with Europe's seemingly inexorable moves towards closer monetary, economic and political union. This division cuts across the political and social spectrum. The British people, geographically detached from Europe but culturally and economically inseparable from it, seem unable to agree on exactly what their relationship with the continent should be.

> **Exchange Rate Mechanism (ERM) and the 1991 Maastricht Treaty**
>
> The ERM was established in 1979 to co-ordinate the exchange rates of the currencies within the European Community. The Maastricht Treaty committed members to full integration of their currencies, foreign policy and defence and changed the name of the community to the European Union.

Activity

Why has Britain's relationship with Europe been so controversial?

Consider the following statements:

a Politicians in Britain were concerned about the impact of closer European ties on national sovereignty.

b Politicians in Britain were concerned about the impact of closer European ties on the relationship with the Empire and Commonwealth.

c Britain was more concerned about a closer relationship with the USA than with Europe.

d It was only the country's weakening economic position that encouraged Britain to become more closely involved in Europe.

Find evidence to support or challenge each of the statements. Which statement do you think best explains why closer relations with Europe have caused such controversy? Write a paragraph to explain your answer.

Why has the British nuclear deterrent been controversial?

What have been the arguments in favour of the British nuclear deterrent?

- The Labour government of the late 1940s decided to build a British nuclear bomb in 1947 because, before the NATO Treaty was signed in 1949, they feared that the USA might be unwilling to defend Europe and that they needed a nuclear weapon to deter the USSR whose conventional forces were much larger than those of Western Europe.
- The British nuclear deterrent continues to contribute to the defence of Western Europe.
- Possession of an independent deterrent maintains Britain's 'great' power status.

What have been the arguments against the British nuclear deterrent?

- Since 1962, when Macmillan persuaded President Kennedy to supply Britain with Polaris missiles to carry British warheads, the British nuclear deterrent has not been independent but reliant on America.
- The British nuclear deterrent is virtually irrelevant when measured against the size of the American and Russian nuclear arsenals.
- The heavy costs in maintaining it reduce government investment in other areas such as education or health services, and conventional forms of defence.

Nuclear weapons as an issue in British domestic politics in the 1950s and 1960s

During the late 1950s and early 1960s, pressure grew for nuclear weapons to be abandoned to make the world safer. In 1958 the Campaign for Nuclear Disarmament (CND) was founded and began a series of annual protest marches from the nuclear weapons plant at Aldermaston in Berkshire to

Trafalgar Square in London. The march in 1960 attracted as many as 100,000 protesters. However, supporters of the nuclear deterrent maintained that Britain needed to be strong to prevent Soviet aggression, even though it was clear by the 1960s that Britain needed US missiles to deliver its bomb. The Labour Party was more divided on the issue of nuclear weapons than were the Conservatives (see page 101).

Britain and international agreements on nuclear technology

In 1963, Britain joined the USSR and the USA in banning nuclear testing in space, under water and in the atmosphere. Britain also signed the 1968 Nuclear Non-Proliferation Treaty by which signatories agreed not to share nuclear technology with other nations. The continued build-up of nuclear-armed missiles by both the USA and the USSR during the 1960s rendered the much smaller British deterrent increasingly insignificant. So much so that Britain played little part when the two superpowers negotiated the two Strategic Arms Limitations Treaties (SALT) in 1972 and 1979.

Britain and nuclear weapons in the 1980s

Britain's role in the nuclear balance between East and West once again became controversial in the 1980s. In the mid-1970s the USSR had begun deploying SS-20 intermediate range missiles capable of hitting targets anywhere in Europe, and in 1979 the NATO powers agreed to deploy US intermediate range cruise missiles in response. This decision:

- Increased the likelihood of Europe becoming a nuclear battleground.
- Prompted a group of women in 1981 to set up a protest camp at the RAF and USAF base at Greenham Common in Berkshire. The camp was for women only and was to demonstrate opposition to the siting of US nuclear weapons on British bases. The camp lasted for nineteen years and became a potent symbol of women's rejection of war and violence.

One woman who did not sympathise with the Greenham Common protest was Prime Minister Thatcher. She was alarmed by President Reagan's willingness, in his discussions with the Soviet leader, Mikhail Gorbachev, to embrace what became known as the 'zero option' – the complete abolition of nuclear weapons on both sides. She told him in December 1984,

'Nuclear weapons have served not only to prevent a nuclear war, but they have also given us forty years of unprecedented peace in Europe. It would be unwise to abandon a deterrence system that has prevented both nuclear and conventional war … If we ever reach the stage of abolishing all nuclear weapons, this would make conventional, biological or chemical war more likely.'

She also believed that the abolition of nuclear weapons would leave Europe exposed to the conventional forces of the USSR, which were much larger than those of NATO. Although the zero option was not adopted, the collapse of the USSR in 1991 did lead to agreements by which both the USA and Russia significantly reduced their nuclear arsenals.

At the end of the century, Britain's nuclear policy remained much like its foreign policy – nominally independent, but in reality dependent on the United States – and debate continued about the cost, ethical issues and viability of the nuclear option.

> ### Britain's nuclear arsenal
>
> The intermediate-range cruise missiles deployed in 1983 were removed as part of the INF (Intermediate-range nuclear forces) Treaty abolishing missiles with a range of 500–5500 km. It was signed by the USA and the USSR in December 1987. Thatcher insisted that the USA supply Britain with Trident submarine-launched missiles to replace the ageing Polaris. At the end of the Cold War, Britain's stockpile of nuclear weapons was reduced to fewer than 200, all of which were assigned to its four Trident submarines, which came into service between 1994 and 1998.

Activity

1 Copy and complete a table like this one to assess Britain's nuclear deterrent:

Arguments in favour of the British nuclear deterrent	Arguments against the British nuclear deterrent

2 To what extent do you think the issues in the debate about Britain's nuclear deterrent changed in the period from 1951 to 1997?

How successfully did Britain deal with the problems of decolonisation and the changing nature of the Commonwealth?

What problems did Britain face in 1951 in its imperial policy?

- The UN Charter, with its emphasis on the 'fundamental freedoms for all without distinction as to race, sex, language, or religion', required Britain to grant independence to its colonies, but Britain also wanted the economic resources of its colonies to assist its recovery after the Second World War.
- British (and US) officials believed that Britain's colonies could not function as independent countries until they had developed their economies and built up their political, administrative and judicial systems. Granting 'premature independence', it was thought, would make the colonies vulnerable to communist take-over.
- Some colonies, for example Cyprus and Malaya, contained racial and religious communities hostile to one another. It was feared they would descend into civil war if the British troops left hastily.
- From the mid-1950s the non-white races of the world challenged white supremacy and anti-British colonial nationalism developed rapidly, especially after the 1956 Suez Crisis when Britain failed to reassert influence over Egypt (see page 188).
- The forces needed to suppress anti-colonial nationalism were costly and any violent confrontations generated bad headlines for Britain and provided material for the anti-colonial propaganda of the USSR and China.

Why did Britain grant independence to the majority of its colonies in the period 1957–64?

Britain wound up its colonial empire for several interlinked reasons:

- The impact of the Second World War.
- Britain's economic weakness.
- The growth of colonial nationalism.
- The impact of the Cold War.

The impact of the Second World War

The war damaged European prestige and changed the relationship between British colonial rulers and the people they ruled:

- The humiliating surrender of Singapore to the Japanese in 1942 and the rapid collapse of the French and Dutch empires in the Far East demonstrated that white European rule was not invincible.
- During the war British colonial administrators tried to exploit the economic resources of the Empire more effectively because food and raw materials were in short supply in Britain. This disrupted many traditional, rural societies. Farmers in Kenya, for example, resented having to sell their crops to the government at a fixed price.
- The colonies were unable to buy manufactured goods from Britain and were often prevented from buying them from elsewhere and this encouraged the rise of nationalist movements and discontent within the colonies.
- The war saw greater unrest in the major British imperial possession, India, and after 1945 there was acceleration of British withdrawal, resulting in independence for India and Pakistan in 1947.

Britain's economic weakness

Britain's post-war economic weakness was so serious that it became government policy to exploit the resources of the colonies even more extensively than during the war. At the end of 1948 the government set up the Colonial Development Corporation and projects such as the East African Groundnut Scheme were established. These schemes often further disrupted colonial communities, increased the resentment of those affected and contributed to the growth of hostility to British rule. Furthermore, British economic weakness also meant that it could no longer supply the colonies with the investment capital and manufactured goods they needed.

The growth of colonial nationalism

The growth of resentment of British rule enabled charismatic, articulate nationalist leaders to emerge who demanded immediate independence. These leaders had usually been educated in the West (often in Britain or the USA), where they studied Western democratic ideals as well as communist anti-colonial theories. They were encouraged by the success of men such as Nasser in challenging British rule, especially as the development of colonial nationalism coincided with a worldwide challenge by non-white races against white supremacy. In the USA, African American people protested against the systematic discrimination that made them second-class citizens and, in 1955, representatives from 25 newly independent countries with developing economies met at Bandung in Indonesia to create the non-aligned movement and denounce European imperialism. When he toured Africa in 1960, British Prime Minister Harold Macmillan recognised the strength of anti-colonial nationalism and told the South African parliament that 'the wind of change is blowing through this continent ... this growth of national consciousness is a political fact'. This had already been seen in the Gold Coast (Ghana) where the Convention's People Party had organised the campaign for independence and in Tanganyika, where the Tanganyika African National Union had insisted that the government of the country must be African. However, in some countries, such as Kenya, the resistance to colonialism was violent. By the end of 1952 there was virtual civil war in Kenya between those who had benefited from colonial rule and those who thought it should be resisted, resulting in over 14,000 individuals being killed and disturbances taking until 1956 to suppress (see page 190).

The impact of the Cold War

In the late 1940s and early 1950s America encouraged Britain to keep their colonial empire, especially in Africa, because they believed that newly independent nations would be too weak to resist communist influence. But, as Britain struggled to control anti-colonial protest in such places as Egypt and Cyprus, both the USA and the USSR produced anti-colonial propaganda designed to win support in Africa and Asia. Winning the propaganda battle became ever more important as the United Nations grew in size and increasingly became a forum for non-white nations to criticise European empires.

How successful were British colonial policies?

Britain hoped that, if they initiated political reform in their colonies, they could turn them into independent nations that would remain within the Commonwealth and the British economic sphere, known as the **sterling area**. This could give Britain the benefits of empire without the costs, difficulties and criticism, both domestic and international, that came with efforts to suppress protest against British rule. Unfortunately, this was not a process they could control, and they usually found themselves handing power over to nationalist leaders they had previously imprisoned as terrorists, such as Kwame Nkrumah in Ghana or Jomo Kenyatta in Kenya.

In a bid to make smaller and weaker colonies economically and politically stronger, the Conservative government attempted to unite adjacent territories into federations. In 1953, the Central African Federation (CAF) was created. A similar policy was adopted for the West Indies in 1958, and for Britain's collection of small territories and protectorates in the Arabian Peninsula in 1963. The policy was not successful and all three federations were short-lived because they made the political divisions among their members worse.

Malaya

Britain's Malayan territories were an invaluable source of tin and rubber and the port of Singapore was strategically important but the colony was ethnically diverse. The population was approximately 45 per cent Chinese, 40 per cent Malay and 15 per cent Indian people. In 1948 Malayan Chinese communists had begun an insurrection against British rule, which lasted until 1960. The guerrilla war against the insurgents involved approximately 40,000 British and Commonwealth troops and was eventually successful because the Malay community was largely Muslim and disliked the atheist communism of the Chinese people. Britain granted independence in August 1957 to a government headed by conservative Malay leaders.

Ghana

In 1948 Britain had responded to riots in the capital city, Accra, by granting universal suffrage and creating an elected parliament, hoping to hand over power to Ghana's conservative nationalists. Instead, they had to deal with the radical nationalist leader, Kwame Nkrumah, who won the elections held in 1951. However, Nkrumah appeased Britain by agreeing to keep Ghana in both the Commonwealth and the British trade bloc – known as the sterling area – and to accept a federal constitution, which devolved some power to the ethnically diverse central and northern regions of the country where Nkrumah had little support. Ghana's independence in March 1957 appeared to be a

The Central African Federation (CAF)

Britain's sub-Saharan African territories – Nyasaland, Northern Rhodesia and Southern Rhodesia – were brought together in the Central African Federation in 1953. But the CAF was never stable because the black African population, especially of Northern Rhodesia and Nyasaland (where there were far fewer white people than in Southern Rhodesia), saw it as the first step in their abandonment by Britain to permanent white minority rule. By 1960, the strength of nationalist protest and unrest in Northern Rhodesia and Nyasaland had convinced the government in London that the CAF had no future. In July 1964 Nyasaland became independent Malawi, and in October 1964 Northern Rhodesia became independent Zambia.

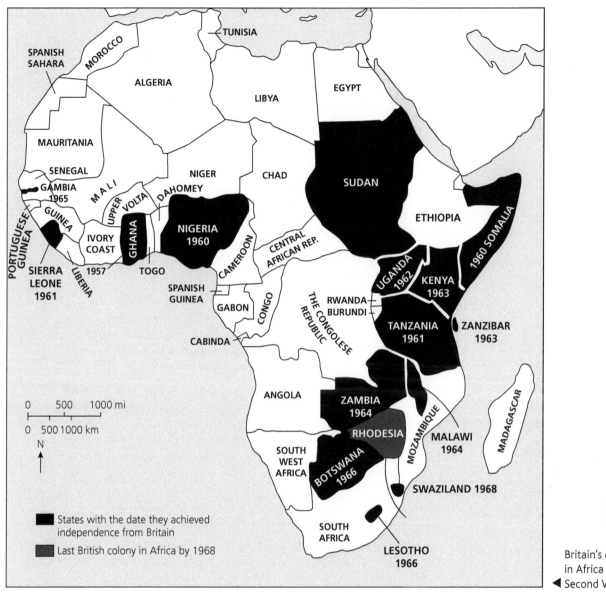

Legend:
- States with the date they achieved independence from Britain
- Last British colony in Africa by 1968

Britain's decolonisation in Africa after the
◀ Second World War.

model of ordered withdrawal because it had been achieved with a minimum of violence. However, Nkrumah's subsequent socialist policies, his active support for black liberation elsewhere in Africa and his authoritarian rule made him controversial and he was overthrown in a military coup in 1966.

Nigeria

Regional differences were even more marked in Nigeria than in Ghana. The north was Muslim, traditional and rural, whereas the south was Christian, more commercial and westernised but was also divided between two different ethnic groups – Igbo in the east and Yoruba in the west. Having imposed a federal constitution, Britain handed over power to a coalition representing the north and the Igbo. Nigeria became independent in October 1960 but its ethnic tensions caused instability and, between 1967 and 1970, the country suffered a bitter and destructive civil war.

Kenya

Kenya was a rich source of coffee and tea and its society was divided between an Asian community which dominated the commercial life of the colony, white settlers who farmed the most productive land, and three indigenous black national groups – Kikuyu, Masai and Luo. In 1952, the Kikuyu people, resentful of their exclusion from the land farmed by the white settlers, began a guerrilla campaign known as the Mau Mau uprising.

For four years this was savagely suppressed by the British authorities but when Macmillan became prime minister in 1957 he realised that the demand for independence was too strong to be resisted. In December 1963 Kenya became independent but, as in Nigeria and Ghana, some of the country's subsequent difficulties stemmed from the failure of the British colonial authorities to tackle the racial divisions and from the haste with which they withdrew.

Cyprus

In April 1955 the Greek Cypriot people began a terror campaign to expel the British authorities and unite the island with Greece. Before long they had tied down 25,000 British troops in a bitter and fruitless campaign in which the cycle of terrorism and arbitrary British justice merely inflamed the uprising. The British response was complicated by the strategic importance of the island as a military base in the eastern Mediterranean and by the fact that 20 per cent of the Cypriot population was Turkish and opposed to union with Greece. In 1960 Macmillan succeeded in persuading the two communities to accept independence under a Greek president and Turkish vice-president. However, continued strife between the two communities and a Turkish invasion of the island in 1974 led to the partition of the island.

Rhodesia

In Southern Rhodesia approximately 200,000 white people monopolised power over more than 3 million black people and in November 1965 the white minority government unilaterally declared the colony independent of Britain. But this was something that London could not accept without destroying the multi-racial Commonwealth and facing the wrath of the United Nations, both increasingly dominated by newly independent non-white nations. Rhodesia divided opinion in Britain more than any other colonial issue. Those on the left wanted the Rhodesian regime crushed, by force if necessary. Right-wingers regarded the Rhodesian white population (most of whom had emigrated from Britain) as 'kith and kin' and recalled that some had fought for Britain in the Second World War.

Harold Wilson (prime minister 1964–70) ruled out the use of force and hoped that British trade sanctions would strangle the Rhodesian economy. But these had little impact and Wilson took the risky decision to try to reach a settlement with the Rhodesian leader, Ian Smith. His efforts failed because Smith would not agree to **majority rule**, even in the distant future. Had Smith agreed to Wilson's terms, it is possible that the Commonwealth would have broken up. The eventual independence of Rhodesia (which became known by its ancient African name of Zimbabwe) occurred in 1980 more because of pressure from South Africa and the USA than from British policy.

How successfully did Britain deal with the changing nature of the Commonwealth?

The Commonwealth had become a diverse and multi-racial association of nations united only by their history as territories formerly ruled by Britain:

- The white-ruled nations of South Africa, Canada, Australia and New Zealand had been granted complete legislative independence in 1931, but retained important economic and strategic ties to Britain.
- India, Pakistan and Ceylon (now Sri Lanka) established a precedent by joining as republics and recognising the British monarch, not as head of state, but merely as head of the Commonwealth.
- During the Korean War, Commonwealth troops fought alongside Britain and America

There were various tensions within the Commonwealth during this period.

- The 1956 Suez Crisis threatened Commonwealth unity because Canada, Australia, South Africa and New Zealand supported Britain but India and Pakistan sympathised with Egypt.
- The rapid dismantling of the British colonial empire in Asia and Africa between 1957 and 1964 considerably changed the nature of the Commonwealth as the newly independent nations joined.
- In 1961 South Africa left the Commonwealth rather than face the criticism of its **apartheid** policies from other members. During the 1970s and 1980s members of the Commonwealth repeatedly criticised Britain for its economic ties with South Africa, particularly the sale of armaments, and Thatcher's government found itself isolated for refusing to impose economic sanctions on the apartheid regime (see page 181).
- The 1962 Commonwealth Immigration Act was particularly resented by the black nations because it was clearly designed to limit immigration of black people into Britain (see page 105).
- Commonwealth unity was again seriously threatened by Britain's handling of the Rhodesian crisis.
- Britain itself sacrificed its preferential trade links with Commonwealth members such as New Zealand by joining the European Community in 1973.

Despite the tensions and difficulties the Commonwealth survived.

- Nelson Mandela's government in South Africa decided to re-join the Commonwealth within a month of being elected in 1994. This suggested that the Commonwealth remained a viable institution.
- In 1995 Mozambique and Cameroon joined and became the first members of the Commonwealth with no historic ties to Britain.
- The 1971 Singapore Declaration condemned racial prejudice, and emphasised members' commitment to democratic values, international peace, equal rights and freedom of the individual. These principles were formally codified in the Commonwealth Charter adopted in 2012. Not all the Commonwealth nations could boast a spotless record in adhering to these principles, and Nigeria's membership was suspended between 1995 and 1999 for violating them.

The Commonwealth has survived into the twenty-first century, in part because its head since 1952, Queen Elizabeth II, is highly regarded by its members for her commitment to it. The Commonwealth, despite its lack of obvious political power, remains a respected medium for cultural and economic exchange and for promoting important democratic values.

Activity

1 Using a scale of 1–6 (with 6 as the top rating), copy and complete the table below in order to assess how well you think Britain handled each of the following issues.

Issue	How was the issue handled?	Mark/6	Reason for mark
Malaya			
Ghana			
Nigeria			
Kenya			
Cyprus			
Rhodesia/ Zimbabwe			
Commonwealth relations			

2 Using your assessments in the table above, answer the following question: 'Britain has skilfully managed the transition from Empire to Commonwealth.' How far do you agree?

Historical debate

Empire to Commonwealth – a well-handled transition?

No one disputes that Britain's power and influence in the world diminished in the period from 1951 to 1997. The debate focuses on the nature of that change, why it occurred and how skilfully it was managed.

Passage 1

In 1939, 1940 and 1941, while Hitler conquered the rest of Europe, Britain mortgaged a large part of its worldwide imperial assets in order to fight single-handed. The bankruptcy brought on by the 1939–45 war – a war the British government knew was beyond its means – was the principal reason why the British Empire ended so much more quickly than anyone expected. Yet bankruptcy was not the whole story. The British bowed out comparatively gracefully because the need to grant self-determination to subject peoples was deeply etched in the Colonial Office mind.

Adapted from Brian Lapping, *End of Empire*, 1989, pages 34–35.

Passage 2

There were many places where the Americans and British successfully co-operated in the post-war period. In Cyprus, Aden, Malaya, Kenya and Iran, British rule was essentially 'underwritten' by the US. This policy reflected the Americans' growing awareness that the Soviet Union posed a far more serious threat to American interests and ideals than the British Empire. But the Suez Crisis revealed that the fundamental American hostility towards the Empire lingered on. And when the Americans exercised their veto, the façade of neo-imperial power collapsed. It was rival empires more than indigenous nationalists who propelled the process of decolonisation forward. As the Cold War entered its hottest phase in the 1960s, the United States and the Soviet Union vied with one another to win the support of independence movements in Africa, Asia and the Caribbean. What Harold Macmillan called 'the wind of change' when he toured Africa in 1960 blew not from Windhoek (in Namibia) or Malawi but from Washington and Moscow.

Adapted from Niall Ferguson, *Empire, How Britain Made the Modern World*, 2004, pages 358–59.

Activity

1 In the light of the two passages and your wider reading, how far do you agree with the view that the hostility of the USA to the British Empire was the most important reason for decolonisation?
2 Using the information in this chapter, find information to support the two following views:
   (i) The transition from Empire to Commonwealth was skilfully handled.
   (ii) British decolonisation was not well handled.
3 Which passage about the reasons for the ending of the British Empire do you find the more convincing? Explain your choice.

Further research

John Dumbrell, *A Special Relationship, Anglo-American Relations from the Cold War to Iraq*, 2006.

Brian Lapping, *End of Empire*, 1985.

W. David McIntyre, *British Decolonisation, 1946–1997*, 1998.

David Reynolds, *Britannia Overruled, British Policy and World Power in the 20th Century*, 2000.

Chapter takeaways

- Britain was involved in the Korean War, but was always a junior partner of the USA. It had little influence on the decisions made, but did help to uphold the UN mandate.
- The Suez Crisis of 1956 was a disaster for Britain and was clear indication of declining status. Britain was pressured to withdraw by the USA who did not support British action; it also encouraged further British decolonisation.
- The Falklands War was a triumph for Thatcher as it helped her to win the 1983 election and restore pride in the nation, but this should be balanced against the cost. Some of the actions were controversial and it is debatable whether the outcomes indicated that Britain was still a great power.
- The First Gulf War brought Britain closer to the USA in upholding the UN agreement. However, long-term success was limited.
- Although Britain had a special relationship with the USA, it has always been the junior partner and there have been times when the USA has ignored Britain. However, in times of crisis the two nations have acted together and Britain has not sacrificed its interests.
- The Soviet Union and communism were viewed as Britain's major overseas concern during the Cold War, but Britain's declining power meant that the Soviet Union often ignored Britain. Relations improved under Gorbachev and Yeltsin.
- Britain played an important role in the UN as a permanent member of the Security Council and in its work in UN agencies.
- Britain's relations with Europe have often been controversial. At the end of the Second World War Britain was involved in a range of agreements, but did not join the EEC until 1973. However, Britain having joined, membership has remained a divisive factor in British politics.
- The British Empire was already being challenged before the Second World War. The period after the war saw decolonisation because of the cost, the growth of nationalist movements and pressure from the UN. However, the Empire has been replaced by the Commonwealth, which has been joined by nations that were not former British colonies.

Study Skills: Writing a conclusion and overall essay writing

The types of question set for AS and A Level essays will be the same and therefore all the advice in this section applies to both examinations.

Writing a conclusion

What is the purpose of a conclusion? A conclusion should come to a judgement that is based on what you have already written and should be briefly supported. It should not introduce new ideas – if they were important they should have been discussed in the main body of the essay. You must also take care to avoid offering a contrary argument to the one you have pursued throughout the rest of the essay as that will suggest to the examiner that you have not thought through your ideas and are unclear as to what you think.

It might be that you are largely re-stating the view you offered in the vital opening paragraph, or in stronger answers there might be a subtle variation to the judgement – you confirm your original view, but suggest, with an example, that there were occasions when this was not always correct.

If the question has named a factor then you should give a judgement about that factor's relative importance, either explaining why it is or is not the most important and the role it played in the events you have discussed. If the question asks you to assess a range of factors, the conclusion should explain which you think is the most important and should support the claim. At first sight a claim might appear to be judgement, but without supporting material it is no more than an assertion and will not gain credit.

Consider the following essay question:

Example

'Economic weakness was the main reason why Britain decolonised.' How far do you agree?

In order to answer this question you may consider:

- Britain's economic weakness at the end of the war.
- The rise of nationalist movements in the Empire.
- The attitude of the USA.
- The impact of the Second World War.
- The impact of the Suez Crisis of 1956.
- Changing political attitudes in Britain.

Now consider this sample conclusion:

> There is no doubt that Britain's economic weakness in the post-war period was a vitally important factor in explaining why the colonial empire was wound up. Britain could hardly sustain imperial rule if it could neither pay for the administration, law and order and defence of its colonies, nor supply them with the other economic resources they needed. However, economic weakness was not the main reason for decolonisation because Britain's economy was at its weakest in the years immediately after the Second World War when government ministers were keen to maintain and exploit the empire, not give it up. The main reason for decolonisation was the dramatic change in attitudes to empire that occurred in the mid-1950s. The rise of non-white protest and colonial nationalism, the growth of the UN and the need to win the propaganda war against the USSR all combined to make the retention of colonies too expensive and troublesome for Britain.

This is an excellent final paragraph because:

- *it focuses immediately on the issue in the question*
- *it provides a clear judgement on that issue*
- *that judgement is supported with good argument and evidence*
- *it briefly summarises what the author believes was the main reason.*

Question practice

In light of these comments and the sample conclusion, write conclusions to the following questions:

- Assess the reasons why Britain joined the EEC in 1972.
- 'Britain's relationship with Europe was always controversial in the period from 1945 to 1997.' How far do you agree?
- 'British influence in international affairs was always limited in the period after the Second World War.' How far do you agree?

You have now covered all the main skills you need to write a good essay. It is worth looking back at these skills before you write each essay you are set. This will help you to build up and reinforce the skills you need for the examination and ensure that you are familiar with the skills needed to do well.

Britain, 1951–97

Revision for the Period Studies essay

It is important, and will be more productive, if you make your revision active rather than simply trying to learn large amounts of factual material about Britain in the period from 1951 to 1997. In revising the material you may gain wider experience of historical study and further develop the skills that you need for this element of the paper:

- focusing on the issue in the question
- analysing the issues
- evaluating the relative importance of the issues and factors
- reaching supported judgements about the issue in the question.

Having studied all four key topics (split into four chapters in this book) you will also be able to see the whole period in its broader context, rather than seeing each key topic in isolation. In light of this you should review some of the judgements you made about the issues and questions raised in the earlier topics.

It might be a good starting point to consider the key questions at the start of each chapter. When you first studied the chapter you may have noted down your view of each question; it would be valuable to go and revisit that view and decide in light of further study whether you want to change it. It would be a good idea to plan an essay answer to each key question. This will not only ensure that you have sufficient material available when you reach the examination room, but will also ensure you have thought about issues around which examination questions are likely to be set.

Remember when planning answers:

- What is your overall view about the question?
- What issues do you need to cover?
- What would be your opening sentences for each paragraph?
- What evidence would you use to support or challenge the idea you have raised in each sentence?

A planning sheet, such as the one on page 198 might provide a structure.

Essay title	
View about question:	

Key ideas:		

Opening sentence	Evidence to support	Evidence to challenge

Judgement:	

You may also have written essays on some of the key questions. Re-read the essays.

■ Do you still agree with the view you put forward?
■ Is the essay balanced? Does it consider both sides of the argument?
■ Is the judgement developed?
■ How would you improve the essay?

In light of this you could produce a new plan or, using the advice in the Study Skills sections of this book, write a new conclusion which develops the judgement.

The Study Skills section in each chapter of this book also contains examples of possible essay questions. You could produce plans for those questions, or write opening or concluding paragraphs for them.

As you can see, all of the suggestions involve you being active and not simply reading through and trying to learn your notes. This approach will help to keep you focused and help to ensure that you have thought about the issues that are likely to be raised in examination questions.

Glossary

Apartheid A system of racial segregation introduced in South Africa from 1948, designed to preserve the status of the white minority which retained all political power. Races were forbidden to intermarry and were allocated separate residential areas and facilities. From 1959 many black people were forced to move to separate homelands established in inhospitable regions of the country.

Appeasement The idea that by offering concessions and meeting reasonable grievances peace can be maintained.

Balance of payments deficit The loss on trade, where imports exceed exports.

Big Three Churchill, Roosevelt and Stalin.

Closed shop Some trade unions insisted that only members of their union could be recruited by employers. This gave unions considerable power over the workforce in some industries.

Cold War The period of tension between the Western powers and the communist powers from 1945–89.

Collective security The idea that countries could act together to prevent war, particularly through the new international body set up in 1920, the League of Nations.

Decolonisation The process by which Britain granted independence to its colonies.

Deflation Falling economic activity and prices.

Dominions These were the self-governing parts of the British Empire, for example Canada, Australia, New Zealand, South Africa.

Eurosceptics A term for those opposed to or doubtful of the benefits of Britain's membership of the European Community.

Gold standard Fixing the amount of money in circulation to the amount of gold in the Bank of England.

Grand Alliance A view that Britain should promote and be part of an alliance of nations to keep the peace and prevent aggression. It became the term for the alliance led by Britain, USA, USSR and China against Germany, Italy and Japan in the Second World War.

Inflation Rising prices.

Interest rate The percentage interest that had to be paid back on a loan.

Iron curtain In 1946 Winston Churchill spoke of an 'iron curtain' across Europe separating the communist states of the East from the democratic countries of the West.

Majority/minority rule Under majority rule every citizen has a vote. In a system of minority rule, only a small section of the population, usually the white-skinned, have a vote.

'Means test' A test made by officials to see if people were poor enough to deserve assistance, which was often considered to be humiliating. This restricted any state benefits if a household had any wealth.

Mixed economy Where the economy is run using a mixture of state or public and private owned industry. It would also mean that there was state intervention in the market.

National sovereignty A sovereign nation is completely self-governing and not subject to any outside authority.

Nationalised industries The industries and utilities that were under state control, including coal mining, civil aviation, telecommunications, transport, electricity, gas and water.

Peaceful co-existence The policy of Soviet leader Nikita Khrushchev (1953–64) to avoid war with the West without ending the Cold War rivalry.

Pickets Striking workers who stand outside their place of work to prevent supplies entering or leaving and to discourage other workers from going to work.

Private sector The section of the economy controlled by a privately run business or industry.

Public sector The section of the economy controlled by the government, either central or local.

Retail Price Index A measure of inflation based on the cost of a basket of retail goods and services. The index takes the price of the basket in a certain year as 100 and shows the extent to which the cost of that basket has changed since then.

Restrictive practices In order to protect jobs, some unions insisted that certain tasks could only be performed by certain workers. Critics argued that this led to overmanning and increased the labour costs of businesses.

Shadow Cabinet The leading figures in the main opposition party together form a 'shadow' Cabinet in which each member specialises in opposing a particular government minister.

Socialism The belief that the power of the state should be used to correct economic injustice and inequalities in society.

Stagflation This combines stagnation and inflation, where industry or the economy declines but prices still rise.

Sterling area The countries that had the British pound as their reserve currency.

Special relationship A term used to signify the supposedly closer relations between the US and Britain than those enjoyed by both these countries' other allies or partners.

Tariffs Taxes imposed on imports. They are usually imposed to make foreign goods more expensive than domestic products but they also provide revenue for the government.

TUC The Trades Union Congress is an umbrella organisation for trade unions to provide a co-ordinated voice for the labour movement.

Unilateralist A one-sided agreement where nothing is done in return.

Unilateral Nuclear disarmament A policy of abandoning nuclear weapons, which Labour adopted in the early 1960s.

Veto The power to say 'no'. Each permanent member of the UN Security Council can prevent a measure being agreed by exercising its veto. This is an important power because Security Council resolutions are binding on all members of the UN.

Welfare State A term meaning that the state takes responsibility for the welfare of its citizens, including their health, housing, environment and employment.

White collar employment White collar workers are those employed in office jobs (who traditionally wore white shirts and ties) in contrast to workers who wore overalls (with blue collars).

Index